The Son of Man as the Last Adam

The Son of Man as the Last Adam

*The Early Church Tradition as a Source
of Paul's Adam Christology*

YONGBOM LEE

☙PICKWICK *Publications* · Eugene, Oregon

THE SON OF MAN AS THE LAST ADAM
The Early Church Tradition as a Source of Paul's Adam Christology

Copyright © 2012 Yongbom Lee. All rights reserved. Except for brief quotations in critical publications or reviews, no part of this book may be reproduced in any manner without prior written permission from the publisher. Write: Permissions, Wipf and Stock Publishers, 199 W. 8th Ave., Suite 3, Eugene, OR 97401.

Pickwick Publications
An Imprint of Wipf and Stock Publishers
199 W. 8th Ave., Suite 3
Eugene, OR 97401

www.wipfandstock.com

Permission was granted by Eerdmans Publishers to reproduce a table from Stephen E. Fowl's *Philippians*. Grand Rapids: Eerdmans, 2005, 116–17. Permission was granted from T. & T. Clark to reproduce Morna D. Hooker's diagram in her article "Adam Redivivus: Philippians 2 Once More," in *The Old Testament in the New Testament: Essays in Honour of J. L. North*, edited by Steve Moyise, 231. Journal for the Study of the New Testament Supplement Series 189. Sheffield, UK: JSOT, 2000.

ISBN 13: 978-1-61097-522-3

Cataloguing-in-Publication data:

Lee, Yongbom.

    The Son of Man as the last Adam : the early church tradition as a source of Paul's Adam Christology / Yongbom Lee, with a foreword by David Wenham.

    xx + 168 pp. ; 23 cm. Includes bibliographical references and index.

    ISBN 13: 978-1-61097-522-3

    1. Jesus Christ—Person and offices—Biblical teaching. 2. Adam (Biblical figure). 3. Son of Man. 4. Paul, the Apostle, Saint. I. Wenham, David. II. Title.

BS2651 L266 2012

Manufactured in the U.S.A.

To My Parents

מה־אנוש כי־תזכרנו
ובן־אדם כי תפקדנו
ותחסרהו מעט מאלהים
וכבוד והדר תעטרהו
תמשילהו במעשי ידיך
כל שתה תחת־רגליו

What is man that you are mindful of him,
    the son of man that you care for him?
You made him a little lower than the heavenly beings
    and crowned him with glory and honor.
You made him ruler over the works of your hands;
    you put everything under his feet.

Psalm 8:4–6 (NIV)

Contents

List of Tables / viii

List of Figures / ix

Foreword by Rev. Dr. David Wenham / xi

Preface / xv

Acknowledgements / xvii

Abbreviations / xix

1 Introduction / 1

2 The Early Church Adam-Jesus Typology as a Source of Paul's Adam Christology / 23

3 The Son of Man Sayings as Sources of Paul's Adam Christology / 96

4 Conclusion / 124

Appendix 1: The Early Church Adam-Jesus Typology in Luke 3:38—4:1 / 127

Appendix 2: Jesus and the Suffering Servant / 136

Bibliography / 142

Scripture Index / 155

Tables

1. Definitions / 14
2. Distinction of the Level of Paul's Allusion to the Early Church Tradition / 20
3. Differences between Rom 5 and Phil 2:6–11 / 54
4. Mark 14:62, Ps 110:1, Dan 7:13, and 1 Cor 15:25 / 78
5. 1 Cor 15:25, 27 / 85
6. Structure of Pre-Pauline Resurrection Tradition / 86
7. Mark 10:45 and 1 Tim 2:5–6 / 98
8. Mark 10:45 and Pauline Parallels / 100
9. Literary Context of Matt 19:28 and Luke 22:30 / 112
10. Matt 19:28, 1 Cor 6:2, and Rom 5:17
11. Dan 7:26, 27 / 116
12. Chiastic Structure in Mark 1:12–13 / 128
13. Adam and Jesus as the Son of God / 130
14. Semantic Relationships among נפח, נשמת, and רוח / 130
15. 1 Cor 15:45 and Gen 2:7 / 133
16. Isa 53:11–12 and Mark 10:45 / 139

Figures

1 Adam and Christ in Phil 2:6–11 / 58
2 The Early Church Adam-Jesus Typology / 87
3 Sources of Paul's Understanding of Jesus' Atoning Death / 108

Foreword

THE QUESTION OF PAUL and Jesus is one that will not go away. It is a hot topic in the popular arena, with wild ideas about Paul founding a new religion being bandied about. But it is also a topic that continues to receive attention in the scholarly world, with established scholars such as James Dunn and Michael Thompson making helpful contributions, but also with research students doing important in-depth studies, for example Maureen Yeung's *Faith in Jesus and Paul* (Tübingen: Mohr, 2002).

The ongoing interest in the subject has been reflected in the work of students in Trinity College Bristol, where I teach. Two students have recently completed significant theses under the supervision of Professor John Nolland: Gerry Schoberg wrote on *Perspectives of Jesus in the Writings of Paul*. Yongbom Lee worked on the central and sensitive area of Christology. Dr. Lee originates from South Korea, which has produced many able New Testament scholars in recent years. One of the most eminent and senior is Professor Seyoon Kim, who has made important contributions to the Paul and Jesus question. Dr. Lee interacts a lot with Professor Kim, appreciatively but critically. Like Professor Kim he argues carefully and confidently, paying admirable attention to detail.

His book's focus on Christology and especially on "Son of Man" in the Jesus tradition and on Adam and Christ in the Pauline tradition is very welcome. One of the most striking differences between Paul and the Jesus of the Gospels is the fact that Jesus typically refers to himself as "Son of Man," but Paul never does so: he speaks of Jesus as Lord, Christ, and Son of God, but not Son of Man. This could be seen as puzzling and as lending weight to the argument of those who do not see Paul as a faithful follower of Jesus. There is a partial parallel in Jesus' use of the concept of the "kingdom of God," since it seems to have been a favorite category of Jesus, but it is not especially prominent in Paul's writings. But the situation is different in scale at least, since Paul does use "kingdom" language, not a lot it is true, but in ways that point to his knowledge of the Jesus tradition. With "Son of Man" there is a deafening silence in Paul's letters.

Or there may be, unless his famous references to Jesus as the second "Adam" can be linked to the Son of Man tradition. That possibility has been strikingly ignored by the majority of scholars, despite the fact that the Hebrew for "son of man" is *ben Adam* (e.g., in Pss 8:5; 80:19, "the one at your right hand . . . the son of *Adam*"). If Jesus spoke of himself as "the son of Adam," then the possibility that this might be connected with Paul's references to Jesus as the second Adam shouts out for consideration.

Interestingly even conservative scholars have failed to make the connection. The failure to make the connection can be explained in all sorts of ways: it is not simply that some scholars are prejudiced against recognizing the probability that Paul knew a lot of Jesus tradition. It is also because there are a whole host of complicated questions and a whole body of scholarly discussion relating both to the Son of Man traditions in the Gospels and to the Adam-Christ teaching of Paul. There are linguistic issues about the Hebrew and Aramaic, historical/exegetical issues (e.g., about the authenticity and meaning of "Son of Man" as used by Jesus), and background issues (e.g., about the Jewish background to Paul's view of Adam). It is by no means clear to most scholars that Jesus' probable use of "Son of Man" has anything to do with Adam, though that in itself does not mean that Paul and others might not have made the connection (the expression does mean something like "the human being" and it would not have been a big leap to Paul's reflection on Jesus as the beginning of a new humanity). Many scholars link Jesus' usage to Daniel 7 and its reference to "one like a son of man" coming on the clouds. The interpretation of Daniel 7 and especially of the "one like a son of man" figure is itself a highly contentious issue among scholars, and, whereas there is an obvious link between the one like a son of man and Israel, there is not such an obvious link with Adam, though recent scholars, such as Tom Wright and Crispin Fletcher-Louis, have made that connection. The complexity of these issues means that a simplistic linking of Jesus' Son of Man sayings and Paul's Adam teaching is impossible; and in the whole discussion of the Jesus/Paul question parallelomania (i.e., making simplistic assumptions about possible parallels being proven links) must be avoided, not least because many parallels could simply reflect Jesus and Paul both coming out of the same Jewish world and making use of common Jewish traditions.

Dr. Lee in this book offers the sort of circumspect study that is necessary if overoptimistic simplifications are to be avoided. He does not try to cover too much ground, but focuses in on a limited number of key texts, engaging with the critical issues that they raise, and offering a particularly interesting exploration of the background to the texts and of the linkages between the relevant Jesus traditions and the Pauline teaching about Adam and Christ. His discussion of Adam and Philippians 2 is important—Philippians 2 is a very interesting passage for the Jesus/Paul question, and has even been linked to the traditions behind John 13—and his exploration of the role of Psalms 8 and 110 in Paul and also in Hebrews is illuminating.

This is not a polemical book flying an unlikely kite, but a serious study of important texts and issues. I warmly commend it as a model of the sort of careful study that is needed if we are to continue to make progress in addressing the question of Paul and Jesus. It has been a personal pleasure to get to know Dr. Lee during his years in Bristol, and to be aware that here is a young scholar who combines a Paul-like commitment to the mission of the church with a commitment to rigorous critical academic thinking. I welcome this first major contribution of his to the study of the New Testament, and look forward to what will follow.

Rev. Dr. David Wenham
Trinity College, Bristol

Preface

WHEN I STUDIED AT Fuller Theological Seminary as a Master of Divinity student in 2003–2006, I fell in love with New Testament studies. I read broadly in New Testament studies in my preparation for a PhD program. One of the books that inspired me was David Wenham's *Paul: Follower of Jesus or Founder of Christianity?* (Grand Rapids: Eerdmans, 1995). When discussing the Jesus-Paul debate, Wenham highlights the theological continuity between Jesus and Paul. On the basis of his observation, Wenham concludes that it is more accurate to call Paul "a follower of Jesus" than "the founder of Christianity." In this study, I also will underscore the theological continuity between the Jesus tradition and Paul in the realm of Christology. Paul demonstrates the so-called "Adam Christology" in Rom 5 and 1 Cor 15. In contrast, there is no explicit reference to Adam Christology in the Synoptic Gospels. Does that mean that Adam Christology is quintessentially Pauline invention? In contrast to the frequent appearances of Jesus' self-designation "the Son of Man" in the Synoptic Gospels, Paul nowhere mentions it in his letters. Does that mean that the Evangelists (or post-Pauline church) have misunderstood the generic sense of the Aramaic idiom *bar nasha* and mistakenly used it as a Christological title in association with Dan 7:13, as some scholars have argued?

I contend that Paul uses the early church tradition as a source of his Adam Christology, particularly, its implicit primitive Adam-Jesus typology and Son of Man saying traditions, reflected in the Synoptic Gospels. In chapter 2, I will argue that Paul in Rom 5 and 1 Cor 15 creatively uses the implicit primitive Adam-Jesus typology of the early church, reflected in Phil 2:6–11; Heb 2:5–11; Mark 14:62. If Phil 2:6–11 reflects some confessional formula of the early church with its implicit primitive Adam-Jesus typology, as I contend, Paul evidently knew about the early church

Adam-Jesus typology and most likely used it as a basis of his explicit and sophisticated Adam Christology in Rom 5 and 1 Cor 15. Also, the fact that both Paul and the writer of Hebrews—despite their general theological differences—quote Ps 8:6 to compare Jesus' eschatological authority with Adam's authority over God's creation in Gen 1:26–30 (1 Cor 15:27; Heb 2:8) signifies that an implicit primitive form of Adam-Jesus typology already existed in the early church. In chapter 3, I will argue that Paul also incorporates two Son of Man saying traditions—Mark 10:45 and Matt 19:28//Luke 22:30—into his Adam Christology in Rom 5.

The minimalists concerning Paul's knowledge of the Jesus tradition may be skeptical about my findings. While Paul rarely refers to the Jesus tradition, he at times occasionally refers to it as authoritative words in support of his instruction (e.g., 1 Cor 7:10–11; 9:14; 11:23–25; 15:3–6; 1 Thess 4:15–17). Considering the creative ways in which Paul cites other authoritative traditions—such as the Old Testament and contemporary Jewish exegetical traditions—and adapts and applies them to the situation (*Sitz im Leben*) of his readers, Paul similarly could have used the early church tradition as a source of his Adam Christology.

Acknowledgments

I DEDICATE THIS STUDY to my parents—Rev. Dr. Heung Joo Lee and Dr. Yong Ja Kim—whose encouragement and support made this work possible. Their Christian faith and dedication to higher education have been my lifelong inspiration.

It was my privilege to study under Professor John Nolland at Trinity College, Bristol, in 2006–10. His constant challenge for clarity and accuracy sharpened this study and trained me as a critical scholar. I had the privilege of working with Dr. Craig A. Evans as my external supervisor. Dr. Evans graciously agreed to see me twice to give me his feedback of my work. Despite our limited time together, he gave me many valuable insights that significantly shaped the final form of this study.

I want to give special thanks to my friend Geoffrey Sutton who is a retired German/French teacher in Bristol, UK. Without his encouragement and help, I could not have engaged in German New Testament scholarship in this study. I want to thank Rev. Dr. David Wenham, Lecturer and Vice-Principal of Trinity College for all his encouragement throughout my doctoratal studies. I want to thank Su Brown, a dear librarian at Trinity College, who has magic and commitment to find any requested item.

I want to recognize my former teachers and mentors at Fuller Theological Seminary, Pasadena, California. I want to thank the late Rev. Dr. David M. Scholer. His *Introduction to the New Testament: Acts-Revelation* was my first class at FTS and ultimately led me to pursue a PhD in New Testament Studies. I want to thank Rev. Dr. Seyoon Kim, a pioneer Korean New Testament scholar. I am only one of many Korean students whom he inspired to study the New Testament critically yet without compromising my evangelical faith. I want to thank Rev. Dr. David L. Matson who taught at FTS as an adjunct professor. I want to thank the late Dean of Students Ruth Vuong and the former Vice-President Howard Wilson for being my mentors, when I worked as All Seminary Council President in 2005–6. I thank my friend Joshua Dutcher who helped me with proofreading of my manuscript. I also want to thank the rest of my family who provided me constant encouragement, especially my parents-in-law, Joseph and Judith Dodson.

Finally, I want to thank my lovely wife, Diana, who married me and left sunny California for gloomy Bristol so that we could be together while I worked on my PhD. Besides her efficient work as Postgraduate Administrator at Trinity College, Bristol, I thank her for supporting me by working full-time. I will never forget watching her walking across the muddy Downs (a big, grassy, and often soggy, area in Bristol) on dark rainy winter days, after a long day of work at the college. Without her encouragement and support, I could not have completed this study.

Above all, I thank God who called me to Christian ministry, without whose strength and wisdom I could not have undertaken and finished this study. I pray that this study would be a humble service to his Kingdom.

Soli Dei Gloria!

Abbreviations

ANRW	H. Temporini and W. Haase, eds. *Aufstieg und Niedergang der römischen Welt: Geschichte und Kultur Roms im Spiegel der neueren Forschung*. Berlin: de Gruyter, 1972–
BDAG	W. Bauer, F. W. Danker, W. F. Arndt, and F. W. Gingrich, *Greek-English Lexicon of the New Testament and Other Early Christian Literature*. 3rd ed. Chicago: The University of Chicago Press, 2000
Bib	*Biblica*
BR	*Biblical Research*
BT	*Bible Translator*
BZ	*Biblische Zeitschrift*
CBQ	*Catholic Biblical Quarterly*
DPL	Ralph P. Martin, Daniel G. Reid, and Gerald F. Hawthorne, eds. *Dictionary of Paul and His Letters*. Downers Grove, IL: InterVarsity, 1993
EDNT	Horst R. Balz and Gerhard Schneider, eds. *Exegetical Dictionary of the New Testament*. 3 vols. Grand Rapids: Eerdmans, 1991
HALOT	L. Koehler and W. Baumgartner, *The Hebrew and Aramaic Lexicon of the Old Testament*. Study Edition. 2 vols. Leiden: Brill, 2001
HTR	*Harvard Theological Review*
JBL	*Journal of Biblical Literature*
JRR	*Journal from the Radical Reformation*
JSHJ	*Journal for the Study of the Historical Jesus*
JSNT	*Journal for the Study of the New Testament*
JTS	*Journal of Theological Studies*

KAI	H. Donner and W. Röllig, *Kanaanäische und aramäische Inschriften: Texte*. 3 vols. Wiesbaden: Harrassowitz, 1962–64
LSJ	H. G. Lidell, R. Scott, and H. S. Jones, *A Greek-English Lexicon*. 9th ed. Oxford: Oxford University Press, 1996
LXX	Septuagint
MT	Masoretic Text
NETS	A. Pietersma and B. G. Wright, eds. *A New English Translation of the Septuagint*. Oxford: Oxford University Press, 2007
NIV	New International Version
NRSV	New Revised Standard Version
NovT	*Novum Testamentum*
NTS	*New Testament Studies*
OTP	James H. Charlesworth, ed. *The Old Testament Pseudepigrapha*. 2 vols. New York: Doubleday, 1983 and 1985
RB	*Revue Biblique*
SNTSU	*Studien zum neuen Testament und seiner Umwelt*
SJT	*Scottish Journal of Theology*
ST	*Studia Theologica*
TDNT	Gerhard Kittel and Gerhard Friedrich, eds. *Theological Dictionary of the New Testament*. Translated by Geoffrey W. Bromiley. 10 vols. Grand Rapids: Eerdmans, 1964–76
TLNT	Ceslas Spicq, *Theological Lexicon of the New Testament*. Translated by James D. Ernest. 2 Vols. Peabody, MA: Hendrickson, 1994
TLOT	Ernst Jenni and Claus Westermann, eds. *Theological Lexicon of the Old Testament*. Translated by Mark E. Biddle. 3 Vols. Peabody, MA: Hendrickson, 1997
TynBul	*Tyndale Bulletin*
VT	*Vetus Testamentum*
ZNW	*Zeitschrift für die neutestamentliche Wissenschaft und die Kunde der älteren Kirche*

1

Introduction

THE PURPOSE OF THIS STUDY

PAUL SELDOM QUOTES THE sayings of Jesus in his letters, which has led some scholars in the past to consider him as "the second founder of Christianity."[1] Despite the scarcity of explicit references to Jesus' earthly life, however, Paul's letters show substantial theological overlap with Jesus' teachings in the Synoptic Gospels.[2] Seyoon Kim argues that Jesus' kingdom gospel had to be replaced or re-presented by Paul's gospel of the death and resurrection of Christ for the post-Easter church and his Hellenistic audience.[3] David Wenham similarly claims that Paul modified Jesus' kingdom preaching according to its spirit.[4] One way to test the theological coherence between the early church tradition and Paul is to compare and contrast the early church Christology—reflected in the Synoptic Gospels—and Paul's Christology in his letters.[5]

---

1. E.g. Wrede, *Paul*, 179; Vermes, *Jesus and the World of Judaism*, 56–57; Casey, *From Jewish Prophet to Gentile God*, 97–120; Lüdemann, *Paulus, Der Gründer des Christentums*, 199–216.

2. Similarly, Wenham, *Paul*, 377–80.

3. Kim, *Paul and the New Perspective*, 275–90.

4. Wenham, *Paul*, 409.

5. Longenecker points out, "It needs also to be recognized that there circulated within the early Christian communities various Christological materials, both written and oral, which brought much of that earlier testimony together and were used by the writers of the New Testament in their portrayals and presentations"; Longenecker, "Christological Materials in the Early Christian Communities," 48. Longenecker recognizes at least four bodies of Christological material from the early Christian communi-

2　The Son of Man as the Last Adam

In this study, I will compare and contrast the early church Christology and Paul's Christology by focusing on the relationship between the early church Adam-Jesus typology—reflected in the Synoptic Gospels and the epistle to the Hebrews—and Paul's Adam Christology in his letters. Although the Evangelists nowhere call Jesus "the Last Adam" as Paul does in 1 Cor 15:45, there are a number of passages in the Gospels that implicitly compare and contrast Jesus and Adam and present Jesus as the eschatological Adam—Mark 2:10, 27–28; 14:62; Luke 3:38—4:1; cf. Heb 2:5–11.[6] Did Paul invent the so-called "Adam Christology" in Rom 5 and 1 Cor 15 out of nothing (*ex nihilo*)? Or, did the early church already possess a primitive form of Adam-Jesus typology that Paul develops into his explicit and sophisticated Adam Christology? Or, have the early church and Paul separately derived Adam Christology from first-century AD Judaism? These questions will be addressed in chapter 2.

Another focus of this book is the relationship between the early church traditions behind the Synoptic Son of Man sayings and Paul's Adam Christology. As I will argue later, Paul in developing his Adam Christology in Rom 5 and 1 Cor 15 incorporates not only the Son of Man saying tradition related to the early church Adam-Jesus typology (Mark 14:62) but also two others that are unrelated (Mark 10:45 and Matt 19:28//Luke 22:30). We cannot find the phrase "the Son of Man" in Paul's letters. Koester claims, "The title was not known to Paul and did not play any role in the corpus of the New Testament epistles."[7] It is difficult to imagine that Paul knew nothing about any Son of Man saying tradition or Jesus' self-designation as בר נשא ("the Son of Man")— the generally accepted Aramaic phrase behind the Greek ὁ υἱὸς τοῦ ἀνθρώπου.[8] As we will see later, Paul most likely knew at least three Son

---

ties: (1) passion narratives and reports, (2) an eschatological tractate and traditions, (3) a Logia or Sayings collection, and (4) confessional portions.

6. I see an allusion to Gen 1:26–28 in the phrase ἐπὶ τῆς γῆς ("on the earth") in Mark 2:10 in which the Son of Man's authority is compared with Adam's authority in God's creation. I see an allusion to Gen 1–2 in Mark 2:27 ("the Sabbath was made for humankind, and not humankind for the Sabbath") in which Jesus' authority is compared with Adam's authority in Gen 1:26–28, as he is compared with David in Mark 2:23–26. Since Paul's Adam Christology shows no specific link with Mark 2:10, 27–28, I will not discuss them in this study. I will discuss the early church Adam-Jesus typology behind Luke 3:38—4:1 in Appendix 1 because of its speculative nature.

7. Koester, *Paul & His World*, 109.

8. Casey points out that there is a general consensus that Jesus spoke Aramaic and the Aramaic phrase behind ὁ υἱὸς τοῦ ἀνθρώπου in the Gospels is בר (א)נש(א) *bar enash(a)*; Casey, *Solution to the 'Son of Man' Problem*, 314; most recently, Hurtado

of Man saying traditions—Mark 10:45; 14:62; Matt 19:28//Luke 22:30—and incorporated them into his Adam Christology in Rom 5 and 1 Cor 15. I will argue in this study that Paul uses the early church tradition as a source of his Adam Christology, particularly, its Adam-Jesus typology and Son of Man saying traditions reflected in the Synoptic Gospels.

LITERATURE SURVEY

Numerous studies exist on the topic of Jesus' Son of Man sayings. Despite such a fact, however, most studies focus on the origin of the Son of Man sayings and only a few studies deal with the relationship between the early church traditions behind the Son of Man sayings and Paul's Adam Christology. There are even fewer studies devoted to the relationship between the early church Adam-Jesus typology and Paul's Adam Christology. I will begin my literature survey with Oscar Cullmann's classic *The Christology of the New Testament* (1959).

While correctly observing the association between the Synoptic Son of Man saying traditions and Paul's Adam Christology, Cullman attributes it to "the common root of the Original Man idea" in ancient Judaism.[9] According to Cullmann, both the early church Son of Man/Adam Christology and Paul's Adam Christology are derived from the Primal Man myth in ancient Judaism and wider ancient Near Eastern thought. Cullmann's view is based on the hypothetical existence of such a myth, which the so-called *religionsgeschichtliche Schule* ("History of Religions School") assumed—influential especially in German-speaking scholarship. The History of Religions School arbitrarily retrojected the Primal Man myth found in Gnosticism to earlier periods. The existence of the Primal Man myth in the first century AD has been largely rejected by English-speaking New Testament scholarship today due to its lack of evidence.

---

notes, "ὁ υἱὸς τοῦ ἀνθρώπου likely represents a careful translation of an equivalent, unusual and distinctive Aramaic expression, probably בר אנשא"; Hurtado, "Summary and Concluding Observations," 174. Lukaszewski voices some reservation about this general consensus: "Until the linguistic data has been mined to this extent [i.e. the wider linguistic milieu: Hebrew and Aramaic], however, no further clarification seems possible with respect to a form, never mind definition, of an Aramaic Son of Man"; Lukaszewski, "Issues Concerning the Aramaic Behind ὁ υἱὸς τοῦ ἀνθρώπου," 26–27.

9. Cullmann, *Christology of the New Testament*, 166–81; similarly, Cortés and Gatti, "The Son of Man or the Son of Adam," 500–502; Bultmann, *Theology of the New Testament*, 1:166–67.

4 The Son of Man as the Last Adam

In "'Der Menschensohn' und die Paulinische Christologie" (1963), Anton Vögtle sums up his discussion of the relationship between the Synoptic Son of Man sayings and Paul's Adam Christology with three statements:

> (1) It is possible, even if it cannot be proven, that the term *bar nasha* was the origin for the Christological use of Psalm 8 . . . (2) The apostle does not use the *bar nasha* expression certainly known to him—ὁ υἱὸς τοῦ ἀνθρώπου or [its] equivalent term— as a Christological title . . . (3) Paul teaches the true coming in the flesh of the pre-existent Son of God.[10]

Vögtle emphasizes the last statement and contrasts it with his observation that the Synoptic Son of Man sayings do not allude to Jesus' pre-existence[11] and concludes: "Even this—admittedly only negative— agreement between Paul and the Synoptics seems to me not without significance, if we take seriously the well-grounded possibility that, in the unique occurrence of the phrase 'Son of Man' in the NT, especially in the Synoptic Jesus-tradition, the knowledge of its special usage continues to have an effect which had to do with Jesus' way of speaking of himself."[12]

Later scholars who deny any relationship between the Synoptic Son of Man saying traditions and Paul's Adam Christology often cite Vögtle's article in support of their view.[13] Vögtle, however, is at least open to the possibility that Paul knew about Jesus' self-designation as בר נשא and its related early church Adam Christology associated with the Christological interpretation of Psalm 8. As I will discuss later, the differences between the Synoptic Son of Man saying traditions and Paul's Adam Christology most likely are due to Paul's creative use of the traditions.

10. My translation of "(1) Es ist möglich, wenn auch keineswegs beweisbar, dass die bar-nascha-Bezeichnung die christologische Verwendung von Ps 8 auslöste . . . (2) Der Apostel verwendet die ihm gewiss bekannte bar-nascha-Bezeichnung—ὁ υἱὸς τοῦ ἀνθρώπου oder Ersatzausdrück—nicht als christologischen Würdenamen . . . (3) Paulus lehrt die wahre Menschwerdung des präexistenten Gottessohnes"; Vögtle, "'Der Menschensohn' und die Paulinische Christologie," 217.

11. Ibid., 217.

12. My translation of "Auch diese—freilich nur negative—Übereinstimmung zwischen Paulus und Synopse erscheint mir nicht bedeutungslos, sofern nur mit der gut begründbaren Möglichkeit ernst gemacht wird, dass im eigenartigen Vorkommen der MS-Bezeichnung im NT und in der synoptischen Jesus-Überlieferung im besonderen das Wissen um eine besondere Bewandtnis nachwirkt, die es mit der Redeweise Jesu vom auf sich hatte"; ibid., 217–18.

13. E.g. Hare, *Son of Man Tradition*, 241–42; Dunn, *Christology in the Making*, 303.

In *Jesus and the Son of Man* (1964), A. J. B. Higgins claims, "Paul is the only New Testament writer, apart from the evangelists, with a consistent and thorough-going Son of Man Christology."[14] Higgins suggests that, in 1 Cor 15:45–49 and Rom 5:12–14, Paul is contradicting "a Jewish doctrine of the two Adams in some form familiar to that known to us from Philo."[15] While correctly recognizing the association between the Synoptic Son of Man saying traditions and Paul's Adam Christology, Higgins does not consider the possibility that Paul uses the early church tradition as a source of his Adam Christology.

In *The Son of Man in the Synoptic Tradition* (1965), H. E. Tödt offers an extensive exegetical analysis of the Synoptic Son of Man sayings in relation to a set of questions rising from the scholarship of his day. Tödt concludes, "There is a Christology in the synoptic tradition the basis of which is not a Christological concept of Jesus' *person*. This Christology conceives of Jesus' *authority on earth*."[16] Tödt suggests a research topic worth pursuing in the future: "It will be necessary to investigate how the early Christology of *exousia* in Q and in other strata of the tradition is related to the Christology in Phil 2 or in Paul's writings,"[17] which this study intends to do.

Robin Scroggs, as his title *The Last Adam: A Study in Pauline Anthropology* (1966) indicates, focuses on Paul's anthropology when looking at his Adam Christology. While discussing the Old Testament, Apocrypha, Pseudepigrapha, and rabbinic literature as the possible backgrounds of Paul's Adam Christology, Scroggs does not consider the possibility of the early church tradition being one of its sources.[18]

In *The Son of Man in Myth and History* (1967), Frederick H. Borsch reservedly accepts the view that the Primal Man myth lies behind Paul's idea of Christ as the Second Man.[19] Commenting on 1 Cor 15:45–49, Borsch claims: "He [Paul] is here converting his own older ideas concerning the Adam-Man speculation, views which he could well have

---

14. Higgins, *Jesus and the Son of Man*, 149.
15. Ibid., 150.
16. Tödt, *Son of Man in the Synoptic Tradition*, 296.
17. Ibid., 296.
18. Scroggs, *Last Adam*, 1–58.
19. Borsch admits, "No one is more conscious than this author of the rather superficial manner in which we have here covered a great sweep of history and the relevant aspects of a number of religions [referring to the Primal Man myth]"; Borsch, *Son of Man in Myth and History*, 242–43.

6 THE SON OF MAN AS THE LAST ADAM

imbibed from his rabbinic background (and perhaps also from sectarian and/or primitive Christian understandings), and he is making these fit his interpretation of the Christ event and its implications."[20] As Borsch suggests, the early church tradition most likely was a source of Paul's Adam Christology but his claim that it reflects the Primal Man myth is unwarranted.

In *The Son of Man in Mark* (1967), Morna D. Hooker provides a careful analysis of the Son of Man sayings in Mark. Hooker claims that the majority of the Markan Son of Man sayings are linked with the question of Jesus' authority,[21] related not only to Dan 7 but also to Gen 1:26–30.[22] Hooker does not investigate the possibility that Paul uses the Son of Man saying traditions as sources of his Adam Christology. Hooker concludes: "Though the title 'Son of Man' itself may not be used in the New Testament epistles, the ideas which are associated with it have nevertheless played a very important part in the formation of New Testament theology: this theme, however, is a subject which demands a study to itself."[23] More than forty years have passed since the publication of Hooker's *The Son of Man in Mark* but there seems to have been no book-length study dedicated to the relationship between the early church tradition and Paul's Adam Christology.[24]

In contrast to many publications concerning the Son of Man sayings in the 1960s in English-speaking scholarship, there seems

---

20. Ibid., 242–43.

21. Hooker, *Son of Man in Mark*, 198.

22. Hooker summarizes her study: "Our examination of Daniel's imagery suggested that the vision of 'one like a Son of man' was not used simply as apocalyptic symbolism, but was intended to express a very real and fundamental truth about the righteous nucleus of Israel. The vindication of those who were faithful to God was certain, because he had acknowledged them as his chosen people, destined to inherit the rule once given to Adam." Hooker goes on, "This same theme of Israel's divine right to rule the earth, a right usurped by other nations, was found in much of the inter-testamental literature, expressed sometime in terms of Adam, though the phrase 'Son of man' is not used"; ibid., 189.

23. Ibid., 198. I met Professor Hooker right after her seminar during Greenbelt Festival 2007 at Cheltenham Racecourse in Cheltenham, UK. I briefly described my research interest to her and she told me that she had the same interest long ago but could not go too far. I hope that she finds this study satisfactory.

24. Despite its date, Hooker's study is important and sparked my own interest in the early stage of my research.

to be a sudden drop in scholars' interest in them since the 1970s.[25] In *Christology in the Making* (1980), James D. G. Dunn rejects the Primal Man myth held by the History of Religions School and argues that the widespread Adam Christology in the 40s and 50s AD is "the most informative and probable background" of Paul's Adam Christology.[26] As I will discuss later, while supporting Dunn's view that the early church Adam Christology was an important source of Paul's Adam Christology, I reject his "through and through" Adam Christology that denies Christ's pre-existence. Dunn's investigation of the relationship between the early church Adam Christology and Paul's Adam Christology is significant but rather limited—only five pages.[27]

In *Adam Christology as the Exegetical & Theological Substructure of 2 Corinthians 4:7—5:21* (1991), C. Marvin Pate argues: "Paul's Adam Christology forms the theological and exegetical foundation, not only for 2 Cor 5:1–10, but for the unit in which it occurs, 2 Cor 4:7—5:21. When this wider context is considered, the following two-fold theme emerges: Paul believes that the primeval glory that the first Adam lost has been restored through the righteous suffering of Christ, the last Adam."[28] Although Paul's Adam Christology possibly operates behind his argument in 2 Cor 5:1–10, it is not as explicit as that in Rom 5 and 1 Cor 15. Also, there is no explicit parallel in the Gospels to the idea that Jesus restores the lost glory of Adam apart from the implicit contrast between Adam's disobedience and Jesus' obedience in the Temptation story in Mark 1:9–13 and its parallels (see Appendix 2). While searching for some earlier Jewish traditions (*Vorlager*) of the restoration of Adam's glory in 2 Cor 5:1–10, Pate does not consider the early church tradition as a source of Paul's Adam Christology.

In *The Climax of the Covenant* (1993), N. T. Wright draws two conclusions on the basis of 1 Cor 15 and Rom 5:

---

25. This may have been due to scholars' rejection of the once popular Primal Man myth of *religionsgeschichte Schule*, which in its own way connects the Synoptic Son of Man sayings and Paul's Adam Christology.

26. Dunn, *Christology in the Making*, 113–15.

27. Ibid., 107–13.

28. Pate, *Adam Christology as the Exegetical & Theological Substructure of 2 Corinthians 4:7—5:21*, 22; Pate sees Paul's allusion to the Adam story in Genesis in the following words in 2 Cor 5:1–10—γυμνός (v. 3; cf. Gen 3:7), στενάζω (vv. 2, 4; cf. Gen 3:16), and ἐνδύω (vv. 2, 4; cf. Gen 3:21); ibid., 115–20.

> First, the apocalyptic belief that Israel is the last Adam is the correct background against which to understand Paul's Adam-Christology. For Paul, Jesus stands in the place of Israel. To him, and to his people, the glory of Adam now belongs in the new Age which has already dawned. But, second, the fact of the cross compelled Paul to rethink the nature of God's plan for his people . . . Jesus, as last Adam, had revealed what God's saving plan for the world really had been—what Israel's vocation had really been—by enacting it, becoming obedient to death, even the death of the cross.[29]

I can only make preliminary comments on Wright's conclusions. Firstly, Wright's claim that the Messiah (Jesus) = Israel = the last Adam is unwarranted.[30] As John R. Levison in his seminal work *Portraits of Adam in Early Judaism* (1988) persuasively illustrates, diversity rather than uniformity characterizes many *Tendenzen* in first-century AD Judaism concerning the portraits of Adam.[31] Such a fact undermines Wright's claim that Israel is equated with Adam in the Old Testament and Jewish intertestamental writings.[32] Paul calls Christ "the last Adam" (1 Cor 15:45) but he never calls Israel "the last Adam." Secondly, Wright's claim that Jesus simply takes what was originally Israel's vocation—"becoming obedient to death, even the death of the cross"—is unconvincing.[33] Wright's claim that Israel-Christology is the background of Paul's Adam Christology is doubtful.

In his unpublished PhD dissertation (1994), Joel William Parkman investigates Adam Christological motifs in the Synoptic traditions.[34] Parkman argues that Paul is not the only New Testament author who adapts Adam Christology (e.g., Rom 5:12–24; 1 Cor 15; Rom 1:18–32; 7:7–11; Phil 2:6–11) but it is implied in various parts of the Synoptic Gospels (e.g., 1:9–13; 2:7; 3:1–6; 10:2–12; Matt 1:28–30). Not every

---

29. Wright, *Climax of the Covenant*, 39–40.

30. Wright also claims, "Paul's Adam-Christology is basically an Israel-Christology, and is predicated on the identification of Jesus as Messiah, in virtue of his resurrection"; ibid., 29.

31. Levison, *Portraits of Adam in Early Judaism*, 145–61.

32. Wright, *Climax of the Covenant*, 21.

33. As I will discuss in chapter 3, Paul incorporates the early church tradition behind Mark 10:45 into his explicit and sophisticated Adam Christology in Rom 5:12–21. Jesus' vicarious suffering itself is not the essence of the early church Adam-Jesus typology that Paul develops in Rom 5 and 1 Cor 15.

34. Parkman, "Adam Christological Motifs in the Synoptic Traditions," 6.

case is equally convincing but his study is unique. As Parkman notes: "There has been no study, monograph or article, fully dedicated to the subject of Adam-Christology in the Synoptic traditions [until 1994]."[35] Commenting on the relationship between the early church Adam Christology and Paul's Adam Christology, Parkman points out: "The fact that Paul's Adam Christology shows signs of being not particularly Pauline but a part of a larger common tradition, plus the appearance of Adam Christology in Hebrews, suggests the widespread existence and importance of this particular theme. The important place in the Pauline tradition that Adam Christology holds and its widespread existence in the New Testament would lead one to expect to find Adam Christology in the synoptic traditions."[36]

Compared to his relatively lengthy discussion of the relationship between the early church Adam Christology and Paul's Adam Christology, Parkman devotes only a few pages to the relationship between the Synoptic Son of Man saying traditions and Paul's Adam Christology.[37] Parkman concludes, "The Adam/Christ comparison was not a uniquely Pauline motif but was an integral part of early Christian speculation about Jesus and left its mark on the synoptic traditions."[38] As we will see later, the findings of this study support Parkman's conclusion. This study examines the relationship between the early church tradition and Paul's Adam Christology on far more exegetical grounds than Parkman's study.

In *The Son of Man Debate* (1999), Delbert Burkett provides a thorough list of the views suggested concerning the so-called "Son of Man Problem" up to that date and his evaluation of them.[39] Burkett's attempt to sum up the most controversial topic in New Testament studies in a short monograph is ambitious. Its natural downside is the author's limited treatment of specific aspects of the Son of Man Problem. In fact, Burkett abruptly claims in the beginning of his study that the Son of Man saying traditions have nothing to do with Adam or Adam Christology, on the basis of his criticism of what he calls "genealogical interpretations."[40] As Burkett notes, to interpret the phrase ὁ υἱὸς τοῦ

35. Ibid., 6.
36. Ibid., 55.
37. Ibid., 55–132 and 154–59.
38. Ibid., 195.
39. Burkett, *Son of Man Debate*.
40. Ibid., 6–12; similarly, Hare, *Son of Man Tradition*, 241–42.

ἀνθρώπου as "the son of Adam" has many problems. As we will see later, however, careful examination reveals significant connections between the Son of Man saying traditions and Paul's Adam Christology.

In *The Origin of Paul's Gospel* (1982), Seyoon Kim concludes: "Paul saw the exalted Christ as the εἰκὼν τοῦ θεοῦ and as the Son of God on the Damascus road. This perception led him to conceive of Christ in terms of the personified, hypostatized Wisdom of God (together with his realization at that time that Christ had superseded the Torah) on the one hand, and in terms of Adam, on the other. Thus, both Paul's Wisdom-Christology and Adam-Christology are grounded in the Damascus Christophany."[41]

In *Paul and the New Perspective* (2002), Kim modifies his original thesis and concludes: "*Paul developed his Adam-christology from his Damascus experience of seeing the exalted Christ appearing in the image of God and by confirming it by Jesus' self-designation as 'the Son of Man' and by Dan 7 and Ps 8.*"[42] Under the heading "The 'Son of Man' Christology Hidden," Kim argues that, although Paul nowhere mentions "the Son of Man" in his letters, he alludes to some of the Synoptic Son of Man saying traditions in various passages in his letters.[43] On the basis of his observation in 1 Cor 15:23–28, Kim claims, "Paul's theologizing process or his theological method: *seeing Jesus' claim (and the early church's kerygma) confirmed by the Damascus revelation, he interpreted the revelation in the light of the Jesus tradition as well as the Scripture, and vice versa.*"[44] While considering the Damascus revelation as an important source of Paul's Adam Christology, I will argue in this study that the early church tradition is another important source of Paul's Adam Christology.

Joel Marcus' two articles (2003) are somewhat related to the subject of this study.[45] Marcus summarizes his thesis:

> The Gospel expression ὁ υἱὸς τοῦ ἀνθρώπου = "the son of the man" means "the son of Adam." The most natural way of construing the double definite article is that it speaks of the son of a particular man, namely Adam, who is called ὁ ἄνθρωπος in Genesis

---

41. Kim, *Origin of Paul's Gospel*, 267.

42. Ibid., 210; Kim's italicization.

43. Kim, *Paul and the New Perspective*, 194–208; cf. Mark 8:38; 13:26–27; 14:62; Matt 10:32–33//Luke 12:8–9; Matt 24:43–44//Luke 12:39–40.

44. Kim, *Paul and the New Perspective*, 206; Kim's italicization.

45. Marcus, "Son of Man as Son of Adam," 38–61; Marcus, "Son of Man as Son of Adam Part II," 370–86.

1–2 LXX. The Adam in question, however, is not just the biblical protoplast but also the figure of later Jewish and Christian legend, who possessed dominion and divine glory, which will be restored to him at the eschaton (cf. the exalted Son of Man sayings), who exercised authority over the created order, which he governed as the earthly representative of the heavenly king (cf. the present authority saying), but who is also associated with the world's present condition of suffering and death (cf. the suffering Son of Man sayings).[46]

Space does not permit me to examine Marcus' thesis in detail. While Marcus' first two claims that "the exalted Son of Man sayings" and "the present authority sayings" are related to Adam (Christology) are convincing, his last claim that "the suffering Son of Man sayings" are related to Adam (Christology) is doubtful.[47] In contrast to Marcus' studies, I do not intend to discover the origin of Jesus' Son of Man sayings *per se* but to examine the relationship between the early church's understanding of them and Paul's Adam Christology.

In "The Origin of Paul's Doctrine of the Two Adams in 1 Corinthians 15.45–49" (2003), Stephen Hultgren convincingly refutes the widespread view that Paul derived his Adam Christology from Philo or Alexandrian traditions and the once popular view that Paul derived his Adam Christology from Gnosticism and its alleged *Urmensch* myth.[48] On the basis of his observation of the striking parallels between 1 Cor 15:45–49 and three particular Rabbinic references that concern the *midrash* of Gen 2:7 (*Gen. R.* 14.2–5; 8.1; *Midr. Teh.* on Ps 139:6),[49] Hultgren suggests that there might have been a earlier Jewish tradition (*Vorlage*) of these rabbinic *midrashim*, which could have influenced Paul.[50] Hultgren

---

46. Marcus, "Son of Man as Son of Adam," 38; similarly, Cortés and Gatti, "The Son of Man or the Son of Adam," 500–502.

47. Marcus supports his last claim by citing *L.A.E.* 47.4 (cf. *Apoc. Moses* 39.2); "[the Lord speaking to Michael] Let him [deceased Adam] be in your custody until the day of dispensing punishment at the last years, when I will turn his sorrow into joy. Then he shall sit on the throne of him who overthrew him"; Johnson, "Life and Adam and Eve," 290; Marcus, "Son of Man as Son of Adam," 60. Marcus' argument here is unconvincing because the supposed tradition behind *L.A.E.* 47.4 was not widely attested in Second Temple Judaism—in contrast to the prevalence of Dan 7:13—to the extent that first-century Christian readers could understand the suffering Son of Man as the deceased first human being, Adam.

48. Hultgren, "Origin of Paul's Doctrine of the Two Adams in 1 Corinthians 15.45–49," 343–70.

49. Ibid., 359–66.

50. Ibid., 363.

claims, "Paul knew Palestinian exegetical traditions about a first and last Adam. His encounter with the risen Christ gave concrete form to that abstract idea."[51] Hypothetically speaking, a certain Jewish exegetical tradition—*midrash* on Gen 2:7—behind these rabbinic references could have existed in the first century AD and Paul creatively incorporates it into his argument in 1 Cor 15:45–49. Considering the much later dates of these three rabbinic sources, however, the contemporary early church tradition probably had more direct impact on Paul's Adam Christology.

In *Christusbekenntnis und Jesusüberlieferung bei Paulus* (2007), Detlef Häusser investigates the extent of Paul's knowledge of the Jesus tradition in a number of passages widely recognized as pre-Pauline: 1 Cor 15:3–8, Rom 1:3–4, Phil 2:6–11, and Gal 4:4–5. Häusser concludes:

> We can accept with certainty Paul's knowledge of the Communion words (cf. 1 Cor 11:23–25), the ransom word of Jesus, the self-designation of Jesus as a son of man, the crucifixion of Jesus, the burial, the location of the empty tomb, and different manifestations of Jesus . . . Paul probably knew the Synoptic saying by the humiliation and exaltation (Luke 14:11 among other things) and the "I have come" and "I was sent" sayings, particularly the sending formula. Paul also probably knew the temptation of Jesus, the controversy saying on the son of God and the son of David and the trial of Jesus, including Jesus' voluntary confession before the Sanhedrin (Mark 14:61–62).[52]

While the findings of this study generally support Häusser's conclusion, it differs from Häusser's at least in two aspects. Firstly, this study strictly focuses on the relationship between the early church tradition and Paul's Adam Christology.[53] Secondly, this study employs a specific

---

51. Ibid., 343.

52. My translation of "Mit *Sicherheit* angenommen werden kann eine paulinische Kenntnis der Abendmahlsworte (vgl. IKor 11,23–25.), des Lösegeldwortes Jesu und damit der Selbstbezeichnung Jesu als Menschensohn, der Kreuzigung Jesu, des Begräbnisses, der Auffindung des leeren Grabes und verschiedener Erscheinungen Jesu . . . *Wahrscheinlich* waren der synoptische Spruch von der Erniedrigung und Erhöhung (Lk 14,11 u.a.) und die Worte vom Gesandten und Gekommenen, besonders die Sendungsformel, Paulus bekannt. Die Versuchung Jesu, das Streitgespräch zur Frage von Gottessohn und Davidssohn und den Prozess Jesu, einschließlich Jesu Selbstbekenntnis vor dem Hohen Rat (Mk 14,61f.), hat Paulus ebenfalls wahrscheinlich gekannt"; Häusser, *Christusbekenntnis und Jesusüberlieferung bei Paulus*, 351–52.

53. For instance, see Häusser's intricate diagram that illustrates the complex history-of-tradition relations of Phil 2:6–11 (Die traditionsgeschichtlichen Beziehungen von Phil 2,6–11); ibid., 290.

methodology in establishing Paul's reference to the early church tradition. Häusser concludes his book with the following comment, "The present study went into the development of the individual aspects of the Christology only on the edge. Here a field is opened for further research, which would expand the perimeter of this work."[54] This study turns out to be such an expansion of Häusser's research.

In "'First Adam' and 'Second Adam' in 1 Cor 15:45–49 in the Light of Midrashic Exegesis and Hebrew Usage" (2010), Menahem Kister suggests:

> Paul's passage employs exegetical techniques, approaches of Scripture, and theological themes comparable to those found in rabbinic texts. Paul wrote Greek and used Hellenistic terms which would be readily understandable to the recipients of the epistle at Corinth. Nevertheless, a similar dualism between earthly and heavenly aspects in human beings is found in those rabbinic parallels, which suggests a Jewish context for Paul's ideas, rather than the non-Jewish Hellenistic one some scholars have proposed. It will be argued that the Pauline idea of Christ as the "last Adam" should be attributed to bilinguial, Greek and Hebrew thinking and results from a midrashic thought model applied to a quasi-rabbinic concept. Thus what may emerge from our paper is a clearer appreciation of Paul's exegetical methods and of the extent to which early Jewish traditions concerning Adam's creation and human resurrection shaped his innovative thinking.[55]

Kister convincingly argues that Paul in 1 Cor 15:45–49 may be creatively incorporating some contemporary Jewish *midrashic* traditions on Gen 2:7. Kister, however, does not consider the possibility of the early church tradition being another source of Paul's Adam Christology.

We have seen that in recent New Testament scholarship—apart from Häusser's study—the possibility that Paul uses the early church tradition as a source of his Adam Christology has not been seriously explored in a book-length study. Without negating other probable sources such as the Old Testament, Jewish exegetical traditions, and the

---

54. My translation of "Nur am Rande ging vorliegende Untersuchung auf die Entwicklung der einzelnen Teilaspekte der Christologie ein. Hier öffnet sich ein Feld für weitere Forschungen, die aber den Umfang dieser Arbeit sprengen würden"; ibid., 364.

55. Kister, "'First Adam' and 'Second Adam' in 1 Cor 15:45–49 in the Light of Midrashic Exegesis and Hebrew Usage," 351.

Damascus Christophany, I will argue in this study that Paul uses the early church tradition as a source of his Adam Christology, particularly, its implicit primitive Adam-Jesus typology and Son of Man saying traditions reflected in the Synoptic Gospels.

METHODOLOGY

Approach

This study approaches its subject mainly with Historical Criticism and partly with Source Criticism and Redaction Criticism. I am not applying to this study more recently developed methods of interpretation such as Canonical Criticism, Structuralism, Narrative (or Literary) Criticism, Rhetorical Criticism, Social (or Socio-cultural) Criticism, and Advocacy (Ideological) Criticism.

Definitions

Term	Definition
The early church	The early Jewish congregations of the followers of Jesus in Palestine, independent of Paul and later Hellenistic development of the church.
The early church tradition	The oral (or written) traditions passed down from the early church, including the Jesus traditions (about the life and teaching of Jesus), some confessional formula, and interpretive traditions.
Authenticity or *authentic*	A certain feature in the Synoptic Gospels is considered to be *authentic* to the early church, when it is not the distinctive work of the Gospel writers but reflects some traditional material from the early church.
Adam-Jesus typology	An implicit primitive scheme of comparison and contrast between Jesus and Adam, which is a diverse and fluid paradigm of thought—not a single coherent doctrine—in the early church.
Rhetorical purposes	Paul's specific goals in persuading his readers in their specific situation in his ethical teaching and pastoral exhortation.[56]
Eschatology or eschatological	The end of time (or the anticipation of the end of time) as the culmination of God's decisive intervention in human history.[57]

In addition to these definitions, I have to make four presuppositions in order to limit the scope of this study.

Presuppositions

Firstly, with regards to the Synoptic Problem, I accept a modified version of the "Two-Source Theory." I accept that Matthew and Luke depended on Mark and Q, and wrote independently of each other.⁵⁸ However, I am also open to the possibility that certain materials in M or L could have been derived from the early church traditions (*ex traditionibus*) rather than having been created by the Evangelists themselves out of nothing (*ex nihilo*).⁵⁹ Although many other interesting theories concerning the Synoptic Problem have emerged in recent scholarship,⁶⁰ I will not consider them as alternatives in this study.

Secondly, I presuppose that the Evangelists worked with various (oral or written) sources within the early church tradition, which were available to them.⁶¹ There exists a wide spectrum of scholarly

---

56. While appreciating many points of what Ben Witherington III and others call "socio-rhetorical criticism," I am not using in this study the term "rhetorical" in particular association with their approaches; Witherington, *What's in the Word*, 1–17.

57. This is the general sense of the word that I use in this study. This is not a study on New Testament eschatology *per se*; since the word "eschatology" is one of the most widely used words in New Testament studies, it is difficult to provide its precise meaning out of its context. See many definitions of the word in Wright, *Jesus and the Victory of God*, 208.

58. Brown, *Introduction to the New Testament*, 114–16; we can never be sure whether a hypothetical source such as Q independently existed as a text or not, despite the recent enthusiasm in Q research; cf. Robinson and Kloppenborg, ed., *Critical Edition of Q*, xv. The question of the independent existence of Q or its form does not seriously affect my discussion in this study, as much as the fact that Matthew and Luke shared certain sources with each other.

59. Similarly, Baum, *Mündliche Faktor und seine Bedeutung für die synoptische Frage*, 415–17; I am critical of Tuckett's implicit assumption that all material unique to Matthew (M) or Luke (L) is inevitably the Evangelist's redaction, simply because it is not attested in Mark or Q; Tuckett, "Synoptic Tradition in 1 Thessalonians?" 176–82.

60. E.g., Burkett, *Rethinking the Gospel Sources*, 133–42; Goodacre, *Synoptic Problem*, 162–66; Farmer, "Case for the Two-Gospel Hypothesis," 97–135; Goulder, *Luke*, 22–23; cf. Tuckett's criticism of the Griesbach hypothesis in Tuckett, *Revival of the Griesbach Hypothesis*.

61. This presupposition is an extension of my first presupposition and is compatible with Baum's hypothetical scenario. There has been escalated scholarly interest in recent

opinions concerning the level of redaction in the Gospels. Although the Evangelists often demonstrate their role and ability as redactors, I presuppose that, on the whole, they took the early church tradition seriously and preserved its essence in their writings—unless the evidence in a particular case indicates otherwise.[62]

Thirdly, I presuppose that the traditions behind many of the Synoptic Son of Man sayings in essence reflect the Christology of the

---

years in the oral transmission of the Jesus tradition from the early church. Although this is an important subject, it goes beyond the scope of this study; cf. Witherington, *What's in the Word*, 121–42; Eddy and Boyd, *Jesus Legend*, 237–308; Bauckham, *Jesus and the Eyewitnesses*, 240–357; Schröter, "Jesus and the Canon," 104–24; Robbins, "Interfaces of Orality and Literature in the Gospel of Mark," 125–46; Dunn, *Jesus Remembered*, 173–254; Gerhardsson, "Secret of the Transmission of the Unwritten Jesus Tradition," 1–18; Byrskog, *Story as History—History as Story*, 254–306.

62. Marcus adds this critique: "Martin Werner's assertion that the agreements between Mark and Paul reflect general early Christian viewpoints is not valid with regard to the theology of the cross, which was a controversial Pauline emphasis and a stress that the later Gospels attenuated in editing Mark"; Marcus, "Mark—Interpreter of Paul," 473–87; cf. Werner, *Einfluss paulinischer Theologie im Markusevangelium*. I will make a few preliminary comments here. Firstly, while Marcus rightly observes the fact that both Paul and Mark portray Jesus as a new Adam, his claim that Mark is interpreting Paul's Adam Christology is troublesome, when we compare the implicit primitive Adam-Jesus typology in Mark with Paul's explicit and sophisticated Adam Christology. If Mark simply follows Paul, Mark would have attested more explicit and sophisticated Adam Christology comparable to Paul's Adam Christology in his letters. Secondly, the fact that both Mark and Paul make negative comments on Peter and Jesus' family members can hardly be evidence that Mark is following Paul, as Marcus suggests. In fact, Paul in Gal 2 never makes any negative comments particularly towards Jesus' family members. Also, we have to remember the fact that Paul in Gal 2 opposes Peter because of his particular action in a specific situation, which hardly suggests that such criticism is why Jesus rebukes Peter in Mark 8:31–33. Thirdly, "that Jesus came not for the righteous but for ungodly sinners (e.g., Mark 2:17; Rom 4:15; 5:18–19)" is one of the characteristics of Jesus' ministry with which most scholars in the study of the historical Jesus agree. Marcus' claim that it is the evidence for Mark's dependence on Paul is hardly convincing. Fourthly, the fact that Ignatius of Antioch—whom Marcus identifies with "a later Paulinist"—puts more emphasis on the Jesus tradition than Paul does not necessarily suggest that Mark incorporated the Jesus tradition into his (Pauline) *kerygma*. It could simply be because "later Paulinists" had access to more accumulative and solidified forms of the Jesus tradition than Paul so that they could make more specific and identifiable references to the Jesus tradition than Paul. Fifthly, Mark's "extraordinary stress on the death of Jesus" is not so unique to Paul's theology of the cross, unless we call both Matthew and Luke "Paulinists." This supposedly "Pauline" theme is definitely not limited to Paul but belongs to the fundamental *kerygma* of the early church, attested throughout the New Testament.

early church.⁶³ Obviously, we cannot verify how close the Christology of the Synoptic Son of Man sayings is to that of the early church. Their Christology may reflect the Christology of Hellenistic Christianity rather than the Christology of the early church. However, since "the Son of Man" never became a Christological title outside of the Gospels in the history of Greek-speaking Christianity, it most likely originated from the early church.⁶⁴ Despite the Evangelists' paraphrasing, I presuppose that Mark 10:45 and Matt 19:28//Luke 22:30 preserve the verbal and conceptual core of the early church Son of Man saying traditions.⁶⁵

Fourthly, I presuppose that Paul as the earliest New Testament writer had access to the same early church tradition as that reflected in the Gospels, because he widely travelled Palestine and interacted with other Jewish believers in the early church during his apostolic ministry.⁶⁶ The four presuppositions that I have mentioned are not universally

63. It goes beyond the scope of this study to discuss which Son of Man saying is dominical and which is not. There has been complicated discussion among scholars on the precise meaning of the odd phrase ὁ υἱὸς τοῦ ἀνθρώπου attested in the Synoptic Gospels. For the purpose of this study, we do not need to engage in such debate. In my opinion, Richard Bauckham's view that Jesus used *bar nasha* in the indefinite sense ("a man," "someone") as "a form of deliberately oblique or ambiguous self-reference" best explains the New Testament evidence; Bauckham, "Son of Man," 29.

64. E.g., Collins, *Mark*, 187–89; Stein, *Mark*, 121; Casey, *Solution to the 'Son of Man' Problem*, 314–19; Boring, *Mark*, 251–52; Hooker, *Gospel According to Saint Mark*, 88–93; Gundry, *Mark*, 456; Nolland, *Luke 9:21—18:34*, 473–74. Recently, Hurtado suggests: "The most likely reason that the Jesus tradition linked Jesus so closely and uniquely with the expression is that he actually used it. That is, Jesus likely made בר אנשא his preferred self-designation, which formed a salient feature of his own speech-practice, his 'voice' or manner of speaking, in linguistic terms, his 'idiolect'"; Hurtado, "Summary and Concluding Observations," 174–75.

65. Hurtado notes: "The origin of the expression [ὁ υἱὸς τοῦ ἀνθρώπου] probably does lie in some Aramaic expression. But the Greek phrasing and probably the underlying Aramaic equivalent were both unusual, and were each intended to connote a particularizing sense. The most economical explanation for the restricted pattern of usage of 'the son of man' in the Gospels is that it reflects a reverential attitude towards Jesus' own distinctive use of an Aramaic equivalent, and an effort to convey that use in the Greek rendition of Jesus' sayings. The evidence of choice in the retention and deployment of the expression in the Gospels probably reflects the aim of the authors (and the tradition on which they drew) to give the sayings of Jesus a certain recognizable verisimilitude, using what had become known as a key feature of Jesus' speech-practice"; ibid., 176–77.

66. Concerning the issue of Pauline authorship, I have my own view but I follow Raymond E. Brown's view in this study in order to engage in broader scholarship. Brown points out that most Pauline scholars take 1 Thessalonians, Galatians, Philippians, Philemon, 1 and 2 Corinthians, and Romans as authentic letters, while

but still widely accepted by critical scholars and provide a foundation and a boundary, which will enable me to pursue more focused and effective investigation.

The Plan of this Study

In chapter 2, section 1 (on Phil 2:6–11), I will discuss the relationship between the early church Adam-Jesus typology and Paul's Adam Christology under three headings:

a. The *Authenticity* of Phil 2:6–11

b. The Early Church Adam-Jesus Typology in Phil 2:6–11

c. Paul's Use of the Early Church Adam-Jesus Typology

Since Pauline authorship of Philippians is universally accepted, if Phil 2:6–11 contains the early church Adam-Jesus typology, as we will see later, Paul creatively uses it in Phil 2:1–18. However, the other cases are not as simple as Phil 2:6–11 and I must discuss whether or not Paul alludes to a particular tradition. In chapter 2, section 2 (on Hebrews 2:5–11) and section 3 (on Mark 14:62), I will discuss the following topics:

a. The *Authenticity* of Heb 2:5–11/Mark 14:62

b. The Early Church Adam-Jesus Typology in Heb 2:5–11/Mark 14:62

c. Paul's Allusion to the Early Church Adam-Jesus Typology

d. Paul's Use of the Early Church Adam-Jesus Typology

In section 4 ("Paul's Adam Christology and First-Century AD Judaism"), I will examine the possibility that Paul derived his Adam Christology exclusively from first-century AD Judaism without any influence of the early church tradition.

When I discuss the *authenticity* of each passage in chapters 2 and 3, my focal point is the early church rather than the historical Jesus.

---

taking 2 Thessalonians, Colossians, Ephesians, and the Pastoral Letters (1 and 2 Tim and Titus) as "deutero-Pauline" writings; Brown, *Introduction to the New Testament*, 5–7. Although Paul's students might have written these "deutero-Pauline" writings, I still consider them as valuable evidence for the development of Pauline theology. I do not include Acts in discussing Paul in this study because Adam Christology does not appear in it and most scholars today question how close Luke's portrait of Paul is to the historical figure. I primarily will focus on the so-called "undisputed" letters in this study.

Also, my investigation will be limited to the specific verse(s) that I will be discussing at the moment. This book is a study about how the New Testament writers adapt the early church tradition. When dealing with the Synoptic Son of Man saying traditions, I am only interested in the ways that the early church understood them—as later reflected in the Gospels—not in discovering or reconstructing the so-called "authentic" Son of Man sayings spoken by the historical Jesus.[67] Unfortunately, commentators do not sharply define what they mean by "editorial" or "redactional" with the Gospel material. The Evangelists often seem to "edit" or "redact" the early church traditions (*ex traditionibus*) rather than creating new materials out of nothing (*ex nihilo*). When I discuss the early church Adam-Jesus typology in each passage in chapter 2, I will present various pieces of evidence for its existence.

When discussing Paul's allusion to the early church Adam-Jesus typology in each passage in chapter 2, sections 1–3, I need an objective and systematic way to determine whether or not Paul refers to a particular early church tradition. I will adapt Michael Thompson's scheme, modified by David Wenham in order to distinguish the level of Paul's Allusion to the early church tradition[68]:

---

67. Both Lindars and Casey identify six "authentic" Son of Man sayings in Mark and Q, in relation to the historical Jesus; Lindars, *Jesus Son of Man*, 29–59; Casey, *Solution to the 'Son of Man' Problem*, 116–43.

68. Thompson, *Clothed with Christ*, 28–36; Wenham, *Paul*, 25–31. Richard B. Hays' pioneering work *Echoes of Scripture in the Letters of Paul* has prompted considerable scholarly interest in the intertextuality in the New Testament. Discussing Paul's references to the Old Testament, Hays identifies "allusions" and "echoes" besides direct quotation. Hays explains, "*allusion* is used of obvious intertextual references, *echo* of subtler ones"; Hays, *Echoes of Scripture in the Letters of Paul*, 29. Hays' category of direct quotation certainly corresponds with "*explicit* reference," while that of *allusion* may correspond with "*verbal* and *formal* similarity" and that of *echo* with "*conceptual* similarity." Hays lists seven tests for "echoes": availability, volume, recurrence, thematic coherence, historical plausibility, history of interpretation and satisfaction; ibid., 29–32. I agree with Sim, "only the first two of them are in fact crucial for establishing an intertextual relationship"; Sim, "Matthew and the Pauline Corpus," 404; similarly, Brawley, *Text to Text Pours Forth Speech*, 13. Since I presuppose that Paul could have had access to the same sources as those that Evangelists used in their Gospels, only the criterion of volume (and not that of availability)—how loud Paul echoes the Jesus traditions—matters.

Level of Allusion	Description
Explicit reference	When Paul clearly refers to a tradition with or without so-called "tradition indicators"
Verbal and *formal* similarity	When Paul echoes the early church traditions with some expressions in common
Conceptual similarity	When, despite the lack of common expressions, Paul displays distinctive ideas in common

In general, *explicit* references provide the strongest evidence of the early church tradition.[69] When dealing with a *conceptual* similarity between a particular early church tradition and Paul's Adam Christology, I will examine whether or not the respective *conceptual* similarity is specific enough to suggest Paul's dependence on that particular tradition. If the *conceptual* similarity between the early church tradition and Paul's Adam Christology is too broad, the case for Paul's dependence on the early church tradition is not persuasive.

Tuckett warns against the potential circular argument of using Pauline evidence in Gospel studies:

> If Paul explicitly cites a tradition about Jesus, it is surely legitimate to use this evidence in seeking to analyse parallel traditions which occur in the Gospels. If, however, Paul only appears to cite a tradition, then it becomes rather harder to justify using the Pauline evidence in this way . . . To point to a possible parallel between Paul and a feature usually regarded as redactional in the Gospels, and then to claim both that Paul is alluding to Jesus tradition *and* that the Pauline evidence shows that the Gospel material is pre-redactional, is to argue in a potentially dangerous circle. In the case of possible implicit allusions to Jesus traditions in Paul, one should perhaps first of all seek to analyse the Synoptic parallels in their own right and only bring the Pauline evidence into the discussion secondarily . . . The simple fact that Paul pre-dates the Gospels should make us at least alive to the possibility that any line of dependency may run from Paul to the Gospels rather than from Jesus (or any early tradition) to Paul and the Gospels separately.[70]

---

69. Wenham warns us about the danger of two extreme positions with regards to discovering Paul's allusions to the Jesus tradition: "parallelmania" and "parallelphobia." The former refers to the tendency that places "great significance in almost every possible parallel between Paul and Jesus" and the latter describes those who "are determinedly sceptical" of any parallel; Wenham, *Paul*, 25.

70. Tuckett, "Synoptic Tradition in 1 Thessalonians?" 162.

Tuckett rightly warns us of the danger of both identifying loose parallels between redacted Synoptic material and Paul and, then, concluding that Paul is alluding to the pre-redactional Synoptic material. However, I need to make a few comments on Tuckett's guidelines.

Firstly, deciding whether Paul in a particular passage cites the early church tradition explicitly or implicitly is not as straightforward as it may sound, because it inevitably involves one's subjective judgment. Some minimalists are even skeptical about a few exceptionally strong cases of Paul's explicit citation of the early church tradition.[71] Secondly, deciding whether or not certain features in the Gospels are redactional also depends on one's subjective judgment to a certain degree.[72] Thirdly, as Tuckett himself admits, since the Pauline evidence pre-dates the Gospels, it is legitimate for us to use it as secondary evidence to reconstruct the early church tradition. Fourthly, we must consider Paul's citation of the early church tradition in the wider context of the early Christian writers' usage of it. As Thompson emphasizes:

> The general lack of appeal to the Jesus Tradition in early Christian writings is no secret, but surprisingly few have seen its significance for the Jesus-Paul debate; minimalists who emphasize the apostle's silence seem oblivious to the data . . . The absence of direct quotation of Jesus in works attributed to people who knew him well (1 Peter, James, Jude) and the rarity of direct citations in writings composed long after our Gospels were written obviate the force of the specific argument that Paul's practice shows he did not know or was not interested in sayings of Jesus.[73]

Unless we make Paul an exception to the norm of how early Christian writers used the early church tradition, we are unjustified to consider only his explicit citation of the early church tradition as evidence and to ignore his possible allusions to or echoes of it. Due to the

---

71. For instance, Francis Watson interestingly argues that Paul in 1 Cor 11:23–25 does not refer to the Jesus tradition concerning Jesus' last supper but to "a revelation to Paul" given by the exalted Lord; Watson, "'I Received from the Lord,'" 103–24. Watson tries to emphasize the continuity between Paul and Jesus in his own terms; however, his argument that Paul himself came up with the Words of Institution in 1 Cor 11:23–25 is unconvincing.

72. Some scholars attribute certain parallels between the Gospels and Paul to the Evangelists' direct dependence on Paul rather than their common sources; cf. Sim, "Matthew and the Pauline Corpus," 411–18; Tuckett, "Synoptic Tradition in 1 Thessalonians?" 168–76.

73. Thompson, *Clothed with Christ*, 62–63.

limited data concerning the early church tradition, unfortunately, I have to frequently use Pauline evidence in discussing whether or not a certain NT passage is *authentic* to the early church. In these cases, however, I will justify my argument in two ways. Firstly, I will refer to an independent (non-Pauline) piece of evidence in addition to Pauline evidence, whenever it is available. Secondly, whenever such evidence is not available, I will emphasize both the convergence and the divergence between each passage and Paul, which make any direct literary dependence on each other unlikely.

In chapter 3, section 1 ("Mark 10:45") and section 2 ("Matt 19:28// Luke 22:30"), I will argue that Paul creatively incorporates the Son of Man saying tradition into his Adam Christology. I will discuss the following topics:

a. The *Authenticity* of Mark 10:45 and Matt 19:28//Luke 22:30

b. Paul's Allusion to the Early Church Tradition behind Mark 10:45 and Matt 19:28//Luke 22:30

c. Paul's Incorporation of the Early Church Tradition behind Mark 10:45 and Matt 19:28//Luke 22:30 into His Adam Christology

d. Paul's Presentation of Jesus' Atoning Death and Isa 53; Paul's Presentation of Jesus' Followers' Eschatological Ruling and Dan 7

e. Paul's Presentation of Jesus' Atoning Death and First-Century AD Judaism; Paul's Presentation of Jesus' Followers' Eschatological Ruling and First-Century AD Judaism

When discussing the second topic, I will use the same method as that in chapter 2 with the category of *"explicit* reference," *"verbal* and *formal* similarity," and *"conceptual* similarity." When discussing the fourth topic, I will examine the possibility that Paul derived the idea of Jesus' atoning death or Jesus' followers' eschatological ruling exclusively from the Scripture (Isa 53 or Dan 7) without any influence from the early church tradition. When discussing the fifth topic, I will examine the possibility that Paul derived the idea of Jesus' atoning death or his followers' eschatological ruling exclusively from first-century AD Judaism without any influence from the early church tradition.

2

The Early Church Adam-Jesus Typology as a Source of Paul's Adam Christology

THE POSSIBILITY THAT PAUL uses the early church tradition as a source of his Adam Christology has not been seriously considered in recent New Testament scholarship. I will argue in this chapter that Paul uses the early church Adam-Jesus typology as a source of his Adam Christology. When developing his explicit and sophisticated Adam Christology, Paul creatively uses the implicit primitive Adam-Jesus typology of the early church as a source of his explicit and sophisticated Adam Christology in Rom 5 and 1 Cor 15. I will discuss Phil 2:6–11, Heb 2:5–11, and Mark 14:62. Since Phil 2:6–11 is an extremely important piece of evidence for the early church Adam-Jesus typology and has been one of the most controversial passages in New Testament studies, I will investigate it far more in depth than the others.

PHILIPPIANS 2:6–11

Gaius Plinius Caecilius Secundus, the appointed governor of Bithynia Pontus by Emperor Trajan in 111 (and died in 113), reports to the Emperor about Christians:

> They [Christians] also asserted that all of their guilt or error was that they used to come together on a certain day before daylight to sing a song with responses to Christ as a god, to bind themselves mutually by a solemn oath (*sacramentum*), not to commit any crime, but to avoid theft, robbery, adultery, not to break a trust or deny a deposit when they are called for it. After these practices it was their custom to separate and then come together again to take food but an ordinary and harmless kind, and they

even gave up this practice after my edict, when, in response to your order, I forbade associations. This convinced me that it was all the more necessary to find out what the truth was by the torture of two female slaves who were called deaconesses. I found nothing else but a depraved and excessive superstition.[1]

Considering Pliny's report that his two captured deaconesses were slaves and that Christians sang a song before daylight on a certain day, there is an interesting possibility that Phil 2:6–11 could have been one of the hymns that they sang. The phrase "taking the form of a slave" in Phil 2:7 and the idea of Christ's humility that runs through in Phil 2:6–8 certainly make such speculation attractive.

Marcus Bockmuehl notes, "Like the proverbial vultures over a carcass, twentieth-century New Testament scholars have tenaciously continued to congregate around the supposed 'hymn' of Phil 2:5–11." He continues, "As a result, this passage is one of the most over-interpreted texts of the New Testament . . . none but the most conceited could claim to have mastered the secondary literature."[2] If Phil 2:6–11 is an early church "hymn" and reflects the early church Adam-Jesus typology, it provides crucial evidence for the Christology of the early church. Unfortunately, the lack of evidence concerning the worship practice of the early church and the scope of this study preclude the possibility of seeking to prove that Phil 2:6–11 is an early church hymn or to interact with every view expressed in contemporary New Testament scholarship concerning its origin. Therefore, I will limit my discussion to the following three topics: (a) the *authenticity* of Phil 2:6–11, (b) the early church Adam-Jesus typology in Phil 2:6–11, and (c) Paul's use of the early church Adam-Jesus typology in the context of his ethical instruction in Phil 2:1–18.[3]

---

1. Benko's translation of Pliny, *Epistula* 10.96; Benko, "Pagan Criticism of Christianity During the First Two Centuries," 1068–76.

2. Bockmuehl, "'Form of God' (Phil 2:6)," 1.

3. Paul does not develop explicit and sophisticated Adam Christology in Phil 2:1–18, as he does in Rom 5 and 1 Cor 15. As we will see shortly, however, Paul alludes to the implicit primitive Adam-Jesus typology of the early church and creatively uses it for his ethical instruction in Phil 2:1–18.

The Early Church Adam-Jesus Typology 25

The Authenticity of Phil 2:6–11

Arguments concerning Form

Ernst Lohmeyer's groundbreaking work *Kyrios Jesus* published in 1928 persuaded many scholars that Paul cites an early church hymn in Phil 2:6–11. Lohmeyer calls Phil 2:6–11 "Stück urchristlicher Psalmdichtung" ("a piece of early Christian poetry-psalm") or "ein *Carmen Christi* in strengem Sinne" ("a hymn to Christ in a strict sense").[4] According to Nikolaus Walter, "The term 'hymn' was accepted later in the 1950s and 1960s, as scholars hoped to be able to identify in the New Testament as many as possible coined phrases as liturgical texts from the early Christian worship service."[5] In contrast to the almost universal acceptance of Lohmeyer's proposal in the previous decades,[6] more and more scholars in recent years have repudiated the view that Phil 2:6–11 is either a hymn or pre-Pauline.[7] After examining their major objections

---

4. Lohmeyer, *Kyrios Jesus*, 7.

5. My translation of "Die Bezeichnung als ‚Hymnus' setze sich später (in den 50er und 60er Jahren), als man hoffte, im NT möglichst viele geprägte Textstücke als liturgische Texte aus dem urchristlichen Gottesdiest identifizieren zu können"; Walter, "Brief an die Philipper," 56.

6. E.g., Bultmann, "Theology of the New Testament," 175; Cullmann, *Christology of the New Testament*, 174–75; Scroggs, *Last Adam*, 90; Deichgäber, *Gotteshymnus und Christushymnus in den frühen Christenheit*, 22–24; Marshall, "Christ-Hymn in Philippians 2:5–11," 113; Sanders, *New Testament Christological Hymns*, 1–5; Murphy-O'Connor, "Christological Anthropology in Phil 2:6–11," 25–29; Dunn, *Christology in the Making*, 128; Parkman, "Adam Christological Motifs in the Synoptic Traditions," 84; Hengel, *Between Jesus and Paul*, 78–96; Martin, *Carmen Christi*, 297–99; Sahlin, "Adam-Christologie im neuen Testament," 26; Wengst, *Humility*, 48; Fitzmyer, "Aramaic Background of Philippians 2:6–11," 483; Kreitzer, "When He at Last Is First!" 111; Dunn, *Theology of Paul the Apostle*, 281; Oakes, *Philippians*, 207–10; Holloway, *Consolation in Philippians*, 122; Williams, *Enemies of the Cross of Christ*, 60–78; Hurtado, *Lord Jesus Christ*, 146–48; Martin and Hawthorne, *Philippians*, lxxiv, 99–100; Longenecker, "Christological Materials in the Early Christian Communities," 71; Thurston and Ryan, *Philippians & Philemon*, 79; Cousar, *Philippians and Philemon*, 53.

7. E.g., Baumert, *Weg des Trauens*, 308; Theobald, "'Der Galaterbrief' und 'der Philipperbrief,'" 379; Reumann, *Philippians*, 374–77; Park, *Submission within the Godhead and the Church in the Epistle to the Philippians*, 12, 16; Silva, *Philippians*, 93; Fowl, *Philippians*, 108–13; Bockmuehl, "'Form of God' (Phil 2:6)," 2; Brucker, *'Christushymnen' oder 'Epideiktische Passagen?'* 318–22; Reed, *Discourse Analysis of Philippians*, 135–36; Fee, *Paul's Letter to the Philippians*, 40–43, 193; Basevi and Chapa, "Philippians 2:6–11," 356; O'Brien, *Epistle to the Philippians*, 198–202; Pate, *Adam Christology as the Exegetical & Theological Substructure of 2 Corinthians 4:7—5:21*, 90; Fowl, *Story of Christ in the Ethics of Paul*, 44–45; Wright, "*Harpagmos* and the Meaning

to Lohmeyer's proposal—that Phil 2:6–11 is a hymn and pre-Pauline—I will argue that, although Phil 2:6–11 may not be a pre-Pauline early church hymn, it evidently reflects some confessional formula of the early church.

Stephen E. Fowl argues against considering Phil 2:6–11 as a hymn for the following reasons. Firstly, Fowl argues that the content of Phil 2:6–11 (or any other supposed hymns in the New Testament) does not fit the definition of ὕμνος in the first-century AD setting. According to Fowl, ὕμνοι in Greek literature have three common features: (a) they are "directed to gods," (b) they begin "by justifying the need to praise," and (c) they "regularly end in a prayer petition."[8] Fowl also claims that, whenever the term ὕμνος appears in the LXX, it is "used to designate a song of praise to God."[9] Fowl concludes, "This would indicate that, for a Greek-speaking Jew, the term could be used in two senses. The first is fairly specific, and similar to that found in Hellenistic texts. The second sense is more generic, referring to a relatively formalized expression directed to God."[10] Since Phil 2:6–11 neither shows the three common features in Hellenistic ὕμνοι nor is directed to God (cf. ὕμνοι in the LXX), Fowl and others argue that it is not a ὕμνος ("hymn").[11]

Fowl and others rightly warn us against the danger of uncritically applying Hermann Gunkel's term "hymn"[12]—one of his seven major types (*Gattungen*) of Psalm—to our understanding of the ὕμνοι mentioned in Col 3:16 and Eph 5:19 or those NT passages that are often assumed to be hymns (e.g., Phil 2:6–11; Col 1:15–20; 1 Tim 3:16).[13] Gordon D. Fee graphically depicts this situation, "This whole matter [of calling Phil

---

of Philippians 2:5–11," 352; Garland, "Composition and Unity of Philippians," 158–59; Kim, *Origin of Paul's Gospel*, 148–49; Häusser, *Christusbekenntnis und Jesusüberlieferung bei Paulus*, 227.

8. Fowl, *Story of Christ in the Ethics of Paul*, 31–32.

9. E.g., 2 Chr 7:6; Neh 12:24, 46, 47; Jdt 15.16; Ps 99:4; 118:171; 148:14; Sir 44.1; 1 Macc 4.33; Fowl, *Story of Christ in the Ethics of Paul*, 32.

10. Fowl, *Story of Christ in the Ethics of Paul*, 33.

11. E.g., ibid., 109; Park, *Submission within the Godhead and the Church in the Epistle to the Philippians*, 12–13; Fee, *Paul's Letter to the Philippians*, 193; Berger, "Hellenistischen Gattungen im Neuen Testament," 1151.

12. Gunkel and Begrich, *Einleitung in die Psalmen*, 32.

13. E.g., Park, *Submission within the Godhead and the Church in the Epistle to the Philippians*, 12–13; Fowl, *Story of Christ in the Ethics of Paul*, 34–37; Berger, "Hellenistischen Gattungen im Neuen Testament," 1151; Fee, *Paul's Epistle to the Philippians*, 193–94.

2:6–11 a 'hymn'] seems to be a case of cross-pollination, whereby the exalted nature of this passage, plus its obvious poetry, is merged with a more contemporary use of the word 'hymn' and then read back into the first century."[14] Despite its validity, Fowl's and others' argument based on their narrow definition of ὕμνος is not entirely convincing, considering the fact that it is extremely difficult to define ὕμνος as a form despite its broadly shared stylistic features and content.[15] Although Phil 2:6–11 fails to include the three common features of Hellenistic ὕμνοι and is not specifically addressed to God, I think that it still can be considered as ὕμνος in a general sense, because it concerns the worship of Jesus (Phil 2:9–11; cf. Isa 45:22–25).[16] The mere fact that it is not addressed to God cannot justify Fowl's and others' claim that it is not a hymn, when we consider the worship of Jesus in Phil 2:6–11 along with its other features that I will discuss shortly.

The second and the most important argument against considering Phil 2:6–11 as a hymn is that it does not follow the formal patterns of Greek hymnody or Hebrew psalmody. Walter comments, "When Lohmeyer spoke of a 'psalm,' he referred to the rules of composition of the Old Testament psalms, with which, admittedly, the construction he accepted in six stanzas of three lines interferes because the two-line *parallelismus membrorum* predominates in Hebrew poetry."[17] However, Fee

14. Ibid., 194; Fowl similarly states, "In calling these passages hymns [Phil 2:6–11; Col 3:16–17; Eph 5:19–20] we are using a term that is the construction of a later, critical community, and not a straightforward translation of ὕμνος in either its specific or generic sense"; Fowl, *Story of Christ in the Ethics of Paul*, 33.

15. Parker points out: "'Hymn' is a simple transliteration of a Greek word; but the relation of Greek to English hymns is not at all simple. ὕμνος has at least three meanings; (1) a song of any kind, (2) any song in honour of a god, (3) a particular type of song in honour of a god. Hymns in this narrow sense may have been principally what the rhetorician Menander was to call 'cletic' or summoning hymns. As a working definition, (2) is the most useful, because the various forms differentiated in (3) probably shared numerous features of style and content"; Parker, "Hymn," 735; cf. Lattke, *Hymnus*, 13–90.

16. As Bauckham notes: "In his eschatological exercise of divine rule and in his bearing of the unique divine name, therefore, Jesus is the one who receives the worship in which the whole of God's creation finally acknowledges God's unique identity. This pattern of thought is not peculiar to Philippians 2 but is shared with a variety of other passages in early Christian literature and must therefore go back to a very early stage of Jewish Christianity"; Bauckham, "Worship of Jesus in Philippians 2:9–11," 136.

17. My translation of "Tatsächlich hatte auch Lohmeyer, als er von einem ‚Psalm' sprach, sich mehr an den Formgesetzen der at.lichen Psalmen orientiert, wobei freilich

notes, "The alleged Semitic parallelism of this piece is unlike any *known* example of Hebrew psalmody."[18] The fact that Lohmeyer and others have to eliminate some parts of it—almost always θανάτου δὲ σταυροῦ in Phil 2:8—to identify a consistent formal pattern in their hypothetical basetext (*Grundtext*) of Phil 2:6–11 in Aramaic or Hebrew signifies its deviation from normal hymnic patterns.[19] Gunter Kennel and others argue that, since Phil 2:6–11 does not follow Greek metrical laws, we should avoid calling Phil 2:6–11 a "hymn" for the sake of clarity.[20]

Klaus Berger and others attempt to identify Phil 2:6–11 with some other Greek literary forms, on the basis of their observation that Phil 2:6–11 does not follow the formal patterns of Greek hymnody. For instance, Berger and others claim that Phil 2:6–11 should be associated with the Greek literary form ἐγκώμιον rather than a hymn.[21] Ralph Brucker finds strong *epideictic* elements in Phil 2:6–11 in common with other Hellenistic rhetorical letters and argues that it has to be understood in relation to "more open categories" such as "style change" and "*epideictic* passages," dismissing the category of "hymn."[22] Walter calls Phil 2:6–11 "Lehrgedicht" ("didactic poem") instead of a "hymn," not

---

der von ihm angenommene Aufbau in sechs Strophen zu je drei Zeilen störte, weil in der hebräischen Dichtung ja eher der zweizeilige Parallelismus membrorum vorherrscht"; Walter, "Brief an die Philipper," 56.

18. Fee, *Paul's Letter to the Philippians*, 41.

19. E.g., Lohmeyer, *Brief an die Philiper*, 90; Jeremias, "Zur Gedankenführung in den paulinischen Briefen," 152–54; Martin, *Hymn of Christ*, 36–37.

20. Kennel, *Frühchristliche Hymn?*, 276; similarly, Fee, *Paul's Letter to the Philippians*, 41; Häusser pushes it further, "According to this research, one can give farewell to the assumption that there is a Christ hymn in Phil 2:6–11"; my translation of "Der Annahme, dass in Phil 2,6–11 ein Christushymnus vorliegt, kann man nach dieser Untersuchung also den Abschied geben"; Häusser, *Christusbekenntnis und Jesusüberlieferung bei Paulus*, 227.

21. Berger, "Hellenistischen Gattungen im Neuen Testament," 1173–4; similarly, Reumann, *Philippians*, 365; Fowl, *Philippians*, 108–9; Basevi and Chapa, "Philippians 2:6–11," 356; Malina and Neyrey define ἐγκώμιον as "a speech of praise" of "another person or some object that would be personified, such as a place or a polis"; Malina and Neyrey, *Portraits of Paul*, 23.

22. "Dabei hat es sich als sehr fruchtbar erwiesen, zunächst auf die hermeneutische Vorgabe ‚Hymnus' zu verzichten und von den offeneren Kategorien ‚Stilwechsel' und ‚epideiktische Passagen' auszugehen"; Brucker, *'Christushymnen' oder 'Epideiktische Passagen?'* 349; similarly, Basevi and Chapa, "Philippians 2:6–11," 338–56.

necessarily supposing Christian worship service as its context but yet considering its poetic formation.²³

In contrast, Edgar Krentz proposes that the supposed NT hymns (including Phil 2:6–11) follow the genre of Hellenistic and early Roman "prose hymns" in the form of the *epideictic encomion*.²⁴ Krentz points out, "Prose hymns [as opposed to earlier Greek hymns with dactylic hexameter] appear as early as the fourth century BC—though we first get examples in the Roman era."²⁵ Krentz also notes, "Greek rhetoricians define the hymn as a sub-category of the *encomion*, itself a form of *epideictic* rhetoric."²⁶ Krentz' proposal directly contrasts with Fee's view that Phil 2:6–11 is "exalted—poetic—prose" but not a hymn.²⁷ Fee argues that the very fact that there is no consensus among scholars on the arrangement of the supposed hymn in Phil 2:6–11 suggests that it is not a hymn.²⁸ While focusing on the distinctive characteristics of traditional Greek hymns, Fee and others seem to overlook another Hellenistic and early Roman genre called "prose hymns" as the potential form of Phil 2:6–11. This is not the place to examine Krentz' proposal in detail. If Krentz is right, however, it effectively undermines the claim that Phil 2:6–11 does not follow the formal patterns of Greek hymnody.

The third argument against considering Phil 2:6–11 as a hymn is that the fact that it is poetic and stands out from its immediate context does not necessarily prove that it is a hymn.²⁹ While admitting that Phil 2:6–11 stands as an independent unit and its language is distinctively poetic, some scholars deny that it is a hymn, using Rom 11:33–36 as

---

23. Walter, "Brief an die Philipper," 57.

24. Krentz, "Epideiktik and Hymnody," 89–93.

25. E.g., the hymns in the ἱεροὶ λόγοι of Ailios Aristides, the Hymns to Zeus in Ps.-Aristotle *De Mundo*, and the Hymn in honor of Isis in *P. Oxy.* 1380; ibid., 55.

26. Ibid.; cf. Quintilian (35–95 AD; *Institutes of Oratory* 3.7.1, 6–9); Alexander son of Numenios (early second century AD; a fragment of Τεχνὴ περὶ ἀφορμῶν ῥητορικῶν); Menander Rhetor (third/fourth century AD; Περὶ τῶν ὕμνων τῶν εἰς τοὺς θεοὺς "hymns directed to the gods" in ΓΕΝΕΘΛΙΩΝ ΔΙΑΡΕΣΙΣ ΤΩΝ ΕΠΙΔΕΙΚΤΙΚΩΝ "Division of Epideictic Speeches").

27. Fee, *Paul's Letter to Philippians*, 41.

28. Ibid., 42–43.

29. E.g., Park, *Submission within the Godhead and the Church in the Epistle to the Philippians*, 11; Fowl, *Philippians*, 111; Fee, *Paul's Letter to Philippians*, 41, 193.

their evidence.[30] While recognizing Paul's ability to cite: "previously formulated material," Fowl insists, "A passage like Rom 11:33–36 argues for the possibility of the composition of poetic speech in the midst of epistolary discourse."[31] Fowl implies here that Phil 2:6–11 is no more a hymn than is Rom 11:33–36. Although Paul uses both Phil 2:6–11 and Rom 11:33–36 "in the midst of epistolary discourse," a more careful reading of them in their immediate contexts reveals an important difference from each other in relation to their rhetorical purposes.

While Paul concludes his long discussion of Israel and the gospel in Rom 9–11 with the poetic doxology in Rom 11:33–36, he uses Phil 2:6–11 as the basis of his core argument in his ethical teaching in Phil 2:1–18. Regardless of whether Phil 2:6–11 is a hymn or not, it evidently has certain authority over the Philippians. Claudio Basevi and Juan Chapa rightly observe that Phil 2:6–11 "lays the foundations for an exhortation to the afflicted community of Christians in Philippi. Knowing what Christ was and what he did, they would be encouraged to stay faithful to the gospel as well as united to Christ, to Paul and amongst themselves."[32] Although Rom 11:33–36 sums up Rom 9–11 in significant ways, Paul does not depend on the authority of Rom 11:33–36 in developing his argument in the same way in which he depends on the authority of Phil 2:6–11 in developing his argument in Phil 2:1–18. Fowl claims, "Since the passage is relatively intelligible in its current context, we are not justified in assuming that Paul presumes the Philippians' prior exposure to it."[33] Fowl and Fee seem to neglect the important rhetorical function of Phil 2:6–11 in discerning its origin.

---

30. E.g., Fowl, *Philippians*, 111; Fee, *Paul's Letter to Philippians*, 41, 194; only Fee mentions 1 Cor 13 as a piece of evidence against the view that Phil 2:6–11 is a hymn. Fee argues that, just as the exalted prose with obvious style changes in 1 Cor 13 does not make it a hymn, the "exalted—poetic—prose" in Phil 2:6–11 does not make it a hymn, because "Paul is capable of especially exalted prose whenever he thinks on the work of Christ"; ibid., 41. In my opinion, as in the case of Rom 11:33–36, we should focus on Paul's rhetorical purposes in 1 Cor 13 rather than on his ability to use exalted prose. Unlike the case of Phil 2:6–11, Paul is not using 1 Cor 13 as an authority in support of his argument. Instead, he is using 1 Cor 13 as a poetic summary of the principles behind his instruction in 1 Cor 12–14 concerning the use of various spiritual gifts in the Corinthian church.

31. Fowl, *Philippians*, 111.

32. Basevi and Chapa, "Philippians 2:6–11," 356.

33. Fowl, *Philippians*, 113.

Fee also contrasts Phil 2:6–11 with Rom 11:33–36, "That Paul is capable of something hymnic is attested by Rom 11:33–36, which, like those in Luke 1 and 2, is a fine mixture of OT words and motifs with his own concerns, and which stands in contrast to this passage, precisely because both its poetry and form are those of a hymn in the first-century use of that word ['hymn']."[34] I agree with Fee that the "poetry and form" of Rom 11:33–36 look more like a hymn—praising God and adopting the two-line *parallelismus membrorum* of the Hebrew poetry—than those of Phil 2:6–11. Paul also demonstrates poetic language in Rom 11:33–36, using rare words such as ἀνεξεραύνητος ("unsearchable"[35])—a *hapax legomenon* word in the New Testament—and ἀνεξιχνίαστος ("inscrutable, incomprehensible"[36])—attested only in Eph 3:8 apart from Rom 11:33. Although Phil 2:6–11 does not follow the two-line *parallelismus membrorum* of Hebrew poetry as Rom 11:33–36 does, as I will discuss later, it appears to be an independent unit with highly poetic language with far more rare expressions than Rom 11:33–36, such as μορφὴ θεοῦ, ἴσα θεῷ, δοῦλος, ὑπερυψόω, ἁρπαγμὸν ἡγέομαι, and καταχθόνιος.[37] Although Phil 2:6–11's self-standing status with poetic language may not necessarily prove that it is a hymn, neither Fee nor anyone else has yet explained satisfactorily why Paul abruptly introduces such distinctive "exalted—poetic—prose," packed with extremely rare words, in the apex of his argument in his ethical instruction in Phil 2:1–18.

To sum up, a number of scholars rightly observe the fact that Phil 2:6–11 does not follow the formal patterns of typical Greek hymnody or Hebrew psalmody. Nonetheless, their argument that Phil 2:6–11 is not a hymn just because it is not directed to God is too simplistic. The fact that Phil 2:6–11 is an independent unit and poetic does not necessarily prove that it is a hymn. Such a fact, however, also does not necessarily prove that it is *not* a hymn. Although Phil 2:6–11 does not fit well into the normal structure of Greek hymns or Hebrew psalms, other characteristics such as the fact that it is a self-standing unit, its poetic language, and the

---

34. Fee, *Paul's Letter to Philippians*, 194.
35. BDAG, 77.
36. Ibid., 77.
37. O'Brien points out that Paul does not use μορφὴ θεοῦ, ἴσα θεῷ, δοῦλος elsewhere in his letters, while ὑπερυψόω and καταχθόνιος are *hapax legomena* in the New Testament and ἁρπαγμὸν ἡγέομαι is a *hapax legomenon* in the entire Greek Bible; O'Brien, *Epistle to the Philippians*, 199.

concentration of rare expressions demand a more satisfactory explanation than attributing them to Paul's "exalted—poetic—prose." Also, most scholars pay no attention to the important rhetorical role of Phil 2:6–11 in Paul's argument in Phil 2:1–18. Unlike the case of Rom 11:33–36 (or 1 Cor 13), Paul's whole argument in his ethical instruction in Phil 2:1–18 depends on the authority of Phil 2:6–11. Regardless of whether or not it is a hymn, it possesses significant authority over Paul and his readers. For the purpose of this study, the question of whether or not Phil 2:6–11 is a hymn is not as essential as its authority and rhetorical function. Even if Phil 2:6–11 is not a hymn but Paul's "exalted—poetic—prose," as Kennel points out, "Most likely, the text could be designated as a worked-out Christological confession text, without the claim of a genre-definition."[38] Or, as Riesenfeld suggests, it could have been "a rhetorically formed Christological teaching piece."[39] As Häusser observes, "Mnemonic aids such as parallelism indicate catechetical material."[40] Häusser notes, "That Phil 2:6–11 is a coherent piece of tradition may be regarded as relatively likely."[41] Phil 2:6–11 probably reflects some traditional piece of the Christological confession of the early church.[42] While recognizing that, form-critically speaking, Phil 2:6–11 does not fit the typical patterns of Greek hymnody or Hebrew psalmnody, I maintain that it contains some traditional elements from the early church. If Phil 2:6–11 is traditional and reflects the implicit primitive Adam-Jesus typology of the early church, as I will argue shortly, it is a definite piece of evidence that Paul was aware of the early church Adam-Jesus typology. I will respond now to some scholars' objections to the view that Phil 2:6–11 is pre-Pauline.

38. My translation of "Am ehesten könnte der Abschnitt noch als durchgeformter christologischer Bekenntnistext bezeichnet werden, ohne daß zunächst damit der Anspruch auf eine Gattungsbestimmung erhoben werden könnte"; Kennel, *Frühchristliche Hymn?* 276.

39. My translation of "Ein rhetorisch geformtes christologisches Lehrstück"; Risenfeld, "Unpoetische Hymnen im neuen Testament? Zu Phil 2,1–11," 168.

40. My translation of "Mnemotechnische Hilfsmittel wie Parallelismen sind auch ein Indiz für katechetisches Material"; Häusser, *Christusbekenntnis und Jesusüberlieferung bei Paulus*, 221.

41. My translation of "Dass es sich in Phil 2,6–11 um ein zusammenhängendes Traditionsstück handelt, darf als relativ wahrscheinlich angesehen warden"; ibid., 221.

42. Similarly, Hooker, "Philippians 2:6–11," 156; Fee, *Paul's Letter to the Philippians*, 193; Basevi and Chapa, "Philippians 2:6–11," 356; Marshall, *Epistle to the Philippians*, 48.

Linguistic Arguments

A number of scholars pose linguistic and theological arguments against the view that Phil 2:6–11 is pre-Pauline. I will examine their linguistic argument first and theological argument later. Some scholars argue that the linguistic evidence in Phil 2:6–11 does not necessarily challenge Pauline authorship. While they do not deny the concentration of unique words in Phil 2:6–11, they argue that it does not prove that Phil 2:6–11 is pre-Pauline.[43] In order to evaluate their argument, I have to discuss now each unusual expression in Phil 2:6–11.

Philippians 2:6

While calling Christ εἰκὼν τοῦ θεοῦ ("the image of God") in 2 Cor 4:4 (cf. Col 1:15), Paul never refers to Christ as ἐν μορφῇ θεοῦ ὑπάρχων ("being in the form of God") apart from Phil 2:6. As Peter T. O'Brien observes, "The theme of Christians being conformed or transformed into the image of Christ appears explicitly only in Paul's letters of the NT (Rom 8:29; 1 Cor 15:49; cf. v. 52; Phil 3:21; Col 3:9, 10; Eph 4:24)."[44] There is a certain connection between Paul's statement that Christ is εἰκὼν τοῦ θεοῦ and that Christians are transformed into his image. However, if Paul is highlighting such a connection in Phil 2:6 (as O'Brien seems to suggest), it is not so obvious why Paul is not using εἰκὼν τοῦ θεοῦ instead of the *hapax legomenon* μορφῇ θεοῦ. It seems more likely the case that Paul or another writer of Phil 2:6–11 is reflecting some traditional elements behind the phrase ἐν μορφῇ θεοῦ ὑπάρχων in Phil 2:6 from a pre-existing confessional formula, as Kennel and others suggest.[45]

Neither the expression τὸ εἶναι ἴσα θεῷ ("equality with God") nor the explicit claim in Phil 2:6 that Christ is equal to God is found anywhere else in the New Testament apart from John 5:18 in which the Jews accuse Jesus of his Sabbath healing and calling God his father. As John Reumann points out, "The 'Judaic tradition' does not let mortals 'think that they are equal to God' (2 Macc 9.12; cf. Philo, *Leg.* 1.49; *Sib. Or.* 5.34; 12.86)."[46] The unusual phrase τὸ εἶναι ἴσα θεῷ in Phil 2:6 certainly

---

43. E.g., Park, *Submission within the Godhead and the Church in the Epistle to the Philippians*, 15–16; Fowl, *Philippians*, 111–12; Fee, *Paul's Letter to the Philippians*, 45–46; O'Brien, *Epistle to the Philippians*, 198–200.

44. Ibid., 200.

45. E.g., Kennel, *Frühchristliche Hymn?* 276; Hooker, "Philippians 2:6–11," 156; Fee, *Paul's Letter to the Philippians*, 193; Basevi and Chapa, "Philippians 2:6–11," 356.

46. Reumann, *Philippians*, 345.

signifies Christian understanding of Jesus' unique identity in relation to God. It is not possible for us here to examine its origin or Christological implications in detail. Considering the fact that it is a *hapax legomenon* in the New Testament, however, Paul more likely is reflecting some early church tradition rather than his own thought as in the case of the phrase ἐν μορφῇ θεοῦ ὑπάρχων.

The noun ἁρπαγμός in Phil 2:6 is a *hapax legomenon* in the entire Greek Bible and also is rarely attested in extra-biblical Greek. It is notoriously difficult to determine the precise sense of the noun in its present context and space does not allow us to discuss its meaning in detail. In his comprehensive survey, Wright lists eighteen different ways of analyzing ἁρπαγμός and subsequent interpretations of μορφή, τὸ εἶναι ἴσα θεῷ, and οὐχ ἁρπαγμὸν ἡγήσατο.[47] Combining C. F. D. Moule's theology and Roy W. Hoover's philology, Wright proposes that οὐχ ἁρπαγμὸν ἡγήσατο has to be understood in the form of a Greek idiom ἁρπαγμὸν ἡγεῖσθαι τι that means "to consider-it-something-to-take-advantage-of."[48] Wright's view presupposes Christ's equality with God, translating Phil 2:6 as "Christ did not consider his equality with God as something to take advantage of."[49] Wright's proposal is widely accepted, not only because it fits well in the *paraenetic* context of Phil 2:6–11 but also because it has strong philological support.[50] Wright claims that, if his proposal is

---

47. Wright, "*Harpagmos* and the meaning of Phil 2:5–11," 342–43.

48. Ibid., 340; Moule argues that ἁρπαγμός signifies the action of the verb, while ἅρπαγμα signifies its result, which leads him to support both the positions of Lightfoot and the Greek Fathers in taking ἁρπαγμός in the abstract sense of "the act of snatching"; Moule, "Further Reflexions on Philippians 2:5–11," 264; on the basis of the various examples of the use of ἁρπαγμός in Greek literature, Hoover concludes that ἅρπαγμον ἡρεῖσθαι τι is a Greek idiom meaning "to regard as something to be taken advantage of" (e.g., Plutarch, *De Alexandri magni fortuna aut virtute* 8.330D; *Marcus Cato* 13.343F; *De liberis educandis* 15.12A; *Amatorius* 2.755B, C; Heliodorus, 4.6; 7.11, 20; 8.7; Vettius Valens 122.1; Strabo, *Geography* 10.4.21; Josephus, *Ant.* 11.5.6; Eusebius, *Hist. Eccl.* 8.12.2; *Vita Constantini* 31.2; Cyril of Alexander, *De Ador.* 1.25); Hoover, "*Harpagmos* Enigma," 95–119.

49. Wright, "*Harpagmos* and the meaning of Phil 2:5–11," 340.

50. Wright's other reasons include: (1) "it explains the relation of vv. 9–11 and vv. 6–8 in a much more satisfying way than the other views," (2) the frequently observed parallel between Phil 2:6–8 and Phil 3:4–6 can be maintained well, (3) his view makes "a characteristically cryptic reference to Adam" not only possible but also helpful, and (4) there are other passages that fits well into his view, e.g., Eusebius' *Historia Ecclesiae* 5.2.2; 8.12.1, Cyril of Alexandria's *De Ador.* 1.25; ibid., 346–52. Ralph P. Martin nominates Wright's essay on ἁρπαγμός as one of three "groundbreaking contributions" on

right, the precise use of a rare Greek idiom in Phil 2:6 such as ἁρπαγμὸν ἡγεῖσθαι τι strongly supports its Pauline authorship.⁵¹

Although the use of a highly sophisticated Greek idiom in Phil 2:6 such as ἁρπαγμὸν ἡγεῖσθαι τι demonstrates the author's familiarity with Greek language, in my opinion, it does not necessarily prove that Phil 2:6–11 is Pauline. Another capable bilingual person could have translated from Phil 2:6 an Aramaic phrase close to חשב שלל—Joseph A. Fitzmyer's reconstruction⁵²—using a sophisticated Greek idiom such as ἁρπαγμὸν ἡγεῖσθαι τι. In Aramaic (as well as in Hebrew), the verb חשב can mean "to consider" (cf. Dan 4:35⁵³), while the noun שלל means "booty, spoil, goods that have been plundered" or "gain, property, wealth."⁵⁴ As we will see shortly, the bilingualism of the author of Phil 2:6–11 becomes more evident in the case of the phrase σχήματι εὑρεθεὶς ὡς ἄνθρωπος in Phil 2:7.

Philippians 2:7

Paul uses the verb κενόω four times in the sense of "to cause to be without result or effect, destroy, render void or of no effect"—1 Cor 1:17; 9:15; 2 Cor 9:3; Rom 4:14; cf. Vettius Valen 90.7.⁵⁵ The phrase ἑαυτὸν ἐκένωσεν ("he emptied himself") in Phil 2:7 simply could be a metaphorical use of the verb. As Joachim Jeremias points out, however, this particular combination of the verb with a reflexive pronoun in the sense of "to make oneself empty" never appears outside of Phil 2:7.⁵⁶ Paul or another writer probably has in mind something close to the Hebrew expression

---

Phil 2:6–11, along with E. Lohmeyer's *Kyrios Jesus* (1928) and E. Käsemann's "Kritische Analyse von Phil 2:5–11" (1950); Martin, "Carmen Christi Revisited," 1. Reumann recently comments, "Wright's interpretation has dominated many Anglo-Saxon commentaries"; Reumann, *Philippians*, 347.

51. Wright, "*Harpagmos* and the meaning of Phil 2:5–11," 352.
52. Fitzmyer, "Aramaic Background of Philippians 2:6–11," 477.
53. All the inhabitants of the earth are accounted as nothing [כלה חשיבין], and he does what he wills with the host of heaven and the inhabitants of the earth"; חשיבין is the peal passive masculine plural participle of the verb חשב, meaning "being considered"; *HALOT*, 1880. I use NRSV as the primary English translation of the Bible and the Apocrypha, unless I indicate otherwise. All italicizations in the citation of primary source-texts in this study are mine for emphasis, unless I indicate otherwise.
54. Ibid., 1531–32.
55. BDAG, 539; LSJ, 938.
56. Jeremias, "Zur Gedankenführung in den paulinischen Briefen," 154.

הערה למות נפשו in Isa 53:12—"he poured out himself to death"—or its Aramaic equivalent.[57]

Paul or any other New Testament writer never calls Jesus δοῦλος ("servant") apart from Phil 2:7, whereas Jesus is called παῖς ("servant") in Matt 12:18; Acts 3:13, 26; 4:27 in association with the עבד יהוה in Isaiah and διάκονος ("servant") in Rom 15:8.[58] Hooker argues, "There is no linguistic evidence for regarding the words ἑαυτὸν ἐκένωσεν . . . μέχρι θανάτου as a reference to Isa 53:11[12]. While κενόω is a possible translation of ערה, it is not used in this sense in the LXX, nor is its primary meaning in this passage the actual death of Christ."[59] Although Hooker is right that the "emptying oneself" in Phil 2:7 concerns Christ's incarnation rather than his redemptive death, it is difficult to deny the link between Phil 2:6–11 and the Servant Songs in Deutero-Isaiah.[60] If the phrase μορφὴν δούλου λαβών ("taking the form of a slave") in Phil 2:7 alludes to the Suffering Servant in Isa 52:13—53:12, however,

---

57. Similarly, Dunn, *Christology in the Making*, 118; Habermann, *Präexistenzaussagen im Neuen Testament*, 129; Häusser, *Christusbekenntnis und Jesusüberlieferung bei Paulus*, 243. The *hiphil* form of ערה means "to uncover" (Lev 20:18), "to lay bare" (Zeph 2:14), or "to tip out [metaphorically, to throw away]" (Isa 53:12). However, in Middle Hebrew and Jewish Aramaic, it also means, "to pour out," which corresponds to the verb κενόω in Phil 2:7; *HALOT*, 881–82.

58. "For I tell you that Christ has become a *servant* of the circumcised on behalf of the truth of God in order that he might confirm the promises given to the patriarchs."

59. Hooker, *Jesus and the Servant*, 121; Hooker concludes, "Jesus himself was not profoundly influenced by the Servant passages in particular"; ibid., 163. While the phrase μέχρι θανάτου (Phil 2:8) is not immediately connected with the verb κενόω (Phil 2:7), as we have noted earlier, the verb ערה in Middle Hebrew and Jewish Aramaic can mean "to pour out" that corresponds with the verb κενόω in Phil 2:7; *HALOT*, 881–82. Hooker's rigid linguistic argument dismisses the fact that Phil 2:6–11 is not a *midrash* on Isa 52:13—53:12 but a Christological confession with possibly multiple allusions to the Old Testament. I cannot examine here Hooker's complex argument. However, even if Hooker is right that Jesus never considered himself as the Suffering Servant, the early church evidently associated Jesus with him (cf. Mark 10:45); see chapter 3 and Appendix 2 ("Jesus and the Suffering Servant").

60. As Fee points out: "Jesus himself interpreted his death in light of Isaiah 53, and Paul and the early church were quick to see that Christ's 'servanthood' was ultimately fulfilled in the 'pouring out of his life unto death' (Isa 53:12) for the sake of others. It is hard to imagine that early Christians, therefore, would not rather automatically have heard this passage [Phil 2:6–11] with that background [Isa 52:13—53:12] in view, especially since that passage begins ([Isa] 52:13) the way this one [Phil 2:9–10; cf. Isa 45:22–25] ends, with the Servant's exaltation by God"; Fee, *Paul's Letter to the Philippians*, 212.

we must wonder why the author of Phil 2:6–11 attests the word δοῦλος rather than παῖς in parallel with the LXX.

Firstly, Paul or another writer may have chosen the word δοῦλος in order to emphasize Christ's humiliation in Phil 2:6–8. As O'Brien points out, "both Greek terms (δοῦλος and παῖς) are used interchangeably in the LXX to render the עבד of Isa 40–55, with a preference for παῖς ([Isa] 42:1; 49:6; 50:10; 52:13; δοῦλος: [Isa] 49:3, 5; cf. 42:19; 48:20)."[61] Nonetheless, in Greek in general, the primary meaning of δοῦλος is "a slave,"[62] while that of παῖς is "a child."[63] Häusser raises an interesting possibility that the word δοῦλος used in Phil 2:7 corresponds not only to the עבד in Isa 52:13—53:12 but also to that in Gen 3:23, linking Christ's humiliation with that of Adam after his expulsion from the Garden of Eden, to which I will come back shortly.[64]

Secondly, Paul or another writer may have chosen the word δοῦλος in Phil 2:7 because it was a part of early Christian *paraenesis*. Larry W. Hurtado rightly observes its connection with Pauline *paraenesis* (e.g., Rom 6:19; 7:6, 25; 12:11; 14:18; 16:18; Gal 5:13; Phil 2:22; 1 Thess 1:9; cf. Col 3:24) and the Jesus tradition of the Gospels (Mark 10:43–45//Matt 20:25–28; Luke 22:24–27; Mark 9:35; Matt 23:11; cf. the δοῦλος imagery in Jesus' foot-washing in John 13:5–7).[65] When we consider Paul's ethical instruction in Phil 2:1–18, Hurtado is probably right to suggest, "The language used to describe Jesus' actions qualitatively in [Phil] 2:6–8 is drawn from the language of early Christian *paraenesis* and possibly from the Jesus tradition of the Pauline period."[66] Paul or another writer probably reflects the early church tradition in calling Jesus δοῦλος in Phil 2:7.

The phrase σχήματι εὑρεθεὶς ὡς ἄνθρωπος ("being found in human form") in Phil 2:7 is awkward in Greek. Following the structure of ἐν μορφῇ θεοῦ ὑπάρχων ("being in the form of God") in Phil 2:6 and μορφὴν δούλου λαβών ("taking the form of a slave") in Phil 2:7, we would expect the phrase σχήματι ἀνθρώπου εὑρεθείς to appear in normal Greek composition. Instead, we have the peculiar form ὡς ἄνθρωπος. As Lohmeyer comments, it is "linguistically impossible" in

61. O'Brien, *Epistle to the Philippians*, 270.
62. LSJ, 447.
63. Ibid., 1289.
64. Hässer, *Christusbekenntnis und Jesusüberlieferung bei Paulus*, 239–41.
65. Hurtado, "Jesus as Lordly Example in Philippians 2:5–11," 126.
66. Ibid.

Greek and it is the literal translation of the Aramaic phrase כבר אנש ("like a human being").⁶⁷

Both Theodotion and the translator of the Old Greek text of Daniel demonstrate a similar effort to preserve the Aramaic phrase כבר אנש in Dan 7:13.⁶⁸ Grammatically speaking, the clause is missing a subject in its nominative form in both translations. Semantically speaking, however, the prepositional phrase ὡς υἱὸς ἀνθρώπου is acting like a subject with a hypothetical indefinite pronoun τις before it. Both translators of Dan 7:13 could have polished the Greek, using another phrase like τις ὅμοιος ἀνθρώπῳ instead of ὡς υἱὸς ἀνθρώπου. Instead, they prefer a more literal rendering of the Aramaic phrase כבר אנש in Dan 7:13.⁶⁹ For the same reason, a literal translation of ὡς ἄνθρωπος is used in Phil 2:8 instead of the polished Greek expression ἀνθρώπου, which possibly reflects an earlier Aramaic tradition (*Vorlage*). Theoretically speaking, it could be the case that the author of Phil 2:6–11 does not reflect an earlier Aramaic tradition (*Vorlage*) but intentionally imitates the unpolished Greek of the Septuagint with Semitic elements. In that case, we must wonder why the author would have done so unless he specifically alludes to Dan 7:13 in the LXX—which is certainly not the case. Regardless of the existence of an earlier Aramaic tradition (*Vorlage*) behind Phil 2:6–11, various pieces of evidence for bilingualism in Phil 2:6–11 that we have observed so far suggest that it maintains some traditional components. If not, there is no reason to use an awkward Greek expression such as σχήματι εὑρεθεὶς ὡς ἄνθρωπος that reflects Aramaism, when writing to Gentile audience.

Philippians 2:9

The verb ὑψόω ("lift up, exalt") is a common word both in the New Testament and the LXX. However, the verb with a prefix ὑπερυψόω ("to raise someone to the loftiest height"⁷⁰) in Phil 2:9 is a *hapax legome-*

---

67. Lohmeyer, *Kyrios Jesus*, 38–40; similarly, Martin, *Hymn of Christ*, 207–9.

68. LXX-Θ: ἰδοὺ μετὰ τῶν νεφελῶν τοῦ οὐρανοῦ ὡς υἱὸς ἀνθρώπου ἐρχόμενος ἦν
LXX-OG: ἰδοὺ ἐπὶ τῶν νεφελῶν τοῦ οὐρανοῦ ὡς υἱὸς ἀνθρώπου ἤρχετο
MT: וארו עם־ענני שמיא כבר אנש אתה הוה

69. Fitzmyer reconstructs the expression σχήματι εὑρεθεὶς ὡς ἄνθρωπος in first-century A.D. Palestinian Aramaic—כבר־אנש משתכח ובחזו. The *hithpeel* participle of שכח ("to be found") is used along with the phrase—preposition ב and the noun חזו ("appearance"; cf. Dan 7:20)—followed by the phrase כבר אנש ("like a human being"); Fitzmyer, "Aramaic Background of Philippians 2:6–11," 478–79.

70. BDAG, 1034.

non in the New Testament. It is used only twice in the LXX (Ps 37:35[71]; 97:9[72]) apart from the *Book of Odes* 8 (*Ode* 8.52, 54, 55, 57–88).[73] The fact that this verb appears only in Psalms and the *Book of Odes* indicates that it is a highly poetic or hymnic expression. While the use of such expression highlights the poetic or hymnic characteristic of Phil 2:6–11, it does not particularly help us to discern whether or not Phil 2:6–11 is Pauline.

Philippians 2:10

The adjective καταχθόνιος ("under the earth") in Phil 2:10 is a *hapax legomenon* in the entire Greek Bible. As Lohmeyer points out, the expression ἐπουρανίων καὶ ἐπιγείων καὶ καταχθονίων in Phil 2:10 is only possible in Greek.[74] The adjective ἐπουράνιος ("heavenly") frequently appears in the New Testament but it is attested only four times in the LXX in Ps 68:14; 2 Macc 3.39; 6.28; 7.6. While the adjective ἐπίγειος ("earthly, terrestrial") is used six times in the New Testament (John 3:12; 1 Cor 15:40; 2 Cor 5:1; Phil 2:10; 3:19; Jas 3:15), it is never used in the LXX, which indicates that ἐπουρανίων καὶ ἐπιγείων καὶ καταχθονίων is essentially a Greek construction. As O'Brien comments, "Ancient man believed in a three-storied universe, and the totality was often expressed by phrases that included all three (e.g., Homer, *Od.* 5.184–86) . . . Paul [or another writer], in proclaiming the universality of the homage offered to Jesus, used the language of his day (cf. Rev 5:13; Ignatius, *Epistle to the Trallians* 9.1)."[75]

As we have seen so far, the linguistic evidence in Phil 2:6–11 is ambivalent. On the one hand, it contains a highly sophisticated Greek

---

71. "I have seen the wicked oppressing, and towering [ומתערה] like a cedar of Lebanon"; the *hithpael* participle of ערה ("to expose himself") here probably is mistaken for that of עלה in the original, meaning "to raise himself"; *HALOT*, 882.

72. "For you, O LORD, are most high over all the earth; you are exalted [נעלית] far above all gods"; the *niphal* perfect of עלה means "to be exalted"; ibid., 829.

73. The *Book of Odes* contains a series of prayers and is included only in Eastern Orthodox Bibles. It is generally considered as a late composition.

74. Lohmeyer, *Brief an die Philipper*, 96.

75. O'Brien, *Epistle to the Philippians*, 244; cf. Rev 5:13 ("Then I heard every creature in heaven and on earth and under the earth [ἐν τῷ οὐρανῷ καὶ ἐπὶ τῆς γῆς καὶ ὑποκάτω τῆς γῆς] and in the sea, and all that is in them"); Ignatius, *Epistle to the Trallians* 9.1 ἀληθῶς ἐσταυρώθη καὶ ἀπέθανεν, βλεπόντων τῶν ἐπουράνιον καὶ ἐπιγείων καὶ ὑποχθονίων ("[Jesus Christ] was truly crucified and died, while those in heaven and on earth and under the earth witnessing [his crucifixion]"; my translation).

idiom such as ἁρπαγμὸν ἡγεῖσθαί τι and a conventional Greek literary phrase like ἐπουρανίων καὶ ἐπιγείων καὶ καταχθονίων. On the other hand, it contains some expressions that are awkward in Greek such as the phrase σχήματι εὑρεθεὶς ὡς ἄνθρωπος and ἑαυτόν ἐκένωσεν. While the latter could have been simply a metaphorical expression, the former most likely reflects the literal translation of the Aramaic phrase כבר אנש. Although another *hapax legomenon* in the New Testament ἐν μορφῇ θεοῦ ὑπάρχων is not peculiar with respect to Greek language, its concept is foreign to the New Testament outside of Phil 2:6–11. As some scholars point out, the appearance of *hapax legomena* and the unusual usage of certain words in Phil 2:6–11 alone do not necessarily prove that it is pre-Pauline. O'Brien claims, "In general, we do not have sufficient material of the apostle's on a wide range of subjects to come to definite conclusions regarding the hymn's authorship; expert linguists claim that a ten thousand-word sampling from an author is usually necessary for making reliable decisions of this kind."[76]

Unfortunately, we do not have the luxury of having a ten thousand-word sampling from Paul. However, even in the limited data we have in Phil 2:6–11, it seems to be the case that the author of Phil 2:6–11 is bilingual in Aramaic and Greek. The author's Aramaism is most evident in the phrase σχήματι εὑρεθεὶς ὡς ἄνθρωπος. This is probably because the author is translating some confessional material from Aramaic into Greek, rather than because he is unskilled in Greek or intentionally imitating the LXX.[77] Considering his use of the highly sophisticated Greek idiom ἁρπαγμὸν ἡγεῖσθαί τι, it is difficult to suppose that the author is not fluent in Greek or intentionally imitates the unpolished Greek of the

---

76. O'Brien, *Epistle to the Philippians*, 199.

77. Häusser points out, "Even if a Semitic basis of Phil 2:6–11 cannot be proved, indeed, one should not immediately conclude that it has a Greek-speaking origin, because this is hardly clear to verify. At least, there are different linguistic observations that suggest rather the supposition of a Semitic tradition of Phil 2:6–11, which would then make the Jewish Christian circle from Jerusalem or Judea a likely location of the composition of this text"; my translation of "Auch wenn sich eine semitische Grundlage von Phil 2,6–11 in der Tat nicht beweisen lässt, sollte man daraus nicht gleich auf einen griechischsprachigen Ursprung schließen, denn dieser ist genauso wenig eindeutig zu verifizieren. Immerhin gibt es verschiedene sprachliche Beobachtungen, die eher die Annahme einer semitischen Vorlage von Phil 2,6–11 nahelegen, die dann einen Abfassungsort dieses Textes im judenchristlichen Kaum von Jerusalem bzw. Judäa wahrscheinlich machen würde"; Häusser, *Christusbekenntnis und Jesusüberlieferung bei Paulus*, 293.

Septuagint with Semitic elements, when writing to his Gentile audience. As I mentioned earlier, the author of Phil 2:6–11's fluency in Greek—cf. his use of a highly sophisticated Greek idiom such as ἁρπαγμὸν ἡρεῖσθαι τι—and his attempt to maintain Aramaism—cf. σχήματι εὑρεθεὶς ὡς ἄνθρωπος—can be best explained by the existence of some traditional elements in Phil 2:6–11. Despite some scholars' valid criticism, when we consider Paul's dependence on the authority of Phil 2:6–11 in developing his argument in Phil 2:1–18, Lohmeyer's proposal that Phil 2:6–11 has an original text (*Urschrift*) in Hebrew or Aramaic and is written in Greek by a poet whose mother tongue was Semitic is still attractive.[78] Obviously, it is impossible for us to know for sure whether or not there existed an earlier Aramaic tradition (*Vorlage*) behind Phil 2:6–11. In spite of this uncertainty, however, Phil 2:6–11 most likely represents some traditional components. I will discuss now some scholars' objections to Lohmeyer's proposal with respect to the theology of Phil 2:6–11 a theology unique to Paul.

Theological Arguments

Some scholars argue that the absence of the characteristics of Pauline soteriology in Phil 2:6–11—(a) the cross and the resurrection of Christ and (b) the redemptive effects of Christ's death for humanity [ὑπὲρ ἡμῶν]—does not prove that it is not Pauline.[79] They rightly criticize those who dismiss the phrase θανάτου δὲ σταυροῦ ("even death on a cross") in Phil 2:8 as Paul's gloss added to the original hymn in their attempts to reconstruct the base-text (*Grundtext*) of Phil 2:6–11 in Aramaic or Hebrew.[80] Otfried Hofius convincingly has demonstrated that the phrase θανάτου δὲ σταυροῦ belongs to the original hymn on the basis of both its form and content.[81] As Hooker suggests, "We must look at the passage

---

78. Lohmeyer, *Kyrios Jesus*, 38–40.

79. E.g., Park, *Submission within the Godhead and the Church in the Epistle to the Philippians*, 16; Fee, *Paul's Letter to the Philippians*, 43–46; O'Brien, *Epistle to the Philippians*, 198–202; Kim, *Origin of Paul's Gospel*, 148; cf. Martin, *Hymn of Christ*, 55–61. Although Martin supports Lohmeyer's proposal that Phil 2:6–11 reflects a pre-Pauline hymn, he still maintains that in it there are certain elements of Pauline doctrine.

80. E.g., Lohmeyer, *Brief an die Philiper*, 90; Jeremias, "Zur Gedankenführung in den paulinischen Briefen," 152–54; Martin, *Hymn of Christ*, 36–37; Reumann interestingly suggests an alternative view that Phil 2:6–11 is an *encomion* composed by the non-Jewish believers in Philippi to which Paul adds the phrase θανάτου δὲ σταυροῦ; Reumann, *Philippians*, 365.

81. Hofius, *Christushymnus Philipper 2,6–11*, 201.

as a whole, and not think that we can pick out the Pauline garnishes to a pre-Pauline structure on the basis of literary form."[82] Since Phil 2:6–11 mentions the cross of Christ in its present form, the "absence" of the cross cannot be evidence against Pauline authorship.

In contrast, the resurrection of Christ is not explicitly mentioned in Phil 2:6–11. As Marshall points out, the Christological scheme of Phil 2:6–11—pre-existence, humiliation, and exaltation; cf. 1 Cor 8:6; 2 Cor 8:9; Col 1:15–20—frequently appears outside of the Pauline corpus in the New Testament (e.g., Luke 24:26; Heb 12:2; 1 Pet 3:18–22; 5:1; Rev 5:12).[83] I agree with Marshall, "It would be wrong to limit the diffusion of the ideas expressed in the hymn [the three-stage Christology] to the Pauline area of primitive Christianity."[84] On the one hand, arguing that Phil 2:6–11 must be pre-Pauline simply because it does not explicitly mention the resurrection of Christ is unwarranted. On the other hand, the fact that the three-stage Christology (with the emphasis on Christ' exaltation) in Phil 2:6–11 is widely shared by various New Testament writers, even with their unique theological perspectives, increases the possibility that it belongs to the Christology of the early church. This is why Marshall contends, "Paul is certainly using pre-formed ideas about Jesus here," although he supports Pauline authorship of Phil 2:6–11.[85]

In addition to the lack of reference to the cross and the resurrection of Christ in Phil 2:6–11, its failure to mention the redemptive effects of Christ's death for humanity (ὑπὲρ ἡμῶν) does not necessarily indicate that it is not Pauline. Kim rightly argues that we should not expect Paul to express his soteriology—that many-sided soteriology—*in toto* whenever he comes to speak of the saving event (cf. Rom 10:6–8).[86] As in the case of the absence of any explicit reference to the resurrection of Christ in Phil 2:6–11, the absence of the redemptive effects of Christ's death for humanity (ὑπὲρ ἡμῶν) alone does not prove that Phil 2:6–11 is not Pauline. Paul is certainly capable of reforming a relevant authoritative

---

82. Hooker, "Philippians 2:6–11," 159; Fee similarly warns, "Any excision of words or lines, so as to reproduce the 'original' hymn is an exercise in exegetical futility"; Fee, *Paul's Letter to the Philippians*, 43.

83. Marshall, "Christ-Hymn in Philippians 2:5–11," 121–22.

84. Ibid., 122.

85. Marshall, *Epistle to the Philippians*, 48.

86. Kim, *Origin of Paul's Gospel*, 148; similarly, Martin, *Hymn of Christ*, 56; O'Brien, *Epistle to the Philippians*, 200–201; Park, *Submission within the Godhead and the Church in the Epistle to the Philippians*, 16.

tradition for his rhetorical purposes and developing his own argument on its basis. When we consider both the linguistic and the theological evidence together in Phil 2:6–11, Paul in Phil 2:6–11 probably is incorporating some pre-existing authoritative traditions and depending on their authority to develop his argument regarding his ethical instruction in Phil 2:1–18 (cf. Rom 10:6–8).

While many scholars maintain that Phil 2:6–11 is Pauline, a few scholars claim that it was written by someone else. For instance, F. W. Beare claims that Phil 2:6–11 "seems to be not a 'pre-Pauline' hymn, but a hymn composed in Pauline circles, under Pauline influence, but introducing certain themes into the proclamation of Christ's victory which are elaborated independently of Paul."[87] Reumann also assumes that "Paul employs in vv 6–11 an encomium the [non-Jewish] Philippians had worked out to use in mission proclamation about Christ and God in their Greco-Roman world."[88] Beare bases his claim on his observation that "in Phil 2:6–11, details fit a Hellenistic syncretistic or more specifically Greco-Roman world."[89] Such a claim not only is impossible to prove—just think about the difficulty of discerning whether or not Phil 2:6–11 is Pauline with the existing data—but also does not explain the Aramaism behind the phrase σχήματι εὑρεθεὶς ὡς ἄνθρωπος in Phil 2:7.[90]

Authenticity: Summary

Martin comments on the issue of the authorship of Phil 2:6–11 in 1967, "When the arguments [Pauline vs. pre-Pauline] are thus set side by side, it may be felt that no clear decision one way or the other is possible.

---

87. Beare, *Commentary on the Epistle to the Philippians*, 78.

88. Reumann, *Philippians*, 33; Schenk, "Philipperbrief in der neueren Forschung," 3299–3308.

89. Beare, *Commentary on the Epistle to the Philippians*, 76; similarly Reumann, *Philippians*, 363; Hellerman, *Reconstructing Honor in Roman Philippi*, 129, 161.

90. Beare claims, "It seems much more likely that the hymn is the work of a disciple of Paul's, and that the teaching of Paul is the middle term between the primitive Christology of the Jerusalem church and this bold adaptation to Jesus of the Oriental myth of the Descent of the Redeemer"; Beare, *Commentary on the Epistle to the Philippians*, 30. Beare also argues, "As E. Käsemann has shown, the terminology is best interpreted within the frame of Hellenistic (syncretistic) religious thought"; ibid., 76. The History of Religions School speculation that the Jewish Son of Man concept is the manifestation of the Oriental Primal Man Myth has long been contested and any argument based on such speculation is no longer convincing.

The issue is finely balanced. Both positions are arguable and neither is absolutely certain."[91] More than forty years have passed since the first publication of Martin's *Carmen Christi*. Although numerous studies on Phil 2:6-11 have appeared since *Carmen Christi*—cf. "the Mt. Everest of Philippians study,"[92] there still is no consensus among critical scholars concerning its genre, authorship, and background. Despite their valid criticism of Lohmeyer's proposal, scholars have not yet provided a satisfactory answer to the question why Paul suddenly introduces "exalted—poetic—prose" with the concentration of extremely rare words and the traces of bilingualism at the apex of his argument in his ethical instruction in Phil 2:1-18. The fact that Paul depends on the authority of Phil 2:6-11 in developing his argument has been largely neglected by commentators. The rhetorical function of Phil 2:6-11 in developing his argument in addition to its linguistic and theological evidence suggests that, although Paul may not be quoting an early church hymn in Phil 2:6-11, he reflects some confessional formula from the early church, with which the Philippians are already familiar.[93] Although we cannot know for sure whether or not Paul quotes a preexisting early church hymn in Phil 2:6-11, linguistic evidence indicates that he reflects some early church tradition.

The Early Church Adam-Jesus Typology in Phil 2:6-11

While many scholars recognize at least some degree of Adam-Jesus typology in Phil 2:6-11,[94] some scholars argue that there is no reference

---

91. Martin, *Carmen Christi*, 61.

92. Reumann, *Philippians*, 333.

93. On the basis of the considerations that I have discussed, I support Baumert's fourth model concerning the authorship of Phil 2:6-11 according to which, "Paul could have found this text as an early church song which he now can incorporate into his train of thought, perhaps supplementing it"; my translation of "Schließlich könnte er diesen Text als urchristliches Lied vorgefunden haben, den er nun in seinen Gedankengang einbaut, vielleicht mit Ergänzungen. Dies Letztere ist die heute herrschende Auffassung." According to Baumert, this is the predominant view today; Baumert, *Weg des Trauens*, 305.

94. E.g., Park, *Submission within the Godhead and the Church in the Epistle to the Philippians*, 23; Silva, *Philippians*, 102; Martin and Hawthorne, *Philippians*, 104–5; Hooker, "Adam Redivivus," 226–27; Martin, *Hymn of Christ*, lxx; Deane, "Obedience and Humility of the Second Adam," 4–12; Wright, *Climax of the Covenant*, 90–97; Sahlin, "Adam-Christologie im Neuen Testament," 26; Kim, *Origin of Paul's Gospel*, 139; Dunn, *Christology in the Making*, 113–25; Hooker, "Philippians 2:6-11," 160–64; Cullmann, *Christology of the New Testament*, 174.

to Adam in Phil 2:6–11 at all. After refuting the view that there is no Adam-Jesus typology in Phil 2:6–11, I will argue that Phil 2:6–11 reflects the implicit primitive Adam-Jesus typology of the early church.

There are four main arguments against the existence of Adam-Jesus typology in Phil 2:6–11. Firstly, some scholars argue that there is no definite linguistic link between Phil 2:6–11 and Gen 1–3.[95] While admitting that there is a general conceptual parallel between Christ in Phil 2:6–11 and Adam in Gen 1–3, they maintain that the lack of any particular linguistic parallel between the two prevents Adam-Jesus typology from being the background of Phil 2:6–11.[96] They criticize those scholars who argue for the semantic interchangeability between εἰκών and μορφή and associate μορφὴ θεοῦ ("form of God") in Phil 2:6 with εἰκὼν τοῦ θεοῦ ("image of God") in Gen 1:27.[97] As we will see shortly, however, the fact that εἰκών and μορφή are not synonyms does not necessarily prove that there is no Adam-Jesus typology in Phil 2:6–11. I will discuss first whether or not εἰκών and μορφή are semantically interchangeable.

Dave Steenburg rightly criticizes Martin's claim that "the LXX often uses μορφή to translate the word צלם in its meaning of 'image, likeness.'"[98] Steenburg argues:

> This is misleading, however, for only once does μορφή translate צלם and it is not in the sense of either "image" or "likeness." צלם in all but one of its occurrences either signifies "idol" or is used to speak of man as being "in the image of God." In almost all of these cases is it translated by εἰκών (26x), exceptions being the resort to ὁμοίωμα (twice) and τύπος (once), both words be-

---

95. E.g., Cousar, *Philippians and Philemon*, 54; Bockmuehl, "'Form of God' (Phil 2:6)," 11; Fee, *Paul's Letter to the Philippians*, 209–10; Hurtado, "Pre-existence," 745; O'Brien, *Epistle to the Philippians*, 197.

96. Bockmuehl calls the *conceptual* parallel "the undeniable counter-analogy between Philippians 2 and Genesis 3 *in general*"; Bockmuehl, "'Form of God' (Phil 2:6)," 11; O'Brien admits, "the contrast between the arrogance and self-seeking of Adam and Christ's humility and self-humbling is evident in general terms"; O'Brien, *Epistle to the Philippians*, 197; similarly, Hurtado, "Pre-existence," 745. It has to be noted that there are also other important Old Testament passages related to Adam such as Ps 8.

97. E.g., Martin and Hawthorne, *Philippians*, 111; Hooker, "Adam Redivivus," 224–26; Dunn, *Theology of Paul the Apostle*, 284; Martin, *Hymn of Christ*, 115–16; Deane, "Obedience and Humility of the Second Adam," 8; Wright, *Climax of the Covenant*, 95; Murphy-O'Connor, "Christological Anthropology in Phil 2:6–11," 41; Kim, *Origin of Paul's Gospel*, 137; Hooker "Philippians 2:6–11," 160–61; Cullmann, *Christology of the New Testament*, 176–77.

98. Martin, *Hymn of Christ*, 107.

ing used in the sense of "idol." The unique occurrence of μορφή as a translation of צלם is found in Dan 3:19, where its Aramaic counterpart is used in the sense of "appearance." Theodotion also avoids εἰκών here by using ὄψις ("face" or "countenance"), a word that, like μορφή, is nowhere else in the LXX used to translate צלם. This suggests rather strongly that μορφή is used, not because it is synonymous with εἰκών, but because it covers a rare portion of צלם's semantic field that εἰκών does not. Therefore, there is no basis for speaking of the interchangeability of the two words in the LXX on the basis of their relationship to צלם.[99]

As Steenburg points out, εἰκών and μορφή are not used as synonyms in the LXX in relation to צלם. When we investigate the root of צלם in Semitic languages and its wide semantic range, however, we soon recognize that it encompasses both the realm of εἰκών and that of μορφή. Wildberger notes that the root צלם in Akkadian refers to "statue, relief, drawing, constellation, cultic figure, physical form," figuratively, "image"—cf. a seventh-century BC burial steles from Nerab with relief depictions and writing in Aramaic, "This is his image [צלם]"; *KAI* no. 225.3, 6, 12; 226.2.[100]

In Biblical Aramaic, the author of Daniel uses צלם to refer not only to "statue" in Dan 2–3 but also to King Nebuchadnezzar's "facial expression" in Dan 3:19.[101] Also, the beauty of Sarah's face is depicted in 1QapGen [or 1 Q20] 20.2 ("How dazzling and pretty is the shape of her face [צלם], and how [. . .]"[102]). We also can detect the proximity between the meaning of "image" and that of "facial expression (or features)" with respect to the Hebrew/Aramaic word צלם in 2 Cor 4:4–6:

> In their case the god of this world has blinded the minds of the unbelievers, to keep them from seeing the *light* of the gospel of the glory of Christ, who is *the image of God* [εἰκὼν τοῦ θεοῦ; cf. צלם אלהים in Gen 1:27]. For we do not proclaim ourselves; we proclaim Jesus Christ as Lord and ourselves as your slaves for Jesus' sake. For it is the God who said, "Let *light* shine out of darkness," who has shone in our hearts to give the *light* of the

---

99. Steenburg, "Case against the Synonymity of μορφή and εἰκών," 79.

100. Wildberger, *TLOT* 2:1080; also, *HALOT*, 1028.

101. Wildberger, *TLOT* 2:1080; cf. "facial features," *HALOT*, 1964.

102. Martínez, *Dead Sea Scrolls Translated*, 233; I am using Martínez' translation as the primary English translation of the Dead Sea Scrolls for this study, unless I indicate otherwise.

knowledge of the glory of God in the *face* [ἐν προσώπῳ; cf. צלם in Dan 3:19; 1QapGen 20.2] of Jesus Christ.

Since there is no particular reason that Paul has to mention the *face* of Jesus Christ in 2 Cor 4:6, I suggest that Paul has the Hebrew/Aramaic concept of צלם in mind and (unconsciously) reflects it in his expression "in the *face* of Jesus Christ." As we can see here, while not being synonyms, εἰκών and μορφή are still closely related to each other in relation to the Hebrew/Aramaic word צלם.

A similar case can be made in 1 Cor 11:3, 7. In 1 Cor 11:3, Paul claims, "Christ is the *head* (κεφαλή) of every man (ἀνδρός), and the husband (ὁ ἀνήρ) is the *head* (κεφαλή) of his wife, and God is the *head* (κεφαλή) of Christ." In 1 Cor 11:7, however, Paul says, "For a man ought not to have his head veiled, since he is the *image* (εἰκών) and reflection (δόξα) of God; but woman is the reflection (δόξα) of man." In relation to 1 Cor 11:3, as Hooker points out, "What Paul *ought* to be saying [but fails to do] in v. 7 is that it is the *head* of man (= Christ) who is the image and glory of God."¹⁰³ We must wonder why Paul uses the word κεφαλή in 1 Cor 11:3 instead of his more conventional expression εἰκών, when referring to the idea that Christ is the image (εἰκών) of God (2 Cor 4:4; cf. Rom 8:28; 1 Cor 15:49; 2 Cor 3:18; Col 1:15). Paul obviously is contrasting here the inevitability of male believers' uncovering of their heads with the necessity of female believers' covering of their heads (cf. 1 Cor 11:3–16). Paul in 1 Cor 10:13 asks a rhetorical question, "Judge for yourselves: is it proper for a woman to pray to God with her *head* unveiled?" Going beyond the surface, however, Paul's argument here is based on the close association between the meaning of "image" (εἰκών) and that of "facial expression (or features)"—cf. "head" (κεφαλή)—intrinsic to the concept of the Hebrew/Aramaic word צלם. That is why Paul in 1 Cor 11:3 can use the word κεφαλή instead of his more conventional expression εἰκών in dealing with the issues related to the propriety of worship in the Corinthian church.

While rightly arguing that εἰκών and μορφή are not synonyms, Steenburg pushes his argument too far and dismisses the proximity of their meanings in relation to the Hebrew/Aramaic word צלם. Steenburg examines the relationship between εἰκών and μορφή in *Sib. Or.* 8.256–73; 8.439–45; Pseudo-Clementine *Homily* 17.7 in which μορφή is used

---

103. Hooker, "Adam Redivivus," 225.

instead of εἰκών in discussing or paraphrasing the Genesis creation account and concludes: "μορφή largely signifies the visible, outward appearance or shape of a thing. εἰκών, being the preferred translation of צלם, like צלם lacks the specifically visual connotation and, therefore, though it is the conventional idiom for expressing man's relationship to God, it is occasionally set aside when the context prefers a more specifically visual definition of the nature of man's representation."[104]

Steenburg's claim that צלם "lacks the specifically visual connotation" contradicts the evidence in Dan 3:19; 1QapGen 20.2. Although εἰκών is the predominant translation of צלם in the LXX, it is not the exclusive one, as צלם is also translated as μορφή (Dan 3:19), ὁμοίωμα (1 Sam 6:5), τύπος (Amos 5:26), and εἴδωλον (Num 33:52; 2 Chr 23:17). When we consider the wide range of the meaning of the Hebrew/Aramaic word צלם that covers both the realm of εἰκών and that of μορφή, the fact that they are not synonyms alone cannot be sufficient ground for denying the existence of Adam-Jesus typology in Phil 2:6–11. The author of Phil 2:6–11 could have had in mind the Hebrew/Aramaic word צלם both in Phil 2:6 and in Phil 2:7 but decided to use μορφή (instead of the usual εἰκών) in order to set the parallelism and the contrast between μορφή θεοῦ (Phil 2:6) and μορφή δούλου (Phil 2:7).[105] The author could not have chosen to use εἰκών both in Phil 2:6 ("the צלם of God") and in Phil 2:7 ("the צלם of slave") for the sake of such parallelism and contrast, because, while εἰκών θεοῦ is the standard translation of צלם אלהים, εἰκών δούλου simply does not work in Greek.

Paul's use of the words related to μορφή in association with εἰκών in describing Christians' transformation also demonstrates their close relationship. In Rom 8:29, Paul writes, "For those whom he foreknew he also predestined to be conformed (σύμμορφος) to the *image* (εἰκών) of his Son, in order that he might be the firstborn within a large family." In 2 Cor 3:18, Paul writes, "And all of us, with unveiled faces, seeing the glory of the Lord as though reflected in a mirror, are being transformed (μεταμορφόω) into the same *image* (εἰκών) from one degree of glory to another; for this comes from the Lord, the Spirit." Steenburg claims: "The use of σύμμορφον and μεταμόρφομαι to describe the believers' transformation into the Lord's εἰκών need not imply synonymity between εἰκών and μορφή. If the suggested distinction between εἰκών and

---

104. Ibid., 84.
105. Similarly, Häusser, *Christusbekenntnis und Jesusüberlieferung bei Paulus*, 280.

μορφή is valid, then the use of σύμμορφον and μεταμόρφομαι with regard to the Lord's εἰκών may convey that the transformation will involve specifically visible appearance—the chosen will come to manifest the divine beauty/splendor. Without these derivatives of μορφή the explicit character of the conformity to the Lord's εἰκών remains ambiguous and unspecified."[106]

As we already have noted, εἰκών and μορφή are not synonyms but they are still closely related to each other, particularly in the case of Rom 8:29 and 2 Cor 3:18. Nothing in the context of Rom 8:29 and 2 Cor 3:18 suggests that Paul distinguishes μορφή from εἰκών in the way that Steenburg does—the former referring to "the visible, outward appearance or shape of a thing," with the latter referring to a general image without "specific visual connotation."[107] Paul certainly is not asserting in Rom 8:29 and 2 Cor 3:18 that each believer (both male and female) will be transformed into the identical "visual [physical] appearance" of Christ.[108] The transformation into Christ's image in Rom 8:29; 2 Cor 3:18 concerns each believer's Christ-like character (cf. Rom 8:3–4; 12–14; 2 Cor 4:7–10; Phil 2:12–18) rather than Christ-like "visual [physical] appearance" (cf. Phil 3:21).

Accepting Steenburg's distinction between εἰκών and μορφή, Bockmuehl claims, "Paul stands in a similar Jewish mystical tradition in which it was possible to speak of the Lord's majesty and greatness by alluding to the inconceivable size and beauty of his bodily appearance."[109] Bockmuehl defends Steenburg's view, based on *b. Ket.* 8a that interprets Gen 1:27 as meaning that God created Man "in the image (צלם) of the likeness (דמות) of his form (תבנית): his 'form' according to the text remains at one remove from his image." According to Bockmuehl, "This confirms the balance of Scripture, where human beings are in God's צלם and in his דמות; both of these terms can mean either an image or like-

---

106. Steenburg, "Case against the Synonymity of μορφή and εἰκών," 85.

107. Häusser also argues, "The understanding of μορφή should not be restricted on the visible figure"; my translation of "Das Verständnis von μορφή sollte nicht auf die sichtbare Gestalt eingeengt werden"; Häusser, *Christusbekenntnis und Jesusüberlieferung bei Paulus*, 271.

108. In 2 Cor 3:18, the present middle participle κατοπτριζόμενοι ("seeing") and the present middle indicative μεταμορφούμεθα ("are being transformed") are used. Their present-tense forms do not support Steenburg's idea of Christians' future physical transformation.

109. Bockmuehl, "'Form of God' (Phil 2:6)," 19.

ness in either two or three dimension. But humanity is never said to be in God's תבנית or, in the LXX, in his μορφή."[110] Bockmuehl's claim is unconvincing for three reasons. Firstly, we do not know the precise date of this particular interpretation. Secondly, there is no evidence that Paul follows the same Jewish mystical tradition as that behind *b. Ket.* 8a, associating the word תבנית with God himself. The word תבנית is never associated with God himself in the Old Testament, while being used for the tabernacle (Exod 25:9, 40), the temple (1 Chr 28:11, 12, 18, 19), the altar of Yahweh (Josh 22:28), and the cherubim (Ezek 10:8). Thirdly, considering that the word תבנית is translated as μορφή only once—Isa 44:13[111]—in the LXX among its total seventeen appearances in the Old Testament,[112] Bockmuehl's claim that Paul has תבנית in mind in Phil 2:6 has slim support.

As we have seen so far, both Steenburg's distinction between εἰκών and μορφή by visibility and Bockmuehl's suggestion of the Jewish mystical background of the phrase μορφή θεοῦ are unconvincing. We should pay attention to the fact that Phil 2:6 claims that Christ is (ὑπάρχω) in the form (μορφή in the translation of צלם) of God (cf. 2 Cor 4:4[113])—in contrast to Gen 1:26–27 in which Adam is created in the image (צלם) of God—as well as the fact that Phil 2:6 uses μορφή instead of εἰκών. Unlike the case of *L.A.E.* 37.3[114]; 39.2–3,[115] Gen 1:26–27 does not claim Adam *is* the image (צלם) of God itself but Adam is created *in* the image of God. On the contrary, Phil 2:6 does not claim Christ is created in the image of God—as Adam is created in it—but Christ himself *is* (ὑπάρχω) in the form (μορφή = צלם) of God, which is related to "equality with God"

---

110. Ibid., 16–17.

111. "The carpenter stretches a line, marks it out with a stylus, fashions it with planes, and marks it with a compass; he makes it in human *form* (תבנית), with human beauty, to be set up in a shrine."

112. Exod 25:9, 40; Deut 4:16, 17, 18; Josh 22:28; 2 Kgs 16:10; Isa 44:13; Ezek 8:3, 10; 10:8; Ps 106:20; 144:12; 1 Chr 28:11, 12, 18, 19.

113. "In their case the god of this world has blinded the minds of the unbelievers, to keep them from seeing the light of the gospel of the glory of Christ, who *is the image of God*."

114. "[Eve speaking to a serpent who came and bit Seth on their way to the gates of Paradise] Cursed beast! How is it that you were not afraid to throw yourself at *the image of God*?"; Johnson, "Life of Adam and Eve," 272.

115. "[Seth speaking to the serpent] "stand back from the image of God!"; ibid., 273.

(τὸ εἶναι ἴσα θεῷ). This fundamental contrast has been largely neglected by commentators.

In addition to the phrase ἐν μορφῇ θεοῦ in Phil 2:6, I see another significant parallel between Phil 2:6–11 and Gen 1–3, which suggests the existence of Adam-Jesus typology in Phil 2:6–11. In Gen 3:4–5, the serpent seduces Eve to eat the fruit of the tree of the knowledge of good and evil, "You will not die; for God knows that when you eat of it your eyes will be opened, and *you will be like God*, knowing good and evil." The LXX translates the phrase "you will be like God" as ἔσεσθε ὡς θεοί (cf. MT והייתם כאלהים). This translation is both formally and conceptually close to τὸ εἶναι ἴσα θεῷ ("equality with God") in Phil 2:6. Spicq points out: "The formula τὸ εἶναι ἴσα θεῷ = 'to be on an equal footing with God' is not synonymous with ἴσος θεῷ = 'to be equal to God' (identity of nature); it places the emphasis on the 'equality of treatment, dignity made manifest and recognized' of the one who was and remained of 'divine condition.' In contrast, the designation ἰσόθεος is applied to kings and eminent persons as a title of honor (cf. Aeschylus, *Persae* 856; Diodorus Siculus 1.2; Dio Cassius 51.20; 52.35)."[116] If Spicq is right, the sense of the phrase τὸ εἶναι ἴσα θεῷ in Phil 2:6 seems to be close to that of the phrase ἔσεσθε ὡς θεοί in Gen 3:5 in which the serpent seduces Adam and Eve, mentioning not the phrase ἔσεσθε θεοί (cf. ἴσος θεῷ) but the phrase ἔσεσθε ὡς θεοί. In contrast to the phrase ἐν μορφῇ θεοῦ in Phil 2:6, the phrase τὸ εἶναι ἴσα θεῷ has not been seriously considered as evidence for Adam-Jesus typology in Phil 2:6–11.

Bockmuehl rejects the view that the phrase ἐν μορφῇ θεοῦ in Phil 2:6 corresponds with the phrase κατ' εἰκόνα θεοῦ in Gen 1:26–27 in the LXX; cf. בצלם אלהים in the MT.[117] Bockmuehl claims, "Corn flakes, toast, and orange juice may be discrete aspects of the same breakfast. In the same way, God's 'form' and his 'glory' are two different things; his 'form' and his 'image' are also two different things."[118] I agree with Bockmuehl and others that the meaning of μορφή ("form") is not particularly related to that of δόξα ("glory").[119] Steenburg rightly criticizes Martin's claim that εἰκών and δόξα are "parallel and equivalent terms" because both

---

116. Spicq, *TLNT* 2:229–30.
117. Bockmuehl, "'Form of God' (Phil 2:6)," 6–11.
118. Ibid., 8.
119. E.g., Bockmuehl, "'Form of God' (Phil 2:6)," 8; Fee, *Paul's Letter to the Philippians*, 204–5, 209; Pöhlmann, "*Morphe*," 443.

are used to translate תמונה[120]; in fact, the LXX never translates תמונה as εἰκών.[121] The Hebrew word תמונה is translated as ὁμοίωμα (Exod 20:4; Deut 4:12, 15, 16, 23, 25; 5:8), δόξα (Num 12:8; Ps 17:15), and μορφή (Job 4:16). Its basic meaning is "form, manifestation" but it "does not indicate a particular shape but refers to the form as an appearance without thereby suggesting a defined outline."[122] The context of Job 4:16 indicates that "a mysterious shape" that stands before Job during the night refers to an angelic being rather than God (cf. Job 4:15–17[123]). The fact that the LXX uses μορφή to translate תמונה in Job 4:16 ("a mysterious shape") undermines Steenburg's claim that μορφή refers to "the visible, outward appearance or shape of a thing." תמונה in Num 12:8; Ps 17:15 does refer to the "manifestation of Yahweh,"[124] which the LXX renders as δόξα. Although both μορφή (Job 4:16) and δόξα (Num 12:8; Ps 17:15) are used in the LXX to translate the Hebrew word תמונה, the fact that תמונה has very different meanings in Job 4:16 and Num 12:8; Ps 17:15 makes it difficult to consider that they are "parallel and equivalent terms." What seems clear, however, is that the meaning of μορφή is closely linked with that of εἰκών ("image"), because both fall in the semantic realm of the Hebrew/Aramaic word צלם. Although they are not synonyms, as Hooker points out, they are closely related to each other in a way that corn flakes, toast, and orange juice are not.[125] Both the phrase ἐν μορφῇ θεοῦ and τὸ εἶναι ἴσα θεῷ in Phil 2:6 support the existence of Adam-Christ typology in Phil 2:6–11.

Recently, Häusser makes an interesting suggestion that the word δοῦλος in Phil 2:7 not only alludes to the word עבד in Isa 52:13—53:12 but also that in Gen 3:23. Häusser points out:

> Secondly, μορφὴ δούλου may be related to Adam after the fall. In my opinion, a connection probably exists between Phil 2:7b and

---

120. Martin, *Hymn of Christ*, 109.

121. Steenburg, "Case against the Synonymity of μορφή and εἰκών," 80–81.

122. *HALOT*, 1746.

123. "A spirit glided past my face; the hair of my flesh bristled. It stood still, but I could not discern its appearance. A form was before my eyes; there was silence, then I heard a voice: 'Can mortals be righteous before God? Can human beings be pure before their Maker? Even in his servants he puts no trust, and his angels he charges with error; how much more those who live in houses of clay, whose foundation is in the dust, who are crushed like a moth.'"

124. *HALOT*, 1746.

125. Hooker, "Adam Redivivus," 221.

Gen 3:23. After the fall, Adam is expelled from Paradise in order to till the soil [עבד את־האדמה]. Adam ([עבד] servant) is associated with the ground that is cursed, which makes the tilling difficult (vv. 17–19). In this respect, עבד has negative connotations and is a reference to the judgment of God. Thus, it stands in stark contrast to עבד in Gen 2:15, where for עבד, the association with a judgment action is absent. We have to reflect even more that Christ who possessed equality with God as δοῦλος voluntarily went the way which Adam was imposed as punishment.[126]

If Häusser's observation is correct, the criticism against the Adam-Christ contrast in Phil 2:6-11—no definite linguistic link between Phil 2:6-11 and Gen 1-3—loses its ground, in which case we have not only a conceptual parallel but also a linguistic parallel between Adam in Gen 1-3 and Christ in Phil 2:6-11.

Secondly, in addition to the lack of a linguistic link between Phil 2:6-11 and Gen 1-3, some scholars argue against the existence of Adam-Jesus typology in Phil 2:6-11 on the basis of their observation that there are real Christological differences between Phil 2:6-11 and Rom 5. On the one hand, Fowl makes a disclaimer that the Christology of Phil 2:6-11 and that of Rom 5 are neither "incompatible" nor "inconsistent" and, therefore, "one can fit both passages into a coherent Pauline Christology."[127] On the other hand, Fowl emphasizes, "There are some real differences of emphasis between the two that ultimately must temper any claims that Phil 2:6-11 exhibits some sort of Adam Christology."[128] While admitting that both Phil 2:6-11 and Rom 5 em-

---

126. My translation of "Zweitens dürfte sich μορφὴ δούλου in der Tat auf den Adam nach dem Fall beziehen. Meines Erachtens besteht nämlich wahrscheinlich eine Verbindung zwischen Phil 2,7b und Gen 3, aber zu V.23. Nach dem Fall wird Adam aus dem Paradies vertrieben, um den Ackerboden zu bestellen. Adams (dienen) ist hier auf den Erdboden bezogen, der verflucht ist, was das Bebauen mühevoll macht (V.17-19). Insofern hat hier *yebed* negative Konnotationen und ist Ausdruck des Gerichts Gottes. Damit steht es in starkem Kontrast zu *yebed* in Gen 2,15, wo für *yebed* die Assoziation eines Gerichtshandelns fehlt. Es wird noch näher zu reflektieren sein, dass Christus, der die Gottgleichheit besaß, als δοῦλος freiwillig den Weg ging, der Adam als Gericht auferlegt wurde"; Häusser, *Christusbekenntnis und Jesusüberlieferung bei Paulus*, 239–40.

127. Fowl, *Philippians*, 116.

128. Ibid.

phasize Christ's obedience, Fowl observes several significant differences between them[129]:

Rom 5	Phil 2:6–11
Explicit contrast with Adam's Disobedience	–
Explicit soteriological emphasis	–
Adam's trespass allows the power of sin to enter the cosmos	–
The cosmic effects of Christ's obedience	The cosmic effects of Christ's obedience
Christ's defeat over the power of sin	Presupposed but not emphasized or made explicit
–	Pre-existence of Christ
Christ's death as a form of submission to sin and death (Rom 5:14, 21) to bring their ultimate defeat (cf. Rom 6:2–14)	Christ's death as the extent of Christ's obedience to God
Christ's obedience results in humanity's *Justification*	Christ's obedience results in his *exaltation* and the *glorification* of God

Highlighting these differences, Fowl concludes, "There are few conceptual parallels between Paul's view of Adam and the account of Christ in Phil 2:6–11."[130]

Fowl's detailed comparison and contrast between Rom 5 and Phil 2:6–11 signify the absence of Paul's explicit and sophisticated Adam Christology in Phil 2:6–11 rather than that of the implicit primitive Adam-Jesus typology of the early church. If such a different Christological emphasis between Phil 2:6–11 and Rom 5 should be used as a piece of evidence against the existence of Adam-Jesus typology in Phil 2:6–11, we also have to conclude that Paul demonstrates a radically different type of Adam Christology in 1 Cor 15, considering its radically different Christological emphasis from that in Rom 5. The focal point of Adam Christology in 1 Cor 15 is the resurrection of Christ that is not addressed at all in Rom 5. Vice versa, neither Adam's disobedience nor Christ's defeat over the power of sin is mentioned in 1 Cor 15. Although Phil 2:6–11 does not mention Adam or explicitly refer to the Creation

---

129. Ibid., 116–17.
130. Ibid., 117.

The Early Church Adam-Jesus Typology 55

account concerning Adam in Gen 1–3, it implicitly contrasts Christ's obedience and Adam's disobedience, using *formal* and *conceptual* parallels such as ἐν μορφῇ θεοῦ,[131] ἁρπαγμὸν ἡγεῖσθαι τι,[132] and τὸ εἶναι ἴσα θεῷ.[133] If we consider Phil 2:6–11 as Pauline, the divergent ways that Paul adopts the implicit primitive Adam-Jesus typology of the early church in Phil 2:6–11 and Rom 5 should not surprise us, given the creative ways that he uses authoritative traditions elsewhere (e.g., Gal 4:21–31; 1 Cor 7:8–16; 9:3–14; 10:1–22; 2 Cor 3:7–18; Rom 10:5–13; 1 Thess 4:13—5:11). Therefore, the different Christological emphasis in Phil 2:6–11 from the Adam Christology in Rom 5 cannot be the decisive evidence against the existence of the implicit primitive Adam-Jesus typology of the early church in Phil 2:6–11.

Thirdly, some scholars argue against the existence of Adam-Jesus typology in Phil 2:6–11, because they suppose that it is incompatible with the concept of the pre-existence of Christ.[134] They criticize Dunn's view that "Phil 2:6–11 is through and through an expression of Adam Christology"[135] according to which Christ's pre-existence was never intended.[136] While rightly criticizing the earlier History of Religions School speculation of the Primal Man myth behind Phil 2:6–11,[137] Dunn applies Adam-Christ typology too rigidly to Phil 2:6–11 to the extent that Christ is not the pre-existent Son of God but simply a "sinless" man

---

131. Cf. κατ' εἰκόνα θεοῦ in Gen 1:27.

132. Cf. Adam's (and Eve's) action to become like God.

133. Cf. ἔσεσθε ὡς θεοί in Gen 3:5.

134. E.g., Fee, *Paul's Letter to Philippians*, 203; O'Brien, *Epistle to the Philippians*, 266–68; Bauckham, "Worship of Jesus in Philippians 2:9–11," 134, 139; Wanamaker, "Philippians 2.6–11," 182–83.

135. Dunn, *Christology in the Making*, 119.

136. Dunn explains, "*Adam precedes Christ.* Adam was not a copy of a pre-existent Christ, but 'a type of *him who was to come*' (Rom 5:14). It would seem therefore that the point of the parallel between Adam and Christ is not dependent on any particular time scale—pre-existence, pre-history, or whatever. *The point focuses rather on the choice confronting Adam and Christ.* The Philippian hymn does not intend to affirm that Jesus was as historical or as prehistorical as Adam, but that the *choice* confronting Christ was as *archetypal* and determinative for mankind as was Adam's; whether the choice was made by the pre-existent Christ or the historical Jesus is immaterial to the Philippian hymn"; ibid.; Murphy-O'Conner similarly concludes, "The original hymn represents an attempt to define the uniqueness of Christ considered precisely as man. This is what one would expect at the beginning of Christian theology"; Murphy-O'Connor, "Christological Anthropology in Phil 2:6–11," 49–50.

137. Dunn, *Christology in the Making*, 114–28.

who makes opposite life-choices to Adam's.[138] As O'Brien observes: "His [Dunn's] interpretation does not do justice to the force of the recapitulatory phrase in v. 7, καὶ σχήματι εὑρεθεὶς ὡς ἄνθρωπος ('and being found in form as man'), which is very strange if it refers to a person who had never been anything else but a man. Further, the contrast clearly expressed between 'being in the form of God' and 'becoming in the form of human beings' is very odd if it is only between two stages in the career of a human being."[139] As Martin notes, "Dunn has failed to press the hymn's 'logic' to inquire what is behind the first Adam's characterization as made in the divine 'likeness' (Gen 1:26–27)."[140] It is impossible to capture the downward movement in Phil 2:6–8 without presupposing Christ's pre-existence (cf. 2 Cor 8:9). Dunn also dismisses the important contrast between Adam's *creation* in the צלם of God (Gen 1:26–27) and Christ's *being* in the צלם of God (Phil 2:6). These observations make Dunn's "through and through" Adam Christology in Phil 2:6–11 unpersuasive.

Wanamaker observes certain parallels between the so-called "Son of God texts" (e.g., Gal 4:4–5; Rom 1:3–4; 8:3–4; 1 Cor 15:24–28) and Phil 2:6–11.[141] In particular, the phrase γενόμενον ἐκ γυναικός ("*born of* a woman") in Gal 4:4 and the phrase ἐν ὁμοιώματι σαρκὸς ἁμαρτίας in Rom 8:3 ("in the *likeness* of sinful flesh") parallel the phrase ἐν ὁμοιώματι ἀνθρώπων γενόμενος ("being *born in* human *likeness*") in Phil 2:7.[142] Wanamaker also notes, "Phil 2:9–11 recalls Rom 1:4 where, according to Paul, the one who is already Son receives power or sovereignty from God after his resurrection from the dead. It also has major similarities with 1 Cor 15:24–28 where Paul employs the Father-Son language in a context which concerns the subjection of the world to Christ and Christ's subjection to God."[143] Relating these parallels to the Hellenistic use of the word μορφή in describing parental relationship (cf. 4 Macc

---

138. Ibid., 120–21.

139. O'Brien, *Epistle to the Philippians*, 267.

140. Martin goes on, "Pauline theology points to humankind's recovery of the *imago Dei* (Rom 8:29; 2 Cor 3:18; Col 3:10; cf. Eph 4:13, 24), which is not what Adam had but lost, but what the heavenly Christ had"; Martin, *Hymn of Christ*, xxi.

141. Wanamaker, "Philippians 2:6–11," 179.

142. Similarly, Hooker, "Adam Redivivus," 229.

143. Wanamaker, "Philippians 2:6–11," 184.

15.4[144]; Philo, *Legat.* 55[145]), Wanamaker argues that Phil 2:6–11 does not express Paul's Adam Christology but his Son of God Christology in which Christ's pre-existence is undeniable.[146] Although Wanamaker is right that the Son of God Christology with the pre-existence of Christ is evident in Phil 2:6–11, that does not necessitate denying the existence of the implicit primitive Adam-Jesus typology of the early church in Phil 2:6–11.

While supporting Dunn's objection to a Gnostic background of Phil 2:6–11, Wright argues, "The presence of Adam Christology, then, says nothing of itself against [Christ's] pre-existence."[147] As Wright points out, the Adam-imagery in Phil 2:6–11 does not contradict Christ's pre-existence in Phil 2:6–11.[148] James W. Aageson aptly observes: "Paul uses Adam and Christ as dialectical figures. They are opposite and yet they are not opposite. There is something similar about them, just as there is something in reality dissimilar about them. The similarity and the dissimilarity between Adam and Christ are discovered in the relational interplay between the two figures."[149] Dunn's logic that, in order for Paul's typology to work, Christ must be a human being—because Adam is a human being—dismisses this *dialectic* of Adam-Christ typology. As Hooker observes, "The chief problem with the idea that Adam is in mind in Phil 2:6 is due to the assumption that Adam and Christ are

---

144. ψυχῆς τε καὶ μορφῆς ὁμοιότητα εἰς μικρὸν παιδὸς χαρακτῆρα θαυμάσιον ἐναποσφραγίζομεν ("We impress upon the character of a small child a wondrous likeness both of mind and of *form*"); the writer of 4 Maccabees comments on parenthood here.

145. ὡς γὰρ αἱ τοῦ σώματος καὶ τῆς ψυχῆς ὁμοιότητες κατά τε τὴν μορφὴν καὶ σχέσεις καὶ κινήσεις βουλάς τε καὶ πράξεις ἐν τοῖς σπερματικοῖς σῴζονται λόγοις ("For the likenesses of the body and the soul, corresponding with the *form* and qualities and emotions and wills and actions, are preserved by means of *the generative principles* [in Stoic philosophy; cf. LSJ, 1627]"; my translation). Philo refers to Gaius' progenitors here as a case of the common wisdom of the ancient world.

146. Wanamaker, "Philippians 2:6–11," 190–91; Hooker points out that Paul contrasts the phrase κατὰ σάρκα with the phrase κατὰ πνεῦμα throughout Rom 1–8 with its summary in Rom 5:12–21, that is, "the contrast between life in Adam and life in Christ." As Hooker argues, "It is only by concentrating on Rom 1:3–4 in isolation and ignoring the argument of Romans 1–8 as a whole that one can deny the relevance of Adam to this passage"; Hooker, "Adam Redivivus," 229–30.

147. Wright, *Climax of the Covenant*, 92; similarly, Hurst, "Christ, Adam, and Preexistence Revisited," 90.

148. Wright, *Climax of the Covenant*, 90.

149. Aageson, *Written Also for Our Sake*, 105–6.

being viewed as equals; they are not."[150] As Hooker notes, in order for the logic of Phil 2:6–11 to work, Christ must be *far greater* than Adam, just as "what happens in Christ is *far greater* than what happens in Adam."[151] Phil 2:6 contrasts with Gen 1:26–27 in that Christ himself *is* (ὑπάρχω) in the form (μορφῇ) [צלם] of God, while Adam *is created* in the צלם of God. Hooker's diagram is most helpful here[152]:

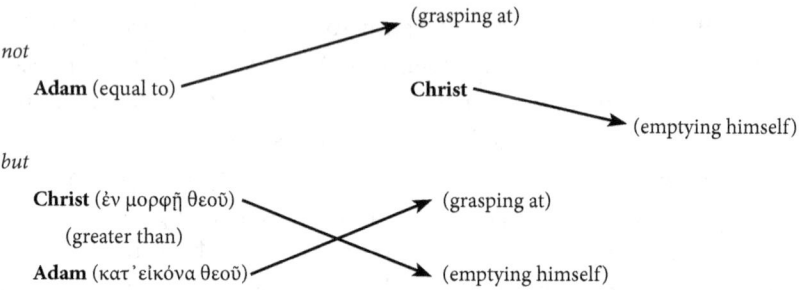

Accepting Bockmuehl's claim that the basic meaning of the word μορφή is "visible form," Hooker distinguishes the phrase ἐν μορφῇ θεοῦ from κατ' εἰκόνα θεοῦ. As Hooker argues, "If Paul has chosen to use the phrase ἐν μορφῇ θεοῦ rather than the one used of Adam in Genesis, that is with good reason, for it would make no sense at all to say that one who was 'in the image of God' (i.e., man) became man! The pre-existent one was *not* κατ' εἰκόνα θεοῦ, but ἐν μορφῇ θεοῦ."[153] While Christ is the true image of God and categorically differs from Adam who is created in that image, the distinction between μορφή and εἰκών based on specificity or visibility is unwarranted. As we have seen so far, in order for Adam-Jesus typology to work in Phil 2:6–11, the pre-existence of Christ is not only possible but as a matter of fact required.[154] Therefore, the pre-existence

---

150. Hooker, "Adam Redivivus," 231.
151. Ibid., 230–31.
152. Ibid., 231.
153. Ibid.
154. Similarly, ibid., 230–31; Wright, *Climax of the Covenant*, 92. Schwindt notes: "The pre-existent status of Christ leads us to Adamic motifs. A link between the μορφή-concept and the εἰκὼν τοῦ θεοῦ from LXX-Gen 1:26–27 is not admittedly proven, but later glorifyings of Adam as a less human than divine *figure* of splendor offer us worthwhile points of reference. Even in the enigmatic expression of 'robbery of divinity' there are resonances of traditions that deal with the expression of overweening pride and the claims to lordship of kingly beings, and which have a basis in LXX-Gen 3:5"; my translation of "So weist der Präexistenzstatus Christi zunächst auf adamitische Motive.

of Christ cannot be the decisive evidence against the existence of the implicit primitive Adam-Jesus typology of the early church, reflected in Phil 2:6–11.

Fourthly, some scholars argue against the existence of Adam-Jesus typology in Phil 2:6–11, because they think that it is incompatible with the second movement of the hymn (Phil 2:9–11[155]) in which the worship of Jesus should be understood in the context of Jewish monotheism (cf. Isa 45:22–25[156]). Richard Bauckham argues, "Phil 2:9–11 cannot be understood as an expression of an Adam Christology. Jesus is not here exalted to the human dominion over other earthly creatures given to humans at creation (Gen 1:28), but to the uniquely divine sovereignty which is acknowledged by all creation when God's sole deity as the one and only God is universally confessed."[157] Besides the obvious allusion to Isa 45:22–25 in Phil 2:9–11, there are similarities between Phil 2:6–8 and the Servant Songs of Deutero-Isaiah, such as the phrase ἑαυτὸν ἐκένωσεν—cf. הערה למות נפשו in Isa 53:12—and particularly the word δοῦλος—cf. עבד (παῖς in the LXX) in Isa 52:13; 53:11. These connections indicate the certain influence of the עבד יהוה concept in Deutero-Isaiah on the Christology of Phil 2:6–11. Criticizing Wright's compromise between Adam Christology and the pre-existence of Christ, Bauckham claims that "an Adam Christology and a full recognition of the monotheistic significance of the allusion to Isa 45:23" are "incompatible."[158]

Eine Verbindung des μορφή-Begriffs mit der εἰκὼν τοῦ θεοῦ aus LXX-Gen 1,26f. ist zwar nicht belegt, doch bieten spätere Glorifizierungen Adams zu einer weniger menschlichen als himmlischen Herrlichkeitsgestalt durchaus Anknüpfungspunkte. Auch in der änigmatischen Aussage vom ‚Raub der Gottgleichheit' klingen Traditionen an, die von der Selbstüberhebung und den Herrschaftsansprüchen königlicher Wesen handeln und in LXX-Gen 3,5 einen Anhalt besitzen"; Schwindt, "Zu Tradition und Theologie des Philipperhymnus," 58.

155. "Therefore God also highly exalted him and gave him the name that is above every name, so that at the name of Jesus *every knee should bend*, in heaven and on earth and under the earth, and *every tongue should confess* that Jesus Christ is Lord, to the *glory* of God the Father."

156. "Turn to me and be saved, all the ends of the earth! For I am God, and there is no other. By myself I have sworn, from my mouth has gone forth in righteousness a word that shall not return: 'To me *every knee shall bow, every tongue shall swear*.' Only in the *LORD*, it shall be said of me, are righteousness and strength; all who were incensed against him shall come to him and be ashamed. In the LORD all the offspring of Israel shall triumph and *glory*."

157. Bauckham, "Worship of Jesus in Philippians 2:9–11," 134–35.

158. Ibid., 139.

Supporting Bauckham's view, Charles B. Cousar claims, "Adam does not figure in Isa 45 at all."[159]

Just as Dunn applies Adam-Christ typology to Phil 2:6–11 too rigidly, Bauckham and Cousar apply the pre-existence of Christ and Jewish monotheism to Phil 2:6–11 too rigidly. The basis of their objection to the existence of Adam-Christ typology in Phil 2:6–11 seems to be the same assumption as Dunn's view that Adam-Christ typology requires that Adam and Christ are equal. In other words, if Adam-Christ typology exists in Phil 2:6–11, Christ cannot be worshipped—because Adam cannot be worshipped. This argument is problematic for two reasons. Firstly, as I have discussed earlier, it is too simplistic a way to apprehend the *dialectic* nature of Adam-Christ typology. Christ is not equal to Adam but *far greater* than him. Secondly, although Adam was never worshipped in the same way in which God was worshipped in first-century AD Judaism, there are some references in Jewish intertestamental literature, which follow Ps 8:6 and venerate Adam as the ruler of the cosmic universe—cf. 4Q381 1.10–11; 4 *Ezra* 6.46, 53–54; 2 *Bar.* 14.18; Wis 10.1–2.[160] Wildberger comments on the phrase צלם אלהים in Gen 1:26–28:

> The human being as God's image should rule over other creatures (רדה) or subdue the earth (כבש). The verbs indicate that humanity is seen as the ruler, one might say as king, over creation. This viewpoint is confirmed, once again, by Ps 8, whose anthropological statements apparently stand in the same stream of tradition as Gen 1:26–27 . . . One may determine, then that the origins of the concept of humanity's divine image are associated with ancient Near Eastern concepts of the king as the son, the representative, viceroy, proxy of God on earth.[161]

Adam Christology is not as immediate a background of the worship of Jesus in Phil 2:9–11 as the עבד יהוה concept in Deutero-Isaiah; however, it still is related to or compatible with the second movement of the hymn.

I have examined so far four main arguments against the existence of Adam-Jesus typology in Phil 2:6–11: (a) no definite linguistic link

---

159. Cousar, *Philippians and Philemon*, 58.

160. Similarly, Bauckham, "Worship of Jesus in Philippians 2:9–11," 139; cf. 4Q381 1.10–11 "[. . .] in them and all his armies and his an[gels . . .] [. . .] *in order to serve man* [לעבד לאדם] and help him and [. . .]."

161. Wildberger, *TLOT* 3:1083.

between Phil 2:6–11 and Gen 1–3, (b) real Christological differences between Phil 2:6–11 and Rom 5, (c) its incompatibility with the pre-existence of Christ, and (d) its incompatibility with the worship of Jesus in Phil 2:9–11. On the one hand, I agree with these arguments that there is no exact linguistic parallel between Phil 2:6–11 and Adam Christology (cf. Gen 1–3; Rom 5; 1 Cor 15). On the other hand, however, there exist a number of significant *verbal* and *conceptual* parallels between the two. Some scholars' verdict that there is no reference in Phil 2:6–11 to Adam-Jesus typology simply does not do them justice. The indirect links between Phil 2:6–11 and Adam Christology may be due to the nature of the implicit primitive Adam-Jesus typology of the early church—from which Paul develops his explicit and sophisticated Adam Christology. Some scholars seem to overlook the existence of Adam-Jesus typology in Phil 2:6–11, because they expect to see Adam Christology as explicit and sophisticated as that in Rom 5 and 1 Cor 15. If Phil 2:6–11 is traditional and contains the early church Adam-Jesus typology, as I contend, it is necessary to examine how Paul uses it in the context of his ethical instruction in Phil 2:1–18.

Paul's Use of the Early Church Adam-Jesus Typology

While Phil 2:6–11 is located in the middle of Paul's ethical instruction in Phil 2:1–18 and stylistically stands out from its context and contains many *hapax legomena* in the New Testament, its logic coheres with Paul's ethical teaching. While Phil 2:6–11 may not be a pre-Pauline early church *hymn*, it certainly reflects some confessional formula from the early church, which contains its implicit primitive Adam-Jesus typology. The genius of Paul lies in his re-shaping of traditional material for his rhetorical purposes and creatively applying it to the situation (*Sitz im Leben*) of his readers.

Paul's main concern in Phil 2:1–18 is that the Philippians have unity among them and humility towards one another. Paul teaches in Phil 2:1–5:

> If then [there is] any encouragement in Christ, if [there is] any comfort from love, if [there is] any sharing of [the] Spirit, if [there are] any affection and compassions, complete my joy *in order that you may think the same* [*thing*] (ἵνα τὸ αὐτὸ φρονῆτε), having the same love, *being united in spirit* (σύμψυχοι), *thinking the* [*same*] *one* [*thing*] (τὸ ἓν φρονοῦντες), [do] nothing according to

selfish ambition or conceit but *in humility* (τῇ ταπεινοφροσύνῃ) considering others better than yourselves, each one not being concerned about the matters of his or her own but [also] those of others. *Think this* (τοῦτο φρονεῖτε) among you, which [was] also in Christ Jesus!¹⁶²

Just as Paul says in Phil 2:5, "think this among you, which [was] also in Christ Jesus," Phil 2:6–11 highlights Jesus' humility and obedience to God—having one mind with God—which he implicitly contrasts with Adam's arrogance and disobedience to God. Although I already have mentioned it, Hurtado's comment is worth citing again: "The language used to describe Jesus' actions qualitatively in Phil 2:6–8 is drawn from the language of early Christian *paraenesis* and possibly from the Jesus tradition of the Pauline period." Hurtado goes on, "This suggests that the tradition of the earthly Jesus was influential in shaping both this description of his actions, and possibly early Christian *paraenesis*."¹⁶³ While we cannot know the exact form of the implicit primitive Adam-Jesus typology of the early church, which Paul is adapting in Phil 2:6–11, he clearly uses it in order to support his ethical teaching. For Paul and his readers, Jesus is not only their savior for whom they live—cf. Phil 1:21—but also their ethical model to follow. Most commentators ignore Paul's rhetorical use of the early church Adam-Jesus typology in support of his ethical teaching in Phil 2:1–18. I will sum up now my discussion of Phil 2:6–11.

It is not my intention in this section to mount "the Mt. Everest of Philippians study" but to discuss three specific topics: (a) the *authenticity* of Phil 2:6–11, (b) the early church Adam-Jesus typology in Phil 2:6–11, and (c) Paul's creative use of the early church Adam-Jesus typology in his ethical teaching in Phil 2:1–18. Concerning the first topic, I contend that, regardless of the identity of the author, Phil 2:6–11 contains some confessional formula from the early church. Paul may

---

162. This is my literal translation of Phil 2:1–5.

163. Hurtado demonstrates that Paul relates the concept of δοῦλος with Christian discipleship and thus uses it far more positively (Rom 1:1; 6:19; 7:6, 25; 12:11; 14:18; 16:18; Gal 1:10; 5:13; Phil 1:1; 2:22; 2 Cor 4:5; Col 3:24; 4:12; 1 Thess 1:9) than negatively with only a few exceptions (Gal 4:3, 7, 8, 9, 25; 5:1; Rom 6:17, 20; 8:21); Hurtado, "Jesus as Lordly Example in Philippians 2:5–11," 126. Similarly, Wolff points out, "Even if Paul does not make an explicit connection, yet he still acts in accordance with Jesus' teaching on humility; in his service he is a follower of Jesus Christ, drawn into the humble self-abasement (Phil 2:8) of the one who 'did not live to please himself' (Rom 15:3)"; Wolff, "Humility and Self-Denial in Jesus' Life and Message and in the Apostolic Existence of Paul," 155.

have cited a pre-Pauline early church hymn more or less in its existing form or substantially modified some traditional material. Considering the rhetorical function of Phil 2:6–11 in the context of Paul's ethical teaching in Phil 2:1–18, the traditional view that Phil 2:6–11 is a pre-Pauline early church hymn is still attractive despite many valid points of its criticism. Some scholars suggest that Paul himself composed an "exalted—poetic—prose" in Phil 2:6–11 similar to Rom 11:33–36; 1 Cor 13:1–13. Considering the specific rhetorical function of Phil 2:6–11, this view is unconvincing.

Concerning the second topic, I contend that Phil 2:6–11 reflects the implicit primitive Adam-Jesus typology of the early church. Some scholars deny the existence of Adam Christology in Phil 2:6–11 on the basis of the lack of any linguistic link between Phil 2:6–11 and Gen 1–3, the different Christological emphasis between Phil 2:6–11 and Rom 5, the pre-existence of Christ in Phil 2:6–11, and the Christological monotheism in Phil 2:9–11. As I have discussed, these objections are not decisive, when we consider the various hints in Phil 2:6–7 to Adam in Gen 1–3 (ἐν μορφῇ θεοῦ ὑπάρχων, τὸ εἶναι ἴσα θεῷ, and μορφὴν δούλου λαβών), the *dialectic* nature of the implicit primitive Adam-Jesus typology, and the fact that it requires—rather than negates—the pre-existence of Christ. Concerning the third topic, Paul creatively uses the implicit primitive Adam-Jesus typology of the early church, reflected in Phil 2:6–11, in support of his ethical teaching in Phil 2:1–5 with emphasis on maintaining unity among believers and submitting to one another in humility. Citing an authoritative tradition, Paul presents the life of Jesus—in contrast to that of Adam—as the ethical model to follow.

HEBREWS 2:5–11

As I will discuss shortly, Heb 2:5–9 and Heb 2:10–11 demonstrate two different aspects of the early church Adam-Jesus typology. Therefore, I will discuss Heb 2:5–9 first and Heb 2:10–11 later with respect to the four topics.

The Authenticity of Heb 2:5–11

Continuing the theme in Hebrews 1 that Jesus the Son of God is superior to angels, the author of Hebrews cites Ps 8:5–7 verbatim from the LXX in Heb 2:6–8a and provides his interpretation in Heb 2:8b–9.[164] It is important to observe that both the author of Hebrews (Heb 2:8) and Paul (1 Cor 15:27) cite Ps 8:6 [7 LXX] in expounding Jesus' eschatological authority. Considering the substantially different theological landscape of Hebrews from that of Paul, any direct literary dependence of Hebrews on Paul or Paul on Hebrews is unlikely. As many commentators note, the author of Hebrews and Paul most likely reflect the early church tradition that Christologically interprets Ps 8:4–6 [5–7 LXX] to explain Jesus' eschatological authority, independently of each other.[165]

Some scholars are skeptical about the view that Heb 2:5–9 is *authentic* to the early church, because the author of Hebrews does not exploit beyond Heb 2:5–9 the Christological connection between the phrase υἱός ἀνθρώπου in Ps 8:4 [5 LXX] and Jesus' characteristic self-designation as ὁ υἱὸς τοῦ ἀνθρώπου.[166] Hurst claims, "There is no evidence that *Auctor* [the author of Hebrews] takes 'Son of Man' in 2:6 in any other sense than as a periphrasis for 'man.' Had he taken it as a 'christological title' he would certainly have explicated it elsewhere."[167] The fact that the author of Hebrews does not use the phrase υἱὸς ἀνθρώπου in Ps 8:4 [5 LXX] as a Christological title, however, does not necessarily suggest that the author of Hebrews created out of nothing (*ex nihilo*) the interpretation of Ps 8:4–6 [5–7 LXX] in Heb 2:5–9. Such a fact simply indicates that the focal point of Hebrews shifts after the second chapter from Jesus' superiority over the angels to his identity as the High Priest according to the order of Melchizedek (Heb 5:6, 10; 6:20; 7:1, 10, 11, 15, 17).[168] Jesus' self-designation as בר נשא most likely is *authentic* to the early church and the

---

164. "In putting everything under him, God left nothing that is not subject to him. Yet at present we do not see everything subject to him. But we see Jesus, who was made a little lower than the angels, now crowned with glory and honor because he suffered death, so that by the grace of God he might taste death for everyone" (NIV).

165. Hooker, "Christ, the 'End' of the Cult," 206–7; Johnson, *Hebrews*, 89–93; Long, *Hebrews*, 35; Lane, *Hebrews 1–8*, 46; Bruce, *Epistle to the Hebrews*, 73; Attridge, *Epistle to the Hebrews*, 72; Dunn, *Christology in the Making*, 111. While recognizing the unique parallel between Heb 2:5–8a and 1 Cor 15:27 in citing Ps 8 in describing Jesus' eschatological authority, many commentators do not consider that both writers depend on the same interpretive tradition of the early church; e.g., Ellingworth, *Epistle to the Hebrews*, 149–57; Hurst, *Epistle to the Hebrews*, 113.

166. E.g., Blomberg, "But We See Jesus," 93; Johnson, *Hebrews*, 90; Lindars, *Theology of the Letter to the Hebrews*, 39; Hurst, *Epistle to the Hebrews*, 110–11.

167. Ibid.; similarly, Attridge, *Epistle to the Hebrews*, 74.

168. Similarly, Sahlin, "Adam-Christologie im Neuen Testament," 30.

author of Hebrews probably was aware of it and its associated traditions. As I will discuss shortly, both the similarity and the dissimilarity of the use of Ps 8:6 [7 LXX] in Heb 2:5–9 and 1 Cor 15:24–28 suggest that the author of Hebrews and Paul independently reflect the implicit primitive Adam-Jesus typology of the early church, when describing Jesus' eschatological authority with allusion to Adam's sovereignty over God's creation. The author of Hebrews does not expound such an allusion as Paul does in 1 Cor 15. The fact that both writers refer to the same Scripture Ps 8:6 [7 LXX] in the context of explaining Jesus' eschatological authority, however, could not have been simply because "Hebrews and Paul are coming out of the same kind of intellectual ferment," as Hurst claims.[169] Although the author of Hebrews does not use the phrase "son of man" in Ps 8:4 [5 LXX] as a Christological title, he most likely does not create the Christological interpretation of Ps 8:4–6 [5–7 LXX] in Heb 2:8b–9 out of nothing (*ex nihilo*) but reflects an earlier tradition (*ex traditione*). Since I have to discuss the *authenticity* of Heb 2:10–11 on the basis of Paul's Adam Christology, I will discuss it when I discuss the third topic ("Paul's Allusion to the early church Adam-Jesus typology") in order to avoid repetition.

The Early Church Adam-Jesus Typology in Heb 2:5–11

Heb 2:5–9 evidently contains the implicit primitive Adam-Jesus typology of the early church—cf. Ps 8:4–6 [5–7 LXX], which compares Jesus' eschatological authority with Adam's sovereignty over God's creation (Gen 1:26–30). Scholars are divided in deciding whether υἱὸς ἀνθρώπου in Ps 8:4 [5 LXX] in Heb 2:6 should be interpreted anthropologically[170] or Christologically.[171] Does the phrase υἱὸς ἀνθρώπου in Heb 2:6 refer to "human beings" in general or Jesus in particular? Blomberg articulates this question and argues:

> At this juncture [Heb 2:9], both main approaches [anthropological and Christological interpretation] agree the writer of Hebrews is applying the psalm to Jesus. But the question is whether Jesus

---

169. Hurst, *Epistle to the Hebrews*, 113.

170. E.g., Blomberg, "But We See Jesus," 88–127; Johnson, *Hebrews*, 90; Lindars, *Theology of the Letter to the Hebrews*, 39–40; Lane, *Hebrews 1–8*, 47; Hurst, *Epistle to the Hebrews*, 112.

171. E.g., Hooker, "Christ, the 'End' of the Cult," 199; Long, *Hebrews*, 35; Ellingworth, *Epistle to the Hebrews*, 150–51; Bruce, *Epistle to the Hebrews*, 72–74; Attridge, *Epistle to the Hebrews*, 72.

has been in view all along [Heb 2:6–8], so that the only transition here is to the explicit mention of Jesus' atoning death, after his pre-existence, incarnation and exaltation have all been rehearsed, or whether the contrast is far more dramatic: God gave humanity a commission which it failed to exercise. Thus we do not see all creation in subjection to humankind. But, miracle of miracles, we see Jesus who remained sinless where we sinned and thus, as a fully human representative of humanity, accomplished what we were intended to have done, and more—making possible our redemption despite our sinful failures.[172]

Blomberg elsewhere claims that the Christological reference to υἱὸς ἀνθρώπου enters into the author's argument only in Heb 2:9.[173] I reject this claim for two reasons. Firstly, the author of Hebrews refers to Jesus' superiority over the angels in Heb 2:5 ("Now God did not subject the coming world, about which we are speaking, to angels"), which has been the recurring theme throughout the first chapter. The author's Christological argument throughout Heb 1:1—2:5 makes Blomberg's view unlikely. Blomberg claims, "There is no necessary reason why the original audience of Hebrews, hearing 2:5 read aloud, would automatically have skipped back over 2:1–4 and thought that the author was resuming the contrast between Christ and the angels."[174] While the author of Hebrews mentions the salvation confirmed to believers in Heb 2:3, his principal Christological argument—that he has been developing since the beginning of his letter—continues to be the superiority of Jesus.[175]

Secondly, as Attridge highlights, "For Hebrews the psalm is not, primarily at least, a meditation on the lofty status of humankind in the

---

172. Blomberg, "But We See Jesus," 96.

173. Blomberg, "Better Things in This Case," 312.

174. Blomberg, "But We See Jesus," 92.

175. Löhr similarly notes: "Clearly, the writer does not have in mind the humanity of Jesus, which is grounded in detail later, in fact, with the ideas that are not totally foreign to the psalm. His mind is fixed here on the eschatological position—not yet perceived—of Jesus above all things. The contrast is not between angels and human beings (a curious thought for the writer of Hebrews) but that between angels and the Son"; my translation of "Dem Verfasser kommt es beim Psalmzitat aber entscheidend zunächst nicht auf die Menschlichkeit Jesu an, die später eigens ausführlich begründet wird, und zwar mit Vorstellungen, die dem Psalm ganz fremd sind. Ihm geht es hier vielmehr um die eschatologische Stellung Jesu über allem, die jetzt noch nicht wahrnehmbar ist. Der Gegensatz ist nicht der zwichen Engeln und Menschen (die wäre ein völlig singulärer Gedanke für den Hebr), sondern weiterhin der zwichen Engeln und dem Sohn"; Löhr, "Anthropologie und Eschatologie im Hebräerbrief," 176–77.

created order, but an oracle that describes the humiliation and exaltation of Jesus."[176] The author of Hebrews evidently interprets Ps 8:4-6 [5-7 LXX] Christologically to refer to the "three stages in the experience of Jesus."[177] The author of Hebrews' selective use of the Scripture affirms this observation. Two cases should be mentioned. When quoting Ps 8:5-7 [LXX] verbatim, the author of Hebrews omits the first clause of Ps 8:7 καὶ κατέστησας αὐτὸν ἐπὶ τὰ ἔργα τῶν χειρῶν σου ("You have given them dominion over the works of your hands"). As Attridge suggests, "That omission was probably made because the clause refers quite clearly to the mastery of humanity over the present world and would make more difficult the interpretation in terms of Christ, his temporary subjection, and his eschatological reign."[178] In order to identify the first clause of Ps 8:5 [6 LXX; MT] with Jesus' incarnation and humiliation (cf. Heb 2:9), the author of Hebrews interprets the phrase βραχύ τι in a temporal sense ("for a little while") in contrast to the most common meaning of the Hebrew expression מעט as "little [in relation to distance and rank]."[179] These cases signify that the author of Hebrews is primarily concerned with the Christological implications of Ps 8. The original meaning of Ps 8 is still important—that υἱὸς ἀνθρώπου refers to Adam who is the representative of humanity—because Jesus is presented as the representative of the new eschatological humanity in Heb 2:5-9.

On the basis of the two reasons that I have discussed—Jesus' superiority over the angels in Heb 2:5 and the author's selective use of Ps 8, I contend that the author associates the phrase υἱὸς ἀνθρώπου in Ps 8:4 [5

---

176. Attridge, *Epistle to the Hebrews*, 72.

177. As Lane points out, "The writer regarded the declarations of Ps 8:6-7 [LXX] as independent statements descriptive of three stages in the experience of Jesus: (A) incarnation and humiliation ('you made him for a little while lower than the angels' [Heb 2:7a]), (B) exaltation ('you crowned him with glory and splendor' [Heb 2:7b]) and (C) final triumph ('you put everything in subjection under his feet' [Heb 2:8a])"; Lane, *Hebrews 1-8*, 44.

178. Attridge, *Epistle to the Hebrews*, 71; similarly, Long, *Hebrews*, 35.

179. Similarly, Attridge, *Epistle to the Hebrews*, 76; Long, *Hebrews*, 36; Bruce, *Epistle to the Hebrews*, 72. מעט does mean, however, "for a short time" in Job 24:24; Ruth 2:7; *HALOT*, 611; cf. Heb 2:9 ("But we do see Jesus, who for a little while was made lower than *the angels* [ἄγγελοι], now crowned with glory and honor because of the suffering of death, so that by the grace of God he might taste death for everyone"); as Lane notes, "It is important to observe that when the line from Ps 8:6a is repeated in v. 9 the word order is changed to bring forward the expression βραχύ τι 'for a little while' into the emphatic position"; Lane, *Hebrews 1-8*, 48.

LXX] with Jesus right from the beginning (Heb 2:6) rather than only in Heb 2:9. In fact, this is the very reason why the author of Hebrews cites Ps 8:4–6 [5–7 LXX] in the first place. What we see in Heb 2:5–9 is most likely the author's reflection of the implicit primitive Adam-Jesus typology of the early church, which compares Jesus' eschatological authority and Adam's sovereignty over God's creation (Gen 1:26–30)—interpreting Ps 8 both Christologically and anthropologically. Since my argument that Heb 2:10–11 contains the early church Adam-Jesus typology is largely based on its parallels in Paul's Adam Christology, I will discuss it together with the next topic in the following sections.

Paul's Allusion to the Early Church Adam-Jesus Typology

I contend that Paul alludes to the early church Adam-Jesus typology reflected in Heb 2:5–9 for the following reason. In 1 Cor 15:12–58, Paul attempts to convince the Corinthian believers of the certainty of their future bodily resurrection. Paul in 1 Cor 15:12 starts his argument saying, "Now if Christ is proclaimed as raised from the dead, how can some of you say there is no resurrection of the dead?" In 1 Cor 15:20–23, Paul argues that, since Christ is the first fruits [ἀπαρχή] of resurrection, each of them will be made alive (or resurrected) in Christ's second coming. Immediately after that, Paul explains what is going to happen in the End-time (1 Cor 15:24–28). Paul cites Ps 110:1 [109:1 LXX] in 1 Cor 15:25 and Ps 8:6 [7 LXX] in 1 Cor 15:27. How Paul modifies these two Scriptural texts will be examined in detail in my discussion of Mark 14:62 later in this chapter. What is significant for us here is the fact that both Paul and the author of Hebrews quote the same Scripture Ps 8:6 [7 LXX] in the context of explaining Jesus' eschatological authority. Paul cites the Scripture to persuade his readers that Christ will subdue every dominion, authority, and power at the End [τέλος] (1 Cor 15:24–28) with the result that they will be made alive, following Christ who is the first fruits of resurrection (1 Cor 15:20–23). As Paul creatively uses Ps 8:6 [7 LXX], the author of Hebrews also creatively uses Ps 8 not only to refer to Jesus' eschatological authority but also to his incarnation and humiliation (Heb 2:8b–9). As Ellingworth points out, "The main distinction between Hebrews' and Paul's reading of the psalm is that Hebrews, with a view to later teaching about Christ's high priesthood, extends the quotation to make it include reference to his humiliation [while Paul does not]."¹⁸⁰ The similarity and the dissimilarity with respect to the use of Ps 8 suggest that Paul and the author of Hebrews adapt the early church Adam-Jesus typology, independently of each other. I will discuss now Paul's allusion to the early church Adam-Jesus typology reflected in Heb 2:10–11.

In contrast to the unique idea that God made Jesus perfect through suffering, the other components of Heb 2:10–11 may be *authentic* to the early church, considering two *conceptual* similarities between Heb 2:10–11 and Paul. Firstly, the statement in Heb 2:10 that Jesus brings many sons into glory has a *conceptual* similarity with Paul's statement in Rom 5:17 that God provides grace and the gift of righteousness to believers through Jesus Christ and lets them reign in life.¹⁸¹ As Attridge points out, "That believers will share eschatologically in Christ's glory is a commonplace" (cf. Phil 3:21; Rom 8:17; 1 Cor 15:43; 1 Pet 1:11).¹⁸² However, the fact that the glorification of believers in the context of the Adam-Jesus typology in Heb 2:5–9 resonates with that in Rom 5:12–17 cannot be taken for granted—cf. 1 Cor 15:22.¹⁸³ Secondly, the statement in Heb 2:11¹⁸⁴—further explicated in Heb 2:17¹⁸⁵—that Jesus sanctifies (ἁγιάζω) his followers has a *conceptual* similarity with Paul's statement in Rom 5:19¹⁸⁶ that Jesus makes his followers righteous (καθίστημι

---

180. Ellingworth, *Epistle to the Hebrews*, 151.

181. Cf. Heb 2:10 ("It was fitting that God, for whom and through whom all things exist, *in bringing many children to glory* [πολλοὺς υἱοὺς εἰς δόξαν ἀγαγόντα], should make the pioneer of their salvation perfect through sufferings"); Rom 5:17 ("If, because of the one man's trespass, death exercised dominion through that one, much more surely will those who receive the abundance of grace and the free gift of righteousness exercise dominion in life [οἱ τὴν περισσείαν τῆς χάριτος καὶ τῆς δωρεᾶς τῆς δικαιοσύνης λαμβάνοντες ἐν ζωῇ βασιλεύσουσιν] through the one man, Jesus Christ").

182. Attridge, *Epistle to the Hebrews*, 83.

183. "For as in Adam all die, so in Christ all will be made alive"; this statement is related to both the glorification of believers and Adam Christology, attested in Heb 2:5–9; Rom 5:12–17.

184. "For *the one who sanctifies* (ὁ ἁγιάζων) and those who are sanctified all have one Father. For this reason Jesus is not ashamed to call them brothers and sisters."

185. "Therefore he had to become like his brothers and sisters in every respect, so that he might be a merciful and faithful high priest in the service of God, *to make a sacrifice of atonement for the sins of the people* (εἰς τὸ ἱλάσκεσθαι τὰς ἁμαρτίας τοῦ λαοῦ)."

186. "For just as by the one man's disobedience the many were made sinners, so by the one man's obedience *the many will be made righteous* (δίκαιοι κατασταθήσονται οἱ πολλοί)."

δίκαιοι) through his obedience.¹⁸⁷ These two *conceptual* similarities can be considered together as the larger theme of Jesus' glorification or sanctification of his followers within the paradigm of "one" and "many" in which both Adam (Ps 8:4-6 cited in Heb 2:6-8a) and Jesus (Heb 2:5-9) function as the representative of humanity.

Although the author of Hebrews does not mention Adam or the universal consequences of his transgression—in contrast to Paul in Rom 5:12-21, it may be implied in correspondence with Jesus' righteous act of obedience and its universal consequence. In order to fully understand the Adam-Jesus typology in Heb 2:10-11, we must go back to Heb 2:5-9. As Blomberg observes:

> Verse 5 uses a simple aorist for what is most naturally interpreted as a simple past event. That God did not subject the coming world to angels implies that he did subject it, in the past, in its entirety, to someone else. The obvious stewards of that subjection were Adam and Eve . . . Within the Genesis narrative, Adam and Eve are being created to have dominion or exercise stewardship over a coming world, the world of all of God's creatures and created things . . . Had they not chosen to sin, a world along the lines of what we only look forward to would have come into being . . .¹⁸⁸

As Bruce points out, the author of Hebrews presents Jesus "as mankind's true representative" who "must share in the conditions inseparable from the human condition"—cf. Heb 2:9.¹⁸⁹ In contrast to Paul in Rom 5:12-21, the author of Hebrews explicitly mentions neither Adam's transgression nor its consequences. Blomberg' observation that the author of Hebrews is concerned with the cosmos of Adam and Eve in Gen 1–3 in citing Ps 8, however, is important. The phrase ἡ οἰκουμένη ἡ μέλλουσα ("the coming world") in Heb 2:5—cf. ἡ οἰκουμένη ("the world") in Heb 1:6—definitely refers to the new eschatological age or realm (with its heavenly realities) which the Son has inaugurated with

---

187. Long points out, "The designation ὁ ἁγιάζων, 'he who consecrates,' seems to reflect the concept of God in the Pentateuch, where he identifies himself with the formula 'I am the Lord who consecrates you' (ἐγὼ κύριος ὁ ἁγιάζων ὑμᾶς; Exod 31:13; Lev 20:8; 21:15; 22:9, 16, 32; cf. Ezek 20:12; 37:28)"; Long, *Hebrews 1–8*, 56. I agree with Long's observation but I contend that the author of Hebrews reflects such a concept not directly from the Old Testament but via the early church tradition.

188. Blomberg, "'But We See Jesus,'" 92–93.

189. Bruce, *Epistle to the Hebrews*, 74; cf. Heb 2:9 ("because of the suffering of death, so that by the grace of God he might taste death for everyone [ὑπὲρ παντός]").

his enthronement and will be consummated in the future.[190] The author of Hebrews may have in mind both God's creation and the eschatological "coming world" in Heb 2:5 at the same time. The gist of Adam-Jesus typology in Heb 2:5–9 is that Adam's subjection of God's creation only partly worked out in contrast to Christ's complete subjection of the eschatological "coming world." This consideration provides an important clue about the Adam-Jesus typology in Heb 2:10–11.

Despite running the risk of *eisegesis* of Heb 2:10–11 through the lens of Rom 5:12–21, I argue that the author of Hebrews here reflects the early church Adam-Jesus typology that Paul independently develops in Rom 5:17, 19. The point of the early church Adam-Jesus typology reflected in Heb 2:5–11 seems to be that Jesus' universal rule glorifies and sanctifies the new eschatological humanity—his followers—in implicit contrast to Adam's failed universal rule—whose disobedience has brought disgrace and made his descendants sinners. The idea in Heb 2:10–11 that Jesus brings his followers to glory and sanctifies them may have belonged to the early church Adam-Jesus typology that Paul independently develops and articulates in Rom 5:17, 19.

Paul's Use of the Early Church Adam-Jesus Typology

I previously discussed this topic when examining Paul's allusion to the early church Adam-Jesus typology. I argued that Heb 2:5–11 contains the early church Adam-Jesus typology on the basis of the parallels in Paul's Adam Christology and that Paul creatively uses the early church Adam-Jesus typology. Against the potential accusation of circular argument, I justify my argument with two considerations. Firstly, as it is generally agreed, Hebrews and Paul's letters demonstrate quite distinctive theological landscapes from each other and any direct influence on one from the other is unlikely. Secondly, both the convergence and the divergence between the Adam-Jesus typology in Heb 2:5–11 and Paul's Adam Christology in 1 Cor 15:27; Rom 5:17, 19 suggest that the author of Hebrews and Paul independently build their ideas upon the implicit primitive Adam-Jesus typology of the early church.

As we have discussed so far, Heb 2:5–11 provides an important piece of evidence for the implicit primitive Adam-Jesus typology of the

---

190. Similarly, Caneday, "Eschatological World Already Subjected to the Son," 28–39; Johnson, *Hebrews*, 90; Lane, *Hebrews 1–8*, 45; Bruce, *Epistle to the Hebrews*, 71–72; Attridge, *Epistle to the Hebrews*, 70.

early church. The author of Hebrews cites Ps 8:4–6 [5–7 LXX] in order to explain Jesus' eschatological authority (Heb 2:8), alluding to Adam's sovereignty over God's creation, in parallel with Paul's citation of Ps 8:6 [7 LXX] in 1 Cor 15:27. While the author of Hebrews cites Ps 8:4–6 [5–7 LXX] in order to explain Jesus' incarnation and humiliation with attention to the fact that Jesus *for a little while* was made lower than the angels (Heb 2:9), Paul only emphasizes Jesus' eschatological authority in 1 Cor 15:27. The author of Hebrews in Heb 2:10–11 expresses similar ideas to Paul's in Rom 5:17, 19, that Jesus' universal rule glorifies and sanctifies his followers in contrast to Adam's failed universal rule. The author of Hebrews and Paul seem to have adapted the implicit primitive Adam-Jesus typology of the early church, independently of each other.

MARK 14:62 (CF. MATT 26:64; LUKE 22:69)

The Authenticity of Mark 14:62

There are a few commentators who seem to consider Mark 14:62[191] as redactional out of nothing (*ex nihilo*). As Brown notes, "*Our best methods do not give us the ability to isolate confidently* [the traditional] *material in its exact wording, assigning pre-Marcan verses and half-verses* from the existing, thoroughly Marcan account" in Mark 14:53–65.[192] Nonetheless, some scholars' view that Mark 14:53–65 as a whole is historically unreliable and is entirely Mark's creation is unwarranted. Adela Yarbro Collins claims:

> A consideration of Jesus' case by the chief priests is mentioned twice (14:53, 55–64, and 15:1). Mistreatment of Jesus by his captors is also mentioned twice (14:65 and 15:16–20a). As noted above, the insertion of the story of Jesus' trial before the council into the account of Peter's denial is a typically Markan literary technique. These observations suggest that Mark added the denial of Peter and the trial before the Judean council to the earlier passion narrative that he used as a source . . .[193]

191. In Mark 14:61 (Matt 26:63; Luke 22:70), in his response to the high priest's question, Jesus openly confesses that he is the Son of God. Matthew follows Mark's order that Jesus speaks about the coming of the Son of Man immediately after his confession. However, in Luke, the council of Sanhedrin asks Jesus if he is the Christ and he replies to them with his prediction of the coming of the Son of Man. Only then he confesses that he is the Son of God.

192. Stein, *Mark*, 676.

193. Collins, *Mark*, 699; similarly, Donahue and Harrington, *Gospel of Mark*, 427.

Collins supports her claim, "This unit [Mark 14:53–72] is one of the clearest examples of the Markan technique of inserting one story within another (intercalation) . . . It is difficult to depict that simultaneity in a narrative, which normally portrays one event after another."[194] Collins' claim that Mark inserted the story of Jesus' trial before the Sanhedrin and that of Peter's denial into "the earlier passion narrative" is unwarranted for two reasons.

Firstly, it is doubtful that the supposed intercalation is due to Mark's literary technique rather than his source. A similar intercalation is found in the account of Jesus' trial in John 18:12–27. Unless one assumes John's direct literary dependence on Mark in John 18:12–27,[195] both John and Mark are independently relying on the same (oral) early church tradition concerning Jesus' trial.[196] Secondly, Collins' argument for Markan redaction based on simultaneity is unwarranted. As Craig A. Evans asks, "Could a story of Peter's denials have circulated with no reference to the interrogation of Jesus taking place inside at the same time?" This very simultaneity supports that the supposed intercalation is *authentic*. Evans points out that there is the evidence of "the literary technique of digression and resumption" in late antiquity texts and claims, "Such a device is just as capable of existence in oral traditions as in written traditions."[197]

---

194. Collins, *Mark*, 698; Collins accepts Dobschütz' argument; Dobschütz, "Zur Erzählerkunst des Markus," 197–98.

195. Cf. Donahue, "Introduction," 9; Dewey, "Peter's Curse and Cursed Peter (Mark 14:53–54; 66–72)," 98, 104.

196. Similarly, Evans, *Mark 8:27—16:20*, 441; as Evans observes, "John 18 has the Jewish hearing at the home of Annas, rather than at the home of Caiaphas; the questions put to Jesus and Jesus' replies are completely different from those of Mark 14; and the details of the questions put to Peter and Peter's replies are almost completely different." With respect to the view of those who suppose John's dependence on Mark, Evans argues, "In essence, we are asked to believe that in depending on Mark 14 the author of John 18 only extracted the literary seam created as the story shifts from Peter, to Jesus, and then back to Peter again. This is not very plausible . . . The problem with this proposal is that evidence of Johannine dependence on Mark or one of the other Synoptics is quite meager, with the result that many, perhaps even a majority, of Johannine scholars think John is literarily independent of the Synoptic tradition"; ibid. ; similarly, Fortna, "Jesus and Peter at the High Priest's House," 375.

197. Evans, *Mark 8:27–16:20*, 441; Evans compares Mark 14:53–72 with a particular example in Achilles Tatius, *Leucippe and Clitophon* 2.2.1–2.12.1; Evans, "'Peter Warming Himself,'" 248–49.

Regardless of the *historicity* of the events in Mark 14:53-72,[198] neither the supposed intercalation nor the simultaneity of the events can be decisive evidence against their *authenticity*.

I find at least two pieces of evidence in support of the *authenticity* of Mark 14:61-62. Firstly, while "the Blessed One" in Mark 14:61 was not a typical Jewish periphrasis for God in the first century AD, as Robert H. Gundry notes, "*1 En.* 77:2 provides some probably pre-Christian Jewish evidence for 'the Blessed One' and thus turns back the argument for inauthenticity that vv. 61-62 reflect a Christology of the church."[199] Marcus argues that "Son of the Blessed One" in Mark 14:61 is not a "non-restrictive synonym" of "Christ" but a "restrictive apposition" to "Christ," qualifying the first title; in other words, the high priest asks

---

198. Many commentators who deny the historicity of Mark 14:53-65 base their judgment on the rules in the mishnaic tractate "Sanhedrin" (*m. Sanh.* 4-7). However, as Stein convincingly argues:

> Yet it must be remembered that the rules found in *m. Sanh.* 4-7 were written down around AD 200 and reflect an idealization of what should have taken place in AD 30. Furthermore, it is questionable whether the Sadducee-dominated Sanhedrin would have followed the idealized rules of the Pharisees found in the Mishnah. Also, the rules of the tractate Sanhedrin often conflict with what Josephus says. Yet even if the rules of the Mishnah were in effect in AD 30, this does not mean that they were followed in the trial of Jesus... Finally, if one must decide between the historicity of the trial accounts in the Gospels and the mishnaic rules in effect at Jesus' trial, why choose the latter over the former? The Passion Narrative existed a century and a half before the Mishnah was written, and many eyewitnesses were still around when the account of the trial in Mark was recorded; Stein, *Mark*, 677.

HAVING considered all the anomalies of Jesus' trial in the Sanhedrin in Mark 14:53-65, Hooker concludes, "Perhaps the most likely explanation of the anomalies is that the proceedings were entirely informal [more like a preliminary hearing] and therefore not bound by the normal rules of procedure, though the evangelists have assumed that it was an official trial." Hooker goes on, "To this we must add the possibility that details may have been altered in the course of retelling the story"; Hooker, *Gospel According to Saint Mark*, 355.

199. Gundry, *Mark*, 909; the reference to God as "the Blessed" is completely ubiquitous and a standard Jewish diction in early rabbinic Judaism as in the phrase "the holy one blessed be he"; cf. *1 En.* 77.2 ("The second is called the South, because the Most High will descend there, indeed because *the Eternally Blessed* will descend there"; Isaac, "1 Enoch," 56); cf. *m. Ber.* 7.3 ("The Holy One, Blessed be He") and its Talmudic commentaries (*b. Ber.* 7.3; *y. Ber.* 7.3). Urbach points out that there is a thin line between epithets and titles, as in the case of the expressions ברך ("Blessed be") and המברך ("the Blessed") closely linked to each other in early rabbinic literature; Urbach, *Sages*, 1:41.

Jesus whether he is "the Messiah-Son-of-David" or the (quasi-divine) "Messiah-Son-of-God." Marcus suggests that Jesus is accused of blasphemy not because he claims to be the Davidic Messiah (cf. 2 Sam 7:14; 4QFlorilegium or 4Q174 1.10–11) but the Messiah-Son-of-God, participating in God's cosmic lordship (cf. Ps 110:1).[200] As Witherington points out, "The allusion to the clouds makes clear that a theophany is being spoken of, with the divine being riding on a cloud chariot said to be Yahweh's vehicle in the OT. Thus Jesus is boldly claiming a status even higher than the high priest has asked about."[201] If Marcus' suggestion and Witherington's observation are correct, they support the *authenticity* of the high priest's question in Mark 14:61. As Boring notes, "The identification of 'Christ' and 'Son of God' was once thought to be a Christian formulation, but now it is often argued, especially on the basis of Qumran evidence [e.g., 4Q174 (or 4QFlorilegium) 1.11; 4Q246 (or 4QAramaic Apocalypse) 2.1; 1QSa (or 1Q28a) 2.11–12], that it is not unhistorical or anachronistic for the high priest to have made this identification."[202] The evidence in 4Q246 is particularly interesting because a messianic figure is specifically called ברה די אל ("son of God"; cf. 2 Sam 7:14) and בר עליון ("son of the Most High"; cf. υἱὸς ὑψίστου in Luke 1:32).[203] I will make a few preliminary comments on the identity of the "son of God" in 4Q246 in the following.

200. Marcus, "Mark 14:61," 125–41.
201. Witherington, *Gospel of Mark*, 385.
202. Boring, *Mark*, 412–13; similarly, France, *Gospel of Mark*, 609; Juel, *Messiah and Temple*, 108–14; Hengel, *Son of God*, 43–45. Dismissing these references mentioned here, Hooker claims, "There is no clear evidence in the literature that has come down to us that 'Son of God' was used by Jews as a synonym for Christ in the first century, though the idea that Israel, the king (and so the future king) and righteous individuals could be described in this way was certainly known"; Hooker, *Gospel According to Saint Mark*, 362; cf. 4Q174 1.11 ("I will be a father to him and he will be a son to me. This (refers to the) 'branch of David'"); 4Q246 2.1 ("He will be called son of God, and they will call him son of the Most High"); 1Q28a 2.11–12 ("This is the assembly of famous men, [those summoned to] the gathering of the community council, when [God] begets the Messiah with them").
203. While עליון is frequently attested in the Old Testament and Jewish intertestamental literature (e.g., Deut 32:8; Isa 14:14; Ps 73:11, 91:9; 107:11; 1Q20 [1QGenesis Apocryphon or 1QapGen ar] 22.15–16), the phrase "son of the Most High" has an exact parallel only in Luke 1:32 (cf. Luke 6:35). Fitzmyer points out, "The absence of definite articles in the Lucan usage is indicative of the Semitism involved, which is not clearly manifest in this Aramaic text"; Fitzmyer, "4Q246," 153–74.

Having listed six different interpretations concerning the identity of the "son of God" in 4Q264, Fitzmyer concludes, "I consider this apocalyptic text to speak positively of a coming Jewish ruler, perhaps a member of the Hasmonian dynasty, who may be a successor to the Davidic throne, but who is not envisaged as a Messiah [cf. 2 Sam 7:14]."[204] Fitzmyer's conclusion, however, is not entirely convincing for the following reason. Despite his thorough analysis of the text on the basis of his reconstruction, Fitzymer does not make much out of its multiple allusions to Dan 7. For example, the phrase in 4Q246 1.8–9 וכלש ישמשון [לה והוא בר אל ר]אב יתקרא—"and they shall all serve [him, (for)] he shall be called [son of] the [gr]eat [God]"[205]—has parallels in Dan 7:10 (the same verb שמש), 14, 18, 27. Also, the verb דוש ("to trample") is used in a similar apocalyptic context both in 4Q246 2.2–3[206] and Dan 7:23[207] and the same can be said for the verb קום ("to arise") used in 4Q246 2.4[208] and Dan 7:17.[209] Most impressively, the phrase מלכותה מלכות עלם ("his kingdom [shall be] an everlasting kingdom") is attested in 4Q246 2.5[210] and Dan 7:27.[211] Also, the phrase שלטנה שלטן עלם ("his dominion [shall be] an everlasting dominion")

---

204. Ibid.

205. Ibid., 157.

206. שני[ן] ימלכון על ארעא וכלא ידשון עם לעם ידוש ומדנה למד[ינ]ה; "For (some) years they shall rule upon the earth and shall *trample* everything (under foot); people shall *trample* upon people, province upon [pro]vince"; ibid., 155.

207. "This is what he said: 'As for the fourth beast, there shall be a fourth kingdom on earth that shall be different from all the other kingdoms; it shall devour the whole earth, and *trample* (ותדושנה) it down, and break it to pieces.'"

208. עד יקום עם אל וכלא ינוח מן חרב ("until there *arises* the people of God, and everyone rests from the sword"); Fitzmyer, "4Q246," 155.

209. "As for these four great beasts, four kings *shall arise* (יקומון) out of the earth."

210. מלכותה מלכות עלם וכל ארחתה בקשוט; "(Then) *his kingdom* (shall be) *an everlasting kingdom*, and all his ways (shall be) in truth"; Fitzmyer, "4Q246," 155.

211. "The kingship and dominion and the greatness of the kingdoms under the whole heaven shall be given to the people of the holy ones of the Most High; their kingdom shall be *an everlasting kingdom, and all dominions shall serve and obey them* (מלכותה מלכות עלם וכל שלטניא לה יפלחון וישתמעון)."

is attested in 4Q246 2.9²¹² and Dan 7:14²¹³ (cf. Dan 4:31). As Dunn observes, "the case for seeing a deliberate echo of Daniel 7 in 4Q246 column 2 is strong enough to provide the basis for further reflection regarding its significance."²¹⁴ If 4Q246 connects the Davidic king in 2 Sam 7:12–14 with the "one like a son of man" in Dan 7:13 in an apocalyptic context, as Kim proposes, "This is the only certain messianic interpretation of Dan 7:13 so far identified in pre-Christian Judaism" much earlier than the *Similitudes* of Enoch or *4 Ezra* 13.²¹⁵ As Martin Hengel notes, the fact that the titles "son of God" and "son of the Most High" are attested in the apocalyptic Qumran writing indicates that they were "not completely alien to Palestinian Judaism."²¹⁶

Secondly, similar to the case of "the Blessed One," while "the Power" in Mark 14:62 was not a recognizable periphrastic title for God, it fits well in the context of 1st century AD Judaism (cf. 1 Chr 29:12; Job 26:12; Ps 54:1, 62:11; 65:6; Isa 40:10; 1QHymnsᵃ [1QHodayothᵃ or 1QHᵃ] 11.10; *Mos.* 1.111).²¹⁷ Some scholars dismiss these pieces of evidence and argue against the *authenticity* of Mark 14:62.²¹⁸ While being open to the possibility of the Evangelist's limited Christological re-working of his source material in Mark 14:53–65 (cf. Mark 1:1), I see no convincing reason to consider it as Mark's own composition of "a historically plausible

---

212. שלטנה שלטן עלם וכל תהומי; "*His dominion* (shall be) *an everlasting dominion*, and none of the abysses of [the earth shall prevail against it]!"; Fitzmyer, "4Q246," 155–56.

213. ". . . *His dominion is an everlasting dominion* (שלטנה שלטן עלם) that shall not pass away, and his kingship is one that shall never be destroyed."

214. Dunn, "'Son of God' as 'Son of Man' in the Dead Sea Scrolls?" 208; cf. Collins, *The Scepter and the Star*, 154–72.

215. Kim, *The 'Son of Man' as the Son of God*, 21–22.

216. Hengel, *Son of God*, 45.

217. On the basis of the evidence in 1QHymnsᵃ 11.10, Flusser raises an interesting possibility that Jesus is interpreting the messianic title "Wonderful Counselor, Mighty God" in Isa 9:5 [LXX; MT] as "Wonderful Counselor with His Might (or Power)"—reflecting the phrase "with His *Power*" in Mark 14:62; Flusser, *Judaism and the Origins of Christianity*, 301–5.

218. E.g., Boring, *Mark*, 413; Perrin, "Mark XIV.62," 150–55. Bock criticizes that Perrin simply ignores the prevalence of allusion to Dan 7 in Second Temple Judaism— e.g., 11QMelch 2.18; Ezekiel the Tragedian; *1 En.* 46.2–4; 48.2; 62.5, 7, 9, 14; 63.11; 69.27, 29; 70.1; 71.14, 17; 4Q491; *4 Ezra* 13—in considering Mark 14:62 as a Christian pesher tradition created by the post-Easter church; Bock, "Use of Daniel 7 in Jesus' Trial, with Implications for His Self-understanding," 87.

narrative,"[219] as some scholars claim. As Hengel notes, "This christological high-point of the Gospel of Mark, which reveals the messianic secret, is certainly not a construct of the author of the gospel—who is sometimes incorrectly portrayed as the first 'Christian novelist'—but contains an 'old form' of Christology which connects the exaltation to the right hand of God and the parousia for the purpose of the last judgment."[220] As Gundry argues, "Mark [in Mark 14:62] is unlikely to have created a chronological problem by putting on Jesus' lips a prediction about the Sanhedrin which failed to reach fulfilment in their lifetimes," which suggests "the traditionality and probably authenticity of the prediction."[221] The pieces of evidence that I have discussed suggest that the crux of Mark 14:62 probably goes back to the early church rather than being created by the Evangelist out of nothing (*ex nihilo*).

The Early Church Adam-Jesus Typology in Mark 14:62

I contend that Mark 14:62 contains the early church Adam-Jesus typology on the basis of two *verbal* and *formal* similarities between the early church tradition behind Mark 14:62 and Paul's Adam Christology.

Mark 14:62	Jesus said, "I am and 'you will see the Son of Man *seated at the right hand of the Power*,' and '*coming with the clouds of heaven*.'"
Ps 110:1 [109:1 LXX]	The Lord says to my lord, "*Sit at my right hand until I make your enemies your footstool*" [NETS].
Dan 7:13 [LXX-Θ]	I was watching in the night visions, and lo, as it were *a son of man coming with the clouds of heaven*. And he came as far as the ancient of days and was presented to him [NETS-Theodotion].
1 Cor 15:25	For he must reign *until he has put all his enemies under his feet*.

The first *verbal* and *formal* similarity between the early church tradition behind Mark 14:62 and Paul's Adam Christology concerns their shared

---

219. Boring, *Mark*, 413; see Bock's response to Boring's skepticism of the *authenticity* of Mark 14:62; Bock, "Use of Daniel 7 in Jesus' Trial, with Implications for His Self-Understanding," 87–88.

220. Hengel, *Studies in Early Christology*, 187.

221. Gundry, *Mark*, 912; while recognizing "the midrashic use of Dan 7:13 in combination with other Scriptural texts [Ps 110:1]" in Mark 14:62, Casey contends that it was Mark who created a new Christological title, the Son of Man, to address the Parousia which was "a major concern of the early church"; Casey, *Solution to the "Son of Man" Problem*, 318.

reference to Ps 110:1 [109:1 LXX]. Having answered the high priest's question affirmatively, Jesus declares in Mark 14:62, "'You will see the Son of Man seated at the right hand of the Power,' and 'coming with the clouds of heaven.'" Jesus' answer here is a combination of Ps 110:1 [109:1 LXX] and Dan 7:13. While the phrase ἐκ δεξιῶν καθήμενον τῆς δυνάμεως ("seated on the right hand of the Power") is derived from the first half of God's speaking to David's Lord in Ps 110:1 [109:1 LXX],[222] both phrases ὁ υἱὸς τοῦ ἀνθρώπου and ἐρχόμενον μετὰ τῶν νεφελῶν τοῦ οὐρανοῦ are derived from Dan 7:13. It is interesting to note the fact that Paul in 1 Cor 15:25 quotes Ps 110:1 [109:1 LXX] in the context of his Adam Christology.

One may argue against the first *verbal* and *formal* similarity between the early church tradition behind Mark 14:62 and 1 Cor 15:25, because the former contains the first four words of Ps 110:1 [109:1 LXX] while 1 Cor 15:25 contains the rest of the verse. Strictly speaking, this is not exactly a *verbal* and *formal* similarity as I defined in chapter 1. However, the parallel between the two texts certainly is far more significant than a *conceptual* similarity, because they cite the same Scripture when describing Jesus' eschatological authority. As Schrage points out:

> In favor of this view [that Paul refers to the tradition linked with Ps 110:1], we could refer to the alteration of ὑποπόδιον τῶν ποδῶν σου of the LXX (thus, e.g., after the LXX also Heb 1:13 and Luke 20:43) into ὑπὸ τοὺς πόδας, which echoes Mark 12:36//Matt 22:44 (ὑποκάτω τῶν ποδῶν). Presumably, even here, we have the influence of Ps 8:7 according to which God has put "everything under his feet" (πάντα ὑπέταξας ὑποκάτω τῶν ποδῶν αὐτοῦ) for man's benefit, which again in verse 27 has been altered to ὑπὸ τοὺς πόδας. Both Old Testament texts from the Psalms, whose theme of lordship is certainly related to each other, are juxtaposed in Eph 1:20–22 and attest in agreement the third person in contrast to κάθου [Ps 109:1 LXX]. This also could

---

222. As Subramanian notes: "The quotation from Ps 110:1 in Mark 12:36 is understood as a prophecy about the Messiah's status as David's Lord, a rank that surpasses the one expected by the scribes who conceive the Messiah as the Son of David. In the original context of Psalm 110, the psalmist utters a divine oracle in which the king is assured of victory over his enemies (cf. Ps 110:1)." Subramanian interestingly suggests, "The Markan presentation of Jesus as the Messiah and the Son of God who will be enthroned on God's right hand as David's Lord in his parousia shows that David's prophetic speech in Ps 110:1 is beginning to be fulfilled in Jesus' death (Mark 15:39) and will be completely realized at his parousia (14:62)"; Subramanian, *Synoptic Gospels and the Psalms as Prophecy*, 64.

argue for a previous link that can be seen in Heb 1:13 and 2:6 and 1 Pet 3:22.[223]

The fact that both Mark and Matthew allude to Ps 110:1 [109:1 LXX] in the phrase ὑποκάτω τῶν ποδῶν—cf. ὑποπόδιον τῶν ποδῶν σου in the LXX—is very interesting. When I discuss the second *verbal* and *formal* similarity between the early church tradition behind Mark 14:62 and Paul's Adam Christology, it will become clear that such variation is not by coincidence but a piece of the evidence for the early church interpretive tradition that combines Ps 110:1 [109:1 LXX] with Ps 8—cf. *gezerah shawah (argument by analogy)*. While the combination of Ps 110:1 [109:1 LXX] and Ps 8:6 [7 LXX] in 1 Cor 15:25–27 is *authentic* to the early church—possibly, a liturgical or catechistic formula—Christ's own submission to God in 1 Cor 15:28 probably is unique to Paul.[224]

One may also argue against the first *verbal* and *formal* similarity, because Ps 110:1 is widely attested throughout the New Testament. As R. T. France notes, "The language about 'sitting at God's right hand' soon became established in Christian tradition to denote the universal sovereignty of the risen Jesus, 'waiting till his enemies be made his footstool' (Heb 10:12–13, and numerous allusions to Ps 110:1 in Hebrews)."[225] However, as Gundry notes, "The combination of sitting at God's right hand and coming with the clouds of heaven does not appear in non-dominical NT materials and therefore seems unlikely to have a Christian origin here [Mark 14:62]. Nor is 'the Son of man' elsewhere as-

---

223. My translation of "Dafür könnte die Veränderung von ὑποπόδιον τῶν ποδῶν σου der LXX (so z.B. nach LXX auch Hebr 1,13 und Lk 20,43) in ὑπὸ τοὺς πόδας sprechen, was an Mk 12,36/Mt 22,44 (ὑποκάτω τῶν ποδῶν) erinnert. Vermutlich liegt schon hier Einfluß von Ps 8,7 vor, wonach Gott dem Menschen »alles unter seine Füße« getan hat (πάντα ὑπέταξας ὑποκάτω τῶν ποδῶν αὐτοῦ)/was in V 27 aber wiederum in ὑπὸ τοὺς πόδας verändert ist. Beide alttestamentlichen Psalmworte, deren sachliche Thematik der Herrschaft eine gewisse Verwandtschaft verrät, stehen auch in Eph 1,20-22 nebeneinander und bieten übereinstimmend die 3. Pers. Gegenüber κάθου. Auch das könnte für eine vorgegebene Verbindung sprechen, die sich zusätzlich durch Hebr 1,13+2,6 und 1Petr 3,22 bestätigen läßt"; Schrage, *Erste Brief an die Korinther (1Kor 15,1—16,24)*, 156.

224. Kreitzer notes: "Both categories of Paul's thought, his belief in the Parousia and Final Judgment as well as his concept of the Messianic Kingdom, contain reflections of a conceptual tension between Christ and God and are thus extremely valuable for investigating the theocentric/christocentric issue"; Kreitzer, *Jesus and God in Paul's Eschatology*, 165–66.

225. France, *Gospel of Mark*, 613.

sociated with sitting at God's right hand; so Christian fabrication again seems unlikely."[226] Darrell D. Hannah claims, "Some early Christians apparently believed that there were two thrones in heaven, one on which God sat and another, lesser throne at his right hand, occupied by the Risen Christ. Such a deduction may owe as much to Daniel 7:9, with its mention of θρόνοι, as to Ps 110:1." Hannah continues, "We know that Ps 110:1 and Dan 7:13 were often combined in early Christianity (e.g., Mark 14:62 pars. Matt 26:64; Luke 22:69; Matt 19:28; 25:31; Acts 7:55–56; *Sib. Or.* 2.241–44; and perhaps Hegesippus)."[227] While Hannah's claim for two heavenly thrones is convincing in the light of the dual reference to Dan 7:13 and Ps 110:1, his claim that both texts "were often combined" overstates the case. Considering the numerous references to Ps 110:1 in the New Testament, the dual reference to Dan 7:13 and Ps 110:1 is unique to the early church tradition behind Mark 14:62—cf. Luke's account of Stephen's speech in Acts 7:55–56. I will come back to this unique combination of Dan 7:13 and Ps 110:1 after discussing the other *verbal* and *formal* similarity between the early church tradition behind Mark 14:62 and Paul's Adam Christology.

The second *verbal* and *formal* similarity between the early church tradition behind Mark 14:62 and Paul's Adam Christology concerns their shared reference to the phrase "son of man." Since Paul nowhere mentions the actual phrase "son of man," one may argue that this *verbal* and *formal* similarity is invalid. Strictly speaking, this criticism is legitimate. As I will demonstrate in the following, however, there is a certain link between the two, far more significant than a *conceptual* similarity. It is generally agreed that the underlying Aramaic phrase behind the Greek expression ὁ υἱὸς τοῦ ἀνθρώπου in the Gospels is בר נשא. As I have discussed earlier ("Heb 2:5–11"), there is evidence for the early church Adam-Jesus typology that links the phrase υἱὸς ἀνθρώπου in Ps 8:4 [5 LXX] with Jesus and compares his eschatological authority with Adam's sovereignty over God's creation in Gen 1:26–30. The early church most likely related Jesus' characteristic self-designation בר נשא not only to the phrase ὡς υἱὸς ἀνθρώπου in Dan 7:13 [LXX] but also to the phrase υἱὸς ἀνθρώπου in Ps 8:4 [5 LXX]. If this is right, the early church associated Jesus' eschatological authority not only with the authority of the "one

---

226. Gundry, *Mark*, 912.
227. Hannah, "Throne of His Glory," 75–76.

like a son of man" in Dan 7:13 but also with that of Adam over God's creation in Gen 1:26–30.

Paul demonstrates his explicit and sophisticated Adam Christology in 1 Cor 15, when he assures the Corinthian believers of their future bodily resurrection. In 1 Cor 15:24–27,[228] Paul highlights Christ's eschatological authority by quoting the second half of Ps 110:1 [109:1 LXX] in 1 Cor 15:25 and Ps 8:6 [7 LXX] in 1 Cor 15:27, comparing Christ's authority with Adam's sovereignty over God's creation in Gen 1:26–30. As I have argued earlier ("Heb 2:5–11"), Paul alludes to the early church Adam-Jesus typology reflected in Heb 2:5–9 and creatively uses it in 1 Cor 15:27. Although Paul does not cite Ps 8:4 [5 LXX] but only Ps 8:6 [7 LXX] in 1 Cor 15:25, Paul must have had in mind the phrase υἱὸς ἀνθρώπου in Ps 8:4—whose feet is the object of the preposition ὑποκάτω ("under") in Ps 8:6. Responding to Dunn's claim that the use of Ps 8:6 in 1 Cor 15:27 reflects Paul's Adam Christology,[229] Kreitzer claims, "we have no way of determining whether or not the larger context of the Psalm has any necessary bearing on Paul's use of [Ps 8:]6b. We simply do not know if Paul had the status of man in mind at all."[230] Contrary to Kreitzer's claim, it is difficult to imagine that Paul in 1 Cor 15:27—when citing Ps 8:6 [7 LXX]—did not have in mind under whose feet everything is subjected. The point of Adam Christology here obviously is not "the status of man (or Adam)" but that of Christ. This does not mean, however, there is no reference to the figure of Adam at all. The use of Ps 8:6 [7 LXX] in 1 Cor 15:27 evidently reflects the implicit primitive Adam-Jesus typology of the early church. As I have discussed earlier, while the Psalmist refers to Adam's sovereignty over God's creation in Gen 1:26–30 and speaks of humanity's rule over the rest of God's creation, Paul and the author of Hebrews Christologically apply Ps 8:6 [7 LXX] to their description of Jesus' eschatological authority. Both of them reflect the early church Adam-Jesus typology, independently of each other. The early church tradition behind Mark 14:62 could have been

---

228. "Then comes the end, when he hands over the kingdom to God the Father, after he has destroyed every ruler and every authority and power. For he must reign *until he has put all his enemies under his feet* [Ps 110:1]. The last enemy to be destroyed is death. For *'God has put all things in subjection under his feet* [Ps 8:6].' But when it says, 'All things are put in subjection,' it is plain that this does not include the one who put all things in subjection under him."

229. Dunn, *Christology in the Making*, 108–11.

230. Kreitzer, *Jesus and God in Paul's Eschatology*, 152.

related to the same early church Adam-Jesus typology as that behind 1 Cor 15:27 and Heb 2:5–9.

Paul most likely was aware of Jesus' characteristic self-designation בר נשא and alluded to it in 1 Cor 15:27, 45. It is difficult to imagine that Paul—a multilingual rabbi who was well versed in the Scripture—was ignorant of the Hebrew equivalent בן אדם (MT; literally, "son of Adam") to the Greek υἱὸς ἀνθρώπου in Ps 8:4 [5 LXX]. Paul probably also knew about its Aramaic translation בר נש (cf. *Tg. Onq.* Ps 8:5[231]). Paul neither refers to Dan 7:13 nor calls Christ בר נשא (or בר נש) but yet he implies in 1 Cor 15:27 that Christ is the very בן אדם (or בר נש) in Ps 8:4 [5 LXX]—cf. "the last Adam" (ὁ ἔσχατος Ἀδάμ) in 1 Cor 15:45. As Hay suggests: "The title ['son of man'] *may* have been in Paul's mind as he wrote 1 Cor 15:25; the Adamic speculation presupposed by the context, and the merging of the ideas of Ps 8 and 110 suggest it. In Heb 2:6–8, there is a quotation of Ps 8 which includes the phrase 'son of man,' and this passage seems to be a continuation of the subjection theme raised in Heb 1:13 with a quotation of Ps 110:1."[232]

Paul's rhetorical purpose of incorporating the early church Adam-Jesus typology into his argument in 1 Cor 15:20–28 is twofold. Firstly, Paul wants to contrast the universality of death in Adam with the universality of life (for those) in Christ because of his resurrection (1 Cor 15:22): ὥσπερ γὰρ ἐν τῷ Ἀδὰμ πάντες ἀποθνῄσκουσιν, οὕτως καὶ ἐν τῷ Χριστῷ πάντες ζῳοποιηθήσονται ("for as all die in Adam, so all will be made alive in Christ"). Secondly, Paul wants to compare the universality of Christ's eschatological rule with the universality of Adam's sovereignty over God's creation in Gen 1:26–30.[233]

Besides the two *verbal* and *formal* similarities between the early church tradition behind Mark 14:62 and Paul's Adam Christology, I have

---

231. Similarly, Bowker, "Son of Man," 36–37.

232. Hay, *Glory at the Right Hand*, 109.

233. Schrage similarly notes: "In the end, God alone can defeat the enemy of all enemies, namely, death. This seems to be indicated in 1 Cor 15:26 as well and is confirmed in 1 Cor 15:54–57. Paul above all still sees that the universality of the rule of Christ has always been contested, ever since Adam and the reign of the destructive power of death (1 Cor 15:21–22), and this is particularly evident in 1 Cor 15:23c"; my translation of "Letztlich kann nur Gott selbst den Feind aller Feinde, nämlich den Tod, besiegen. Das scheint auch V 26 zu zeigen und wird durch V 54–57 bestätigt. Paulus sieht vor allem noch in der seit Adam bestehenden (V 21f) Herrschaft der Unheilsmacht des Todes die Universalität der Herrschaft des Christus bestritten, was nach V 23c besonders auffällt"; Schrage, *Erste Brief an die Korinther (1Kor 15,1—16,24)*, 178.

to highlight the unique combination of Ps 110:1 [109:1 LXX] (1 Cor 15:25) and Ps 8:6 (1 Cor 15:27) in parallel with that of Ps 110:1 [109:1 LXX] (Heb 1:13) and Ps 8:4–6 (Heb 2:6–8a). The difference between Paul and the author of Hebrews is that Paul puts the two texts together by means of *gezerah shawah* but the author of Hebrews does not. When quoting Ps 110:1 [109:1 LXX], Paul seems to make a few modifications—presuming that his Scriptural text was similar to the critical editions of the LXX such as Rahlfs, Cambridge, and Göttingen. Firstly, Paul in 1 Cor 15:25 skips the first half, κάθου ἐκ δεξιῶν μου ("Sit at my right hand"). Secondly, Paul changes the first person singular aorist subjunctive verb θῶ (from τίθημι "to put") to the third person singular form θῇ. Paul in 1 Cor 15:25 does not quote Ps 110:1 [109:1 LXX] verbatim but modifies God's speaking to David's lord. Thirdly, Paul slightly changes the expression ὑποπόδιον τῶν ποδῶν σου ("your footstool") to ὑπὸ τοὺς πόδας αὐτου ("under his feet"), dropping the word ὑποπόδιον in the original, with the result that it creates a parallel with Ps 8:6 cited in 1 Cor 15:27. Fourthly, Paul adds the adjective πᾶς ("all") to modify the noun οἱ ἐχθροί and emphasizes ἔσχατος ἐχθρὸς καταργεῖται ὁ θάνατος ("the last enemy, Death, is destroyed [by Christ]") in 1 Cor 15:26.

When citing Ps 8:6 in 1 Cor 15:27, Paul seems to change the second person singular aorist indicative verb ὑπέταξας (from ὑποτάσσω "to submit, subject") to the third person singular form ὑπέταξεν. The subject of both Ps 8:6 and 1 Cor 15:27 remains the same—God. Confusingly, unlike in the case of 1 Cor 15:25, the agent of subjection is God and not Christ.[234] Paul slightly modifies the expression ὑποκάτω τῶν ποδῶν αὐτοῦ ("under his feet") to ὑπὸ τοὺς πόδας αὐτοῦ ("under his feet") for the sake of the intended parallelism between 1 Cor 15:25 and 27[235]:

---

234. As Schrage points out: "Since the subject of ὑποτάξαντος ('submitting') in 1 Cor 15:27b clearly is God, Christ functions as the representative delegated by God to govern for him, whose unlimited authority is due to God alone. This explains the clear parallelism with 1 Cor 15:25, which deals with Christ"; my translation of "Da Subjekt des ὑποτάξαντος in V 27b in jedem Falle Gott ist, fungiert Christus als der von Gott delegierte Statthalter und Repräsentant, dessen unbegrenzte Machtfülle sich allein Gott selbst verdankt (vgl. 11,3). Damit erklärt sich auch der sachliche Parallelismus zu V 25, der von Christus handelt"; ibid., 182. Thiselton comments, "It is important, however, to recognize that since God and Christ as Lord are 'One,' this emphasis is not upon a 'discontinuation' of Christ's Lordship as such, but upon its culmination within the terms of its purpose for this world and Christ's kingdom here"; Thiselton, *First Epistle to the Thessalonians*, 1231; similarly, Garland, *1 Corinthians*, 713.

235. Stanley cannot find any particular reason why Paul prefers ὑπό to the original ὑποκάτω in his quotation of Ps 8:6 in 1 Cor 15:27. Stanley concludes, "Though a

	Texts in Parallel
1 Cor 15:25	For he must reign until *he has put all his enemies under his feet.*
Ps 110:1 [109:1 LXX]	The Lord said to my lord, "Sit on my right until *I make your enemies a footstool for your feet*" [NETS].
1 Cor 15:27	For "God *has put all things in subjection under his feet.*"
Ps 8:6 [7 LXX]	And you set him over the works of your hands; *you subjected all under his feet* [NETS].

Paul demonstrates *gezerah shawah*—Ps 110:1 [109:1 LXX] and Ps 8:6 [7 LXX]—with focus on the phrase ὑπὸ τοὺς πόδας αὐτοῦ to elucidate Christ's eschatological authority.

While Paul may have been responsible for the *gezerah shawah*, the unique combination of the two psalms in the context of Adam Christology (1 Cor 15:25–27; Heb 1:13; 2:6–8a) reflects the early church tradition. As Dunn points out, "It is unlikely that they [1 Cor 15:25–27; Eph 1:20–22; Heb 1:13–2:8; Mark 12:36; Matt 22:44; 1 Pet 3:22] all derived it from Paul independently."[236] De Boer similarly notes:

> The frequent citation and adaptation of these two Psalm texts (especially of Ps 110:1) elsewhere in the NT suggest that Paul may not be citing (or alluding to) "Scripture" but a christological tradition in which the language of Ps 110:1 and Ps 8:6b had already come to play a prominent and relatively fixed role. This surmise finds weighty support in the parallels to 1 Cor 15:20–28 in Ephesians (1:20–23), 1 Peter (3:21b–22), and Hebrews (1:3, 13; 2:8; cf. 8:1; 10:12–13; 12:2). These three works juxtapose language derived from Ps 110:1 and Ps 8:6b and they do so in contexts having to do with Jesus' resurrection (explicitly mentioned in Eph 1:20 and 1 Pet 3:21b), which is portrayed as his exaltation over principalities, powers, or angels. This is precisely the context in which Paul "cites" or makes use of this material.[237]

Striking *verbal* and *formal* similarities can be detected in the following verses.[238]

---

pre-Pauline origin cannot be ruled out, all the evidence seems to favor the view that Paul has (perhaps unconsciously) adapted the wording of this common quotation to conform to his own linguistic usage"; Stanley, *Paul and the Language of Scripture*, 207.

236. Dunn, *Christology in the Making*, 108–9.

237. De Boer, "Paul's Use of a Resurrection Tradition in 1 Cor 15:20–28," 642; similarly, Fitzmyer, *First Corinthians*, 578; Black, "Πᾶσαι ἐξουσίαι αὐτῷ ὑποταγήσονται," 75.

238. Cf. De Boer, "Paul's Use of a Resurrection Tradition in 1 Cor 15:20–28," 643.

1 Cor 15:20–28	Eph 1:20–23	1 Pet 3:21b–22	Heb 1:3; 2:8
Χριστὸς ἐγήγερται ἐκ νεκρῶν	[θεός] ἐγείρας αὐτόν ἐκ νεκρῶν	δι' ἀναστάσεως Ἰησοῦ Χριστοῦ	
πᾶσαν ἀρχὴν καὶ πᾶσαν ἐξουσίαν καὶ δύναμιν	ὑπεράνω πάσης ἀρχῆς καὶ ἐξουσίας καὶ δυνάμεως καὶ κυριότητος	ὅς ἐστιν ἐν δεξιᾷ θεοῦ πορευθεὶς εἰς οὐρανόν	ἐκάθισεν ἐν δεξιᾷ τῆς μεγαλωσύνης ἐν ὑψηλοῖς, τοσούτῳ κρείττων γενόμενος τῶν ἀγγέλων
δεῖ γὰρ αὐτὸν βασιλεύειν ἄχρι οὗ θῇ πάντας τοὺς ἐχθροὺς ὑπὸ τοὺς πόδας αὐτοῦ	[θεός] καθίσας ἐν δεξιᾷ αὐτοῦ ἐν τοῖς ἐπουρανίοις	ὑποταγέντων αὐτῷ ἀγγέλων καὶ ἐξουσιῶν καὶ δυνάμεων	πάντα ὑπέταξας ὑποκάτω τῶν ποδῶν αὐτοῦ
πάντα γὰρ ὑπέταξεν ὑπὸ τοὺς πόδας αὐτοῦ	καὶ πάντα ὑπέταξεν ὑπὸ τοὺς πόδας αὐτοῦ		
πάντα ἐν πᾶσιν	τὰ πάντα ἐν πᾶσιν		

On the basis of the similarities and the dissimilarities among these passages, De Boer correctly recognizes a shared pre-Pauline "resurrection tradition."[239]

This "resurrection tradition" seems to reflect the early church Adam-Jesus typology. Responding to the high priest's life-threatening question, "Are you the Messiah, the Son of the Blessed One?" Jesus answers, "I am; and 'you will see the Son of Man seated at the right hand of the Power,' and 'coming with the clouds of heaven.'" Although Jesus does not explicitly mention his resurrection in Mark 14:62, his reply to the high priest anticipates his post-mortem vindication that he previously alluded to in Mark 8:31; 9:31; 10:33–34. The two *verbal* and *formal* similarities between the early church tradition behind Mark 14:62 and Paul's Adam Christology in 1 Cor 15:25–27 in addition to the unique combination of Ps 110:1 and Ps 8 in the latter suggest that this "resurrection tradition" was linked with the early church Adam-Jesus typology—cf. Mark 14:62; 1 Cor 15:25–27; Heb 1:3; 2:6–8a. Kim points out:

239. Ibid., 646–47.

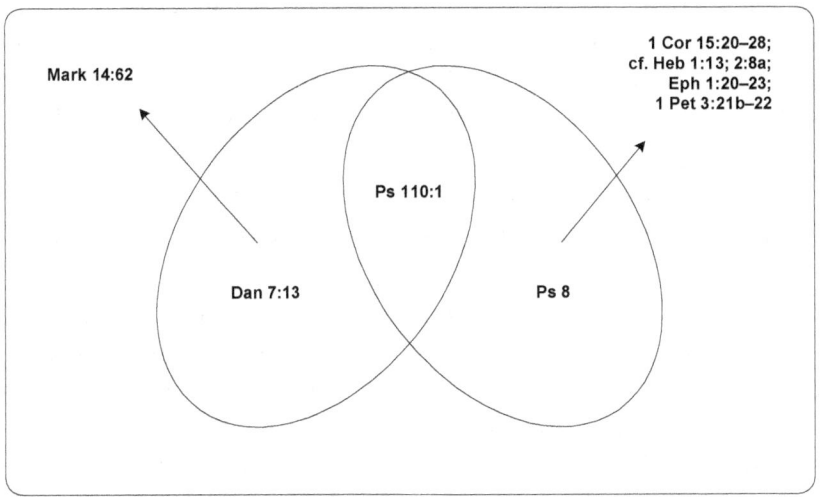

Then, the main idea of this passage [1 Cor 15:23–28], the temporary entrusting of God's kingly reign to Christ until he subjugates all those enemy forces, reflects Dan 7:13–14 as well as Ps 110:1 and 8:7 . . . So the "Son of Man" saying of Mark 14:62 and parallels join Dan 7:13–14 and Ps 110:1 in its scriptural allusion. Even if Paul did not know the saying of Mark 14:62, he himself could have taken the Danielic and Psalm passages together. Then they could have drawn Ps 8:7 into a further combination, because the latter also speaks about the "son of man" being given dominion (=Dan 7:14) and God subjecting all things under his feet (=Ps 110:1/Dan 7:14).[240]

Kim rightly highlights the importance of the text of Dan 7 in the link between Mark 14:62 and 1 Cor 15:23–28. Considering the multiple manifestations of the combination of Dan 7:13; Ps 110:1; Ps 8 and their related Christological ideas with respect to Jesus' eschatological authority, however, such a combination was most likely *authentic* to the early church.

I have discussed so far two *verbal* and *formal* similarities between the early church tradition behind Mark 14:62 and Paul's Adam Christology—Ps 110:1 and the phrase "son of man"—and the unique combination of Ps 110:1 and Ps 8 in 1 Cor 15:25–27 and Heb 1:13—2:8a. The diagram below visualizes these observations:

240. Kim, *Paul and the New Perspective*, 196–97.

88 THE SON OF MAN AS THE LAST ADAM

These rather complicated connections can be best explained when we assume the early church Adam-Jesus typology that compares Jesus' eschatological authority with Adam's sovereignty over God's creation in Gen 1:26–30, citing a set of Scriptures: Dan 7:13, Ps 110:1, and Ps 8.[241]

Paul's Allusion to the Early Church Adam-Jesus Typology

I already have argued in detail that Paul alludes to the early church Adam-Jesus typology reflected in Mark 14:62 in 1 Cor 15:25–27. I have argued that Mark 14:62 contains the early church Adam-Jesus typology based on Pauline evidence and concluded that Paul is creatively using the early church Adam-Jesus typology. Against the potential accusation of circular argument, I defend my argument with two considerations. Firstly, I am using not only Pauline evidence (1 Cor 15:25–27) but also the evidence in Hebrews (Heb 1:13; 2:6–8a). Secondly, it is difficult to suppose any direct influence among Mark 14:62, 1 Cor 15:25–27, and Heb 1:13; 2:6–8a, considering the fact that they apply the early church Adam-Jesus typology to their settings distinctively.

Paul's Use of the Early Church Adam-Jesus Typology

Paul creatively uses the early church Adam-Jesus typology reflected in Mark 14:62 in developing his explicit and sophisticated Adam Christology in 1 Cor 15:20–28. In his attempt to assure the Corinthian believers of their bodily future resurrection, Paul in 1 Cor 15:20 calls Christ "the first fruits" (ἀπαρχή) of resurrection and continues: "For since death came through a human being, the resurrection of the dead has also come through a human being; for as all die in Adam, so all will be made alive in Christ. But each in his own order: Christ the first fruits, then at his coming those who belong to Christ" (1 Cor 15:21–23). Having assured the Corinthian believers of their future resurrection, Paul describes what is to happen in the End-time, emphasizing Christ's eschatological authority:

> Then comes the end, when he hands over the kingdom to God the Father, after he has destroyed every ruler and every authority and power. For he must reign until he has put all his enemies under his feet. The last enemy to be destroyed is death. For "God has put all things in subjection under his feet." But when it says,

---

241. Cf. Albl, "And Scripture Cannot Be Broken," 236.

"All things are put in subjection," it is plain that this does not include the one who put all things in subjection under him. When all things are subjected to him, then the Son himself will also be subjected to the one who put all things in subjection under him, so that God may be all in all (1 Cor 15:24–28).

When highlighting Christ's eschatological authority, as I pointed out earlier, Paul interprets Ps 110:1 [109:1 LXX] in 1 Cor 15:25 and Ps 8:6 [7 LXX] in 1 Cor 15:27 together by means of *gezerah shawah*, focusing on the phrase ὑπὸ τοὺς πόδας αὐτοῦ. As I proposed, Paul has at least two goals for incorporating the early church Adam-Jesus typology into his argument in 1 Cor 15:20–28—(a) to contrast the universality of death in Adam with the universality of life in Christ through resurrection and (b) to compare Christ's eschatological authority with Adam's sovereignty over God's creation. Both Paul's allusion to the phrase υἱὸς ἀνθρώπου ("son of man") in Ps 8:4 [5 LXX] and his Adam Christology starting from 1 Cor 15:20 illuminate that he is comparing Christ's eschatological authority with Adam's sovereignty over God's creation in Gen 1:26–30.

As I have discussed so far, regardless of the *historicity* of the events in Mark 14:53–72, there is no strong reason to doubt the *authenticity* of Mark 14:62 in relation to the early church's understanding of who Jesus is, reflected in his answer to the high priest's question in Mark 14:61. Despite the popularity of Ps 110:1 in early Christianity, the combination of Dan 7:13 and Ps 110:1 is unique to the early church tradition behind Mark 14:62. Although Paul does not allude to Dan 7:13 but only to Ps 110:1 [109:1 LXX] and Ps 8:4–6 [5–7 LXX] in 1 Cor 15:25–27 (cf. Heb 1:13; 2:6–8a), his reference to Ps 110:1 in the context of his comparison of Jesus' eschatological authority with Adam's sovereignty over God's creation in Genesis could not have been coincidental. Although Paul nowhere mentions the phrase "son of man," his citation of Ps 8:6 [7 LXX] in 1 Cor 15:27 indicates that he identifies Jesus with בן אדם in Ps 8:4 [5 LXX], which is translated as בר נש in the Targums. This parallels the supposed Jesus' self-designation בר נשא in Mark 14:62. These pieces of evidence suggest that Mark, Paul, and the author of Hebrews independently reflect the early church Adam-Jesus typology.

PAUL'S ADAM CHRISTOLOGY AND FIRST-CENTURY AD JUDAISM

This is a broad topic that requires another study for thorough investigation.[242] I will discuss this topic within certain confines under two headings: (a) the diversity of Adam portraits in Second Temple Judaism and (b) the uniqueness of the early church Adam-Jesus typology.

The Diversity of Adam Portraits in Second Temple Judaism

As Kreitzer points out, despite the limited number of references to the OT figure of Adam, Paul uses it as an important vehicle to expound crucial theological truths in his letters.[243] Kreitzer underscores that a number of first-century Jewish and Christian documents show the same fascination with the figure of Adam.[244] In his seminal contribution *Portraits of Adam in Early Judaism*, Levison argues:

> The thesis of this book can be stated negatively: the "motifs" of an "Adam speculation" or "Adam myth" which the last generation of scholars discerned in Early Judaism do not exist . . . the use of early Jewish texts to provide background material for Paul's letters led to an unwarranted emphasis upon certain dominant Pauline motifs, such as "Adam: the Original Sin and Death", or "the presentation of the two Adam-men as contrasting, corresponding universal figures." This approach squeezed the early Jewish data into the mold of Pauline concepts and motifs—the *Tendenz* of Paul and not of individual early Jewish authors became the interpretative key for organizing the ideas of these various texts, leading to a distortion of the meaning of Adam in Early Judaism and a failure to recognize the diversity of interpretations.[245]

I agree with Levison that, when we examine various references to Adam in their particular literary contexts, there is no one "Adam speculation" or "Adam myth" in Second Temple Judaism but many different *Tendenzen*. Nonetheless, an author's exposure to a particular *Tendenz* could have influenced the depiction of Adam in his or her literary work. The diversity of the portrait of Adam in Second Temple Judaism signi-

---

242. See Levison, *Portraits of Adam in Early Judaism*.
243. Kreitzer, "Adam and Christ," 9.
244. Ibid.
245. Levison, *Portraits of Adam in Early Judaism*, 13.

fies the fact that Paul's Adam Christology should be understood in the context of many portraits of Adam in Second Temple Judaism.

It goes beyond the scope of this study to examine Adam speculations in Second Temple Judaism in detail. It suffices for us to recognize that, as Levison summarizes, the portraits of Adam in Second Temple Judaism fall into four general categories: (1) the creation of Adam—with reference to Gen 1:26–28 [the image of God; male and female; Adam's dominion] and Gen 2:7, (2) the original nature of Adam, (3) the transgression of Adam, and (4) the effects of Adam's transgression.[246] The findings of this chapter elucidate what seem to be four main domains of the early church Adam-Jesus typology:

a. Jesus' eschatological *authority* (using Dan 7:13; Ps 110:1; 8:4–6; cf. Mark 14:62; Heb 1:13–2:11; 1 Cor 15:25–27) in comparison with Adam's superiority over God's creation in Gen 1:26–28

b. Jesus' *obedience* (cf. Phil 2:6–11; Rom 5:19) in contrast to Adam's disobedience

c. Jesus' *solidarity* with his followers (cf. Rom 5:17; 1 Cor 15:22; Heb 2:10) in comparison with Adam as the representative of humankind

d. Jesus' *sanctification* of his followers (cf. Rom 5:19; Heb 2:11, 17) in contrast to the consequences of Adam's transgression

As we can see here, various *Tendenzen* with respect to the portraits of Adam in Second Temple Judaism have broad thematic parallels with the early church Adam-Jesus typology. The early church could have been familiar with these *Tendenzen* and similarly interpreted various Adamic Scriptures—such as Gen 1:26–28; 2:7; Ps 8—when explaining who Christ is in relation to Adam.

The Uniqueness of the Early Church Adam-Jesus Typology

As I have argued earlier, the unique combinations of Scriptures—Dan 7:13; Ps 110:1 (Mark 14:62) and Ps 110:1; Ps 8 (1 Cor 15:25–27; Heb 1:13–2:8a)—in explaining Jesus' eschatological authority can be best explained by the early church Adam-Jesus typology. In the following I want to demonstrate further the uniqueness of the early church Adam-

---

246. Ibid., 145.

Jesus typology. Hengel claims, "The affinity between Ps 110 and the figure of the son of man which is alluded to for the first time in Dan 7:13 and broadly developed in the *Similitudes*, is also present in the answer of Jesus to the question of the high priest about the messiah in Mark 14:62."[247] While correctly recognizing the unique dual reference to Dan 7:13 and Ps 110:1 in Mark 14:62, Hengel's claim that Ps 110:1 "is alluded to for the first time in Dan 7:13 and broadly developed in the *Similitudes*" is problematic. Form-critically speaking, nothing alludes specifically to Ps 110:1 in Dan 7:13. Hengel lists four references (*1 En.* 51.3; 55.4; 61.8; 62.1–2) as the examples of "the affinity between both texts [Dan 7:13 and Ps 110:1]" in the *Similitudes* of Enoch.[248] There are certain allusions to the Danielic Son of Man on the *conceptual* level in these references. Nonetheless, any specific link with Ps 110:1 cannot be established in them, not to mention the unique combination of Dan 7:13 and Ps 110:1. In other words, the connections between Ps 110:1 and the four references in the *Similitudes* of Enoch are not specific enough to support Hengel's claim. As Hengel himself admits, "The sitting at the right hand of God, which so clearly expresses the communion with God, is missing in the *Similitudes*."[249]

On the basis of his view that the *Similitudes* of Enoch are not later than early Christianity, dating between 40 B.C. and 70 AD, Hengel contends that "a direct—even a mutual—influence is possible" between the two.[250] While supporting the early dating of the *Similitudes* of Enoch in general, in my opinion, there is no evidence for any direct or mutual influence of the *Similitudes* of Enoch on the early church tradition behind Mark 14:62.[251] As I have argued earlier, the combination of Dan 7:13 and Ps 110:1 seems unique to the early church tradition behind Mark 14:62 and 1 Cor 15:25, 27.

---

247. Hengel, *Studies in Early Christology*, 186.

248. Ibid., 185.

249. Ibid., 188.

250. Ibid., 185–86.

251. Hannah claims, "In all probability the Similitudes stand entirely alone within Second Temple Judaism in placing a divine mediator on the divine throne [itself]"; Hannah, "Throne of His Glory," 88. Space does not permit us to examine Hannah's claim here. If Hannah is right, however, there is no possibility that the *Similitudes* of Enoch may have influenced the early church tradition behind Mark 14:62, as Hengel seems to suggest. The absence of the *Similitudes* at Qumran also makes such a possibility less likely.

Although there are many references to the eschatological judgment—cf. *1 En.* 45.6; 54.6; *2 En.* 58.6; 65.6; *Sib. Or.* 4.183–84; *2 Bar.* 54.21; *T. Jud.* 45.5–6; *T. Ab.* 13.7; *L.A.E.* 49.3—and various Adam speculations in Jewish intertestamental literature, only *T. Ab.* 13.1–8 [A[252]] designates the agent of the eschatological judgment as "the son of Adam":

> And Abraham said, "My lord Commander-in-chief [Michael], who is this all-wondrous judge? . . . "Do you see, all-pious Abraham, the frightful man who is seated on the throne? This is the son of Adam, the first-formed, who is called Abel, whom Cain the wicked killed. And he sits here to judge the entire creation, examining both righteous and sinners. For God said, "I do not judge you, but every man is judged by man." On account of this he gave him judgment, to judge the world until his great and glorious Parousia . . . For every person has sprung from the first-formed, and on account of this they are first judged here by his son. And at the second Parousia they will be judged by the twelve tribes of Israel, both every breath and every creature. And, thirdly, they shall be judged by the Master God of all . . . And thus the judgment and recompense of the world is made through three tribunals. And therefore a matter is not ultimately established by one or two witnesses, but *every matter shall be established by three witnesses*.[253]

It is impossible to know the exact date of the Testament of Abraham. Sanders dates it approximately around 100 AD and considers its content in both recensions as "unmistakably Jewish."[254] Recently, James R. Davila challenges its Jewish origin and supports its Christian authorship.[255] Only the longer recension A includes *T. Ab.* 13.1–8 and it is difficult to know whether its *Urtext* was Jewish or Christian. Davila lists some reasons to consider the Jewish origin of *T. Ab.* 13.1–8: (a) the two *parousiai* and three eschatological judgments, (b) the lack of reference to Jesus, and (c) the judgment by the twelve tribes of Israel. Davila also lists other reasons

252. This is the longer recension in Rumanian.

253. Sanders, "Testament of Abraham," 889–90; Sander's own italicization to indicate a Scriptural citation—Deut 19:15.

254. Ibid., 875.

255. Davila claims, "To my mind, Christian authorship of the *Urtext* offers few difficulties, but authorship by a Jew or a gentile God-fearer remains quite possible. In any case, both recensions have been heavily reworked in different ways and if a pre-Christian original ever existed, it cannot be recovered without a fortuitous discovery of the data." Davila, *Provenance of the Pseudepigrapha*, 207.

to consider the Christian origin of *T. Ab.* 13.1–8: (a) the abundance of Christian terminology, (b) the lack of a parallel in the shorter recension B [chapter 11], which is probably more original, (c) the lack of interest in Jewish culture and institutions, and (d) its universalistic eschatology.[256]

If the core of *T. Ab.* 13.1–8 is derived from a Jewish source, theoretically speaking, Paul could have known its earlier tradition (*Vorlage*) and reflected it in his Adam Christology in Rom 5 and 1 Cor 15. However, there are at least two fundamental differences between *T. Ab.* 13.1–8 and Paul. Firstly, there is no particular reference to Abel in Rom 5 or 1 Cor 15. Secondly, Paul mentions neither the tribunal system of the eschatological judgment nor three separate Parousiai—the coming of Abel, that of the twelve tribes of Israel, and that of God himself—implied in *T. Ab.* 13.1–8. These fundamental differences between *T. Ab.* 13.1–8 and Paul's Adam Christology make any direct and exclusive link between the two doubtful. Considering the various connections between what I consider as the early church Adam-Jesus typology and Paul's Adam Christology—which I have discussed so far, Paul most likely did not derive his Adam Christology exclusively from first-century AD Judaism but through the early church tradition.

CONCLUSION

In the beginning of this study, I asked the question, "Did Paul invent the so-called Adam Christology out of nothing (*ex nihilo*) or develop the implicit primitive Adam-Jesus typology of the early church?" Although we cannot know the precise form of the early church Adam-Jesus typology, there exist several pieces of evidence in the New Testament. In this chapter, I have examined three passages (Phil 2:6–11; Heb 2:5–11; Mark 14:62) exploring the relationship between the implicit primitive Adam-Jesus typology of the early church and Paul's explicit and sophisticated Adam Christology.

While these three passages obviously are not verbatim quotations of the early church tradition, they reflect certain traditional elements that I identify with the early church Adam-Jesus typology. Paul does not create his Adam Christology out of nothing (*ex nihilo*) in building up his argument in Phil 2:1–18; 1 Cor 15:25, 27, 45; Rom 5:17, 19 but creatively develops an early church Adam-Jesus typology, applying it

---

256. Ibid., 203–7.

to the situation (*Sitz im Leben*) of his readers. One may argue that the Old Testament passages such as Dan 7:13, Ps 110:1, and Ps 8:4–6 were used simply as messianic proof-texts in the New Testament and do not necessarily reflect a coherent Adam Christology in the early church. On the one hand, we certainly do not have evidence for a single coherent Adam Christology, as if it were an already established doctrine in the early church. On the other hand, however, as I have discussed in this chapter, those Old Testament passages can hardly be random messianic proof-texts but provide the pieces of evidence for the multifaceted early church Adam-Jesus typology. Paul most likely knew about the implicit primitive Adam-Jesus typology of the early church and expanded it to his explicit and sophisticated Adam Christology, creatively applying it to his argument in Rom 5 and 1 Cor 15. The early church employed Adam-Jesus typology in explicating Jesus' eschatological *authority* (cf. Adam's authority over God's creation in Gen 1:26–28), Jesus' *obedience* (*contra* Adam's disobedience), Jesus' *solidarity* with his followers (cf. Adam as the representative of humankind), and Jesus' *sanctification* of his followers (*contra* the consequences of Adam's transgression).

3

The Son of Man Sayings as Sources of Paul's Adam Christology

IN CHAPTER 2, I examined the relationship between the early church Adam-Jesus typology and Paul's Adam Christology. The four topics discussed in chapter 2 were (a) the *authenticity* of Phil 2:6–11; Heb 2:5–11; Mark 14:62, (b) the early church Adam-Jesus typology in each passage, (c) Paul's allusion to the early church Adam-Jesus typology, and (d) Paul's creative use of the early church Adam-Jesus typology. In this chapter, I will investigate the relationship between two particular early church traditions (reflected in Mark 10:45 and Matt 19:28//Luke 22:30) and Paul's Adam Christology. These traditions do not concern the early church Adam-Jesus typology *per se*. As we will see shortly, however, Paul incorporates them into his Adam Christology. In parallel with chapter 2, I will discuss in this chapter the following topics: (a) the *authenticity* of Mark 10:45 and Matt 19:28//Luke 22:30, (b) Paul's allusion to the early church tradition behind Mark 10:45 and Matt 19:28//Luke 22:30, (c) Paul's incorporation of the early church tradition behind Mark 10:45 and Matt 19:28//Luke 22:30 into his Adam Christology, (d) Paul's presentation of Jesus' atoning death / Jesus' followers' eschatological ruling and the Scriptures, and (e) Paul's presentation of these ideas and first-century AD Judaism.

MARK 10:45 (CF. MATT 20:28; LUKE 22:27)

The Authenticity of Mark 10:45

Most commentators recognize the uniqueness of Mark 10:45 and suggest that Mark is depending on his source material.[1] In contrast, Müller claims:

> Mark 10:45 could still be authentic, in which, "the Son of Man" likewise happens to be an exclusive designation for Jesus—indeed, without the following clause of the "ransom," has no parallel in the authentic Jesus tradition. In any case, the judgment cannot be made that all ἦλθεν/sayings are due to summarization or to the apparently retrospective post-Easter character. Mark 10:45 could come from Jesus, in so far as in the ἦλθεν-phrase the Aramaic way of speaking continues to have an effect, which signifies, "to intend," "to want," or "to have the task of."[2]

As I will explain shortly, Müller's claim that Mark 10:45 is *authentic* to the early church tradition except for the "ransom" clause is unconvincing. Marcus claims, "This ransom saying is of central importance in Mark's narrative because it is the clearest Markan reflection on the saving purpose of Jesus' death (cf. 14:24)."[3] Mark 10:45 probably is not merely the Evangelist's own reflection on the redemptive death of Jesus for two reasons. Firstly, the conciseness of Mark 10:45 and its lack of the mention of the cross or resurrection undermine Marcus' claim.[4]

---

1. E.g., Collins, *Mark*, 500–504; Donahue and Harrington, *Gospel of Mark*, 313; Evans, *Mark 8:27—16:20*, 119-25; Stein, *Mark*, 487-89; Gnilka, *Das Evangelium nach Markus (Mk 8:27—16:20)*, 104.

2. My translation of "Authentisch könnte noch Mk 10,45 sein, wo, der Menschensohn' ebenfalls als exklusive Bezeichnung für Jesus begegnet—allerdings ohne den Nachsatz vom ‚Lösegeld', der in der authentischen Jesustradition ohne Parallele ist. Jedenfalls darf nicht pauschal geurteilt werden, alle ἦλθεν/-Sprüche seien wegen des zusammenfassenden bzw. angeblich rückblickenden Charakters nachösterlich. Mk 10,45 könnte von Jesus stammen, insofern in der ἦλθεν-Wendung aramäische Sprechweise nachwirkt, die die Bedeutung ‚beabsichtigen,' ‚wollen,' oder ‚die Aufgabe haben' besitzt"; Müller, "Jesus als ‚der Menschensohn,'" 106.

3. Marcus, *Mark 8-16*, 757; Marcus considers Mark as a follower of Paul and argues that he reflects many distinctive Pauline ideas in his Gospel; Marcus, "Mark—Interpreter of Paul," 473-87.

4. Similarly, Stein, *Mark*, 757; Marcus emphasizes the centrality of the theology of the cross in Mark's Gospel, which he attributes to Paul; Marcus, "Mark—Interpreter of Paul," 479. If that is the case, it is strange that Mark fails to mention the cross in a soteriologically important passage such as Mark 10:45.

Secondly and more importantly, the Semitic-like form of Mark 10:45 strongly supports its *authenticity*.

Jeremias and others correctly identify the Hellenized form of Mark 10:45 in 1 Tim 2:5–6 with the following parallels:[5]

	Mark 10:45	1 Tim 2:5–6
(a)	ὁ υἱὸς τοῦ ἀνθρώπου	ἄνθρωπος
(b)	δοῦναι τὴν ψυχὴν αὐτοῦ	ὁ δοὺς ἑαυτόν
(c)	λύτρον	ἀντίλυτρον
(d)	ἀντὶ πολλῶν	ὑπὲρ πάντων

Jeremias explains these parallels: "It can be seen that 1 Tim 2:6 has given Mark's Semitic wording a more pronounced Greek flavour in every word. 1 Tim 2:6 confirms the result of the literary analysis that Mark 10:45b was originally a *logion* in independent circulation. Anyone who regards the nucleus of the Eucharistic words as genuine will have no hesitation in deriving the substance of this *logion* from Jesus."[6] When we compare the Semitic-like form of Mark 10:45 with the Hellenized form of 1 Tim 2:5–6, as Evans points out, Mark 10:45 can hardly be a Pauline formula or some other Hellenized formula.[7] The same features of polished Greek also can be seen in Paul's "indisputable" letters. For instance, (b) is apparent behind παραδόντος ἑαυτὸν ὑπὲρ ἐμοῦ ("who gave himself for me") in Gal 2:20. The addition of a prefix before λύτρον, (c), is attested in Paul's use of ἀπολύτρωσις in Rom 3:24. Also, as in (d), Paul translates in 2 Cor 5:14–15 the Semitic expression of רב ("many") into the Greek expression of πᾶς ("all")—cf. its literal translation πολύς in the LXX. These observations provide a strong case of the Evangelist's and Paul's dependence on the same early church tradition, independent of each other.[8]

---

5. Jeremias, *New Testament Theology*, 294; Stuhlmacher, *Reconciliation, Law, & Righteousness*, 18; Evans, *Mark 8:27—16:20*, 124.

6. Jeremias, *New Testament Theology*, 293–94.

7. Evans, *Mark 8:27—16:20*, 124.

8. Collins similarly notes, "It is unlikely that Mark is depending on Paul on v. 45. It is more likely that they drew independently upon similar earlier traditions"; Collins, *Mark*, 503; also, Breytenbach, *Versöhnung*, 208–9; Kraus, *Tod Jesu als Heiligtumsweihe*, 261; Taylor, *New Testament Essays*, 60–71.

The Son of Man Sayings as Sources of Paul's Adam Christology 99

These observations make an exceptionally strong case for the *authenticity* of Mark 10:45.[9] If Mark or another "creative mind" created Mark 10:45 based on Jewish martyrdom ideology, as Barrett suggests,[10] the author would have composed Mark 10:45 in polished Greek (cf. 1 Tim 2:5-6) for his Gentile readership. Barrett's claim is unlikely, unless we assume that Mark is an incompetent Greek writer or that Mark is intentionally imitating Semitic expressions in Mark 10:45 to make it sound like the very words (*ipsissima verba*) of Jesus.

Paul's Allusion to the Early Church Tradition behind Mark 10:45

In order to demonstrate Paul's allusion to the early church tradition behind Mark 10:45, I have to present my argument in the following logical steps. Firstly, Paul clearly depends on the early church tradition in Rom 5:8 Χριστὸς ὑπὲρ ἡμῶν ἀπέθανεν ("Christ died for us")—cf. Rom 5:6; 4:25. As Dunn comments on Rom 5:6, 8, "ἀποθανεῖν ὑπέρ, (Christ) 'died for the sake/benefit of,' is well established in the evangelistic and creedal language inherited by Paul (14:15; 1 Cor 15:3; 2 Cor 5:15; 1 Thess 5:10; cf. 1 Pet 3:18)."[11] Paul bases his statements in Rom 5:15, 19 on "the evangelistic and creedal language" in Rom 5:6, 8. Secondly, if this early church tradition is represented anywhere in the Synoptic Gospels, we have only three possibilities: the early church tradition behind (a) Mark 10:45, (b) the Words of Institution (Mark 14:22-25; Matt 26:26-29; Luke 22:15-20; cf. 1 Cor 11:24-25), and (c) Jesus' Passion predictions (Mark 8:31; 9:31; 10:33-34, and their parallels).

Thirdly, while the phrase οἱ πολλοί ("the many") in Rom 5:15, 19 may have been influenced by the early church tradition behind the Words of Institution, the early church tradition behind Mark 10:45 has a much wider range of links with Pauline material. A number of passages in the Pauline Corpus reflect the early church tradition behind Mark 10:45, which I will discuss shortly. The following chart visualizes multiple links between the early church tradition behind Mark 10:45 and Paul:

---

9. See more arguments for the *authenticity* of Mark 10:45 in Riesner, "Back to the Historical Jesus through Paul and His School (the Ransom Logion—Mark 10:45; Matthew 20:28)," 171-99.

10. Barrett, "Background of Mark 10:45," 15.

11. Dunn, *Romans 1-8*, 255, 257; similarly, Byrne, *Romans*, 171.

Mark 10:45	δοῦναι τὴν ψυχὴν αὐτοῦ	λύτρον ἀντὶ πολλῶν
Undisputed Pauline Letters		
Rom 3:24	δικαιούμενοι δωρεὰν τῇ αὐτοῦ χάριτι [ ]	[διὰ τῆς ἀπολυτρώσεως τῆς ἐν Χριστῷ Ἰησοῦ]
Rom 4:25	ὃς παρεδόθη [ ]	[διὰ τὰ παραπτώματα ἡμῶν]
Rom 5:6	Ἔτι γὰρ Χριστὸς ὄντων ἡμῶν ἀσθενῶν ἔτι κατὰ καιρὸν [ ] ἀπέθανεν	[ὑπὲρ ἀσεβῶν]
Rom 5:8	ὅτι ἔτι ἁμαρτωλῶν ὄντων ἡμῶν Χριστὸς [ ] ἀπέθανεν.	[ὑπὲρ ἡμῶν]
Rom 5:15	πολλῷ μᾶλλον ἡ χάρις τοῦ θεοῦ καὶ ἡ χάρις τοῦ θεοῦ καὶ ἡ δωρεὰ ἐν χάριτι τῇ τοῦ ἑνὸς ἀνθρώπου Ἰησοῦ Χριστοῦ [ ] ἐπερίσσευσεν.	[εἰς τοὺς πολλούς]
Rom 5:19	ὥσπερ γὰρ διὰ τῆς παρακοῆς τοῦ ἑνὸς ἀνθρώπου ἁμαρτωλοὶ κατεστάθησαν [ ], οὕτως καὶ διὰ τῆς ὑπακοῆς τοῦ ἑνὸς δίκαιοι κατασταθήσονται [ ].	[οἱ πολλοί] [οἱ πολλοί]
Rom 8:32	ὅς γε τοῦ ἰδίου υἱοῦ οὐκ ἐφείσατο ἀλλὰ [ ] παρέδωκεν αὐτόν	[ὑπὲρ ἡμῶν πάντων]
1 Cor 15:3	Χριστὸς ἀπέθανεν [ ]	[ὑπὲρ τῶν ἁμαρτιῶν ἡμῶν]
2 Cor 4:11	ἀεὶ γὰρ ἡμεῖς οἱ ζῶντες εἰς θάνατον παραδιδόμεθα [ ]	Cf. [διὰ Ἰησοῦν]
Gal 2:20	τοῦ ἀγαπήσαντός με καὶ παραδόντος ἑαυτον [ ]	[ὑπὲρ ἐμοῦ]
Disputed Pauline Letters		
Eph 5:2	ὁ Χριστὸς ἠγάπησεν ἡμᾶς καὶ παρέδωκεν ἑαυτὸν [ ]	[ὑπὲρ ἡμῶν]
Eph 5:25	ὁ Χριστὸς ἠγάπησεν τὴν ἐκκλησίαν καὶ ἑαυτὸν παρέδωκεν [ ]	[ὑπὲρ αὐτῆς]

Fourthly, considering the multiple parallels between the early church tradition behind Mark 10:45 and Pauline material, the former is the strongest candidate to have influenced the latter. Fifthly, the fact that Paul prefers the preposition ὑπέρ to the preposition ἀντί in the passages listed above cannot be the decisive evidence against his allusion to the early church tradition behind Mark 10:45. The preposition ἀντί naturally goes with the noun λύτρον, however, without the latter, the former is awkward and the preposition ὑπέρ becomes the most serviceable preposition. Sixthly, it is likely that the passages that attest the verb παραδίδωμι with Christ as its object (Rom 4:25; 8:32) have been influenced not only by the early church tradition behind Mark 10:45 but also by that behind Jesus' Passion predictions. Finally, as I will discuss shortly, Paul in various passages seems to have merged the early church tradition behind Mark 10:45, the Words of Institution, and Jesus' Passion predictions. On the one hand, such a creative use of various authoritative traditions should not surprise us—cf. Gal 4:21–31; 1 Cor 7:8–16; 9:3–14; 10:1–22; 2 Cor 3:7–18; Rom 10:5–13; 1 Thess 4:13—5:11. On the other hand, the early church tradition behind Mark 10:45 shows a much wider set of features parallel with Pauline material than the tradition behind the Words of Institution—limited to the phrase οἱ πολλοί[12]—or the tradition behind Jesus' Passion prediction—limited to the verb παραδίδωμι with Christ as its object.

One may argue that the absence of the word λύτρον in Rom 5 provides evidence against Paul's allusion to the early church tradition behind Mark 10:45. Although the word λύτρον ("ransom") is not a rare word in Greek, it is attested in the New Testament only in Mark 10:45 and its parallel in Matt 20:28. Does this mean that the idea of the death of Christ as a ransom is unique to the Evangelists? As Gundry points out, "It is untrue that the rest of the New Testament does not make the notion of a ransom part of Jesus' salvific work."[13] Although Paul never

12. Stuhlmacher refutes Roloff's claim that the motif of serving in Mark 10:45 was directly derived from the Lord's Supper tradition—cf. Roloff, "Anfänge der soteriologischen Deutung des Todes Jesu (Mark 10:45 und Luke 22:27)," 62—in the following: "Neither λύτρον, the word so particularly characteristic of Mark 10:45 (Matt 20:28), nor the concise formulation ἀντὶ πολλῶν is typical of the New Testament Lord's Supper texts. These speak of the covenantal blood of Jesus, poured out ὑπὲρ πολλῶν (also περὶ πολλῶν); they avoid the word λύτρον (or ἀντίλυτρον). Also missing in the Lord's Supper context are the title Son of man and the saying about Jesus' 'serving' (= διακονεῖν). But one should expect a christological formulation alleged to have grown out of the early Christian Lord's Supper tradition to reflect clearly the language of this tradition! The Lord's Supper texts and Mark 10:45 (Matt 20:28) overlap only in a single word, πολλῶν, which in my view points to Isa 53:10–12. There is really no compelling evidence for deriving Mark 10:45 from the Lord's Supper context"; Stuhlmacher, *Reconciliation, Law, and Righteousness*, 18–19.

13. Gundry, *Mark*, 590.

uses λύτρον in his letters, related words like ἀπολύτρωσις ("redemption, acquittal"; Rom 3:24; Eph 1:7; Col 1:14), ἀντίλυτρον ("ransom"; 1 Tim 2:6) and λυτρόω ("to ransom, redeem"; Titus 2:14) are attested throughout the Pauline corpus.

Paul's use of the word ἀπολύτρωσις in Rom 3:24 is particularly significant. In Rom 3:22–25, Paul writes:

> For there is no distinction, since all have sinned and fall short of the glory of God; they are now justified by his grace as a gift, through the *redemption* that is in Christ Jesus, whom God put forward as *a sacrifice of atonement* [ἱλαστήριον] by his blood, effective through faith. He did this to show his righteousness, because in his divine forbearance he had passed over the sins previously committed.

The word ἀπολύτρωσις originally means "'buying back' a slave or captive, i.e., 'making free' by payment of a ransom (λύτρον, q.v.; prisoners of war could ordinarily face slavery) . . . usage may diverge freely from the original meaning," such as "release, redemption, deliverance."[14] The meaning of the verb develops progressively from "the activity of being released (or buying back)" to "means of release" and then to "release" without completely losing its original sense. Therefore, although the word λύτρον is not mentioned in Rom 3:22–25, its sense has not deviated too far from the original meaning. Although it is difficult to know the precise sense of the word ἱλαστήριον in Rom 3:25—which is used only in Heb 9:5 apart from here—Paul in Rom 3:22–25 evidently implies the idea of Jesus' death as a ransom and presupposes it in his later statement in Rom 5:6, 8 that Christ died for sinners. As we can see here, although Paul does not use the word λύτρον in Rom 5, Paul certainly identifies Jesus' death as a ransom for the many in parallel with the early church tradition behind Mark 10:45.

Paul's Incorporation of the Early Church Tradition behind Mark 10:45 into His Adam Christology

I contend that Paul incorporates the early church tradition behind Mark 10:45 into his Adam Christology in Rom 5:6, 8, 15, 19 for his rhetorical purposes, on the basis of his creative use of it elsewhere. Although Paul nowhere quotes the exact phrase in Mark 10:45 "to give his life a ransom

---

14. BDAG, 117.

for many," he seems to have modified it and creatively applied it to the situation (*Sitz im Leben*) of his readers. In the following, I will highlight how Paul creatively uses the early church tradition behind Mark 10:45 in each passage that I have listed, in order to support my argument that Paul creatively incorporates the early church tradition behind Mark 10:45 into his Adam Christology in Rom 5:6, 8, 15, 19.

Romans 4:25

Paul in Rom 4:25 uses the verb παραδίδωμι instead of the verb δίδωμι in Mark 10:45 and a single verb παρεδόθη instead of the Semitizing poetic expression δοῦναι τὴν ψυχὴν αὐτοῦ. Many commentators note that Paul most likely depends on the early church tradition in Rom 4:25.[15] What Dunn calls "the two sections" of Paul's argument reflect Paul's adaptation of two separate traditions: the tradition behind Mark 8:31; 9:31; 10:33-34 ("Jesus *was handed over* and [they killed him and] *arose* after three days") and the tradition behind Mark 10:45 ("Jesus *gave* his life [a ransom] *for many*").[16]

Paul's phrase διὰ τὰ παραπτώματα ἡμῶν ("for our transgressions") compliments the phrase λύτρον ἀντὶ πολλῶν ("a ransom for many") in Mark 10:45. Although Paul nowhere calls Jesus' death "a ransom for many," he highlights its significance. In contrast, while calling Jesus' death "a ransom for many," Mark 10:45 does not spell out its implication concerning the issue of sin. This complimentary relationship between Mark 10:45 and Rom 4:25 suggests that both Paul and the Evangelist rely on the same early church tradition, independently of each other. Paul in Rom 4:25 follows the actual wording of Isa 53:12 [LXX] more closely than Mark 10:45, using the verb παραδίδωμι ("to hand over") and the phrase διὰ τὰ παραπτώματα ἡμῶν ("for our trespasses). Could Paul have derived these expressions exclusively from Isa 53:12 [LXX] without any influence from the early church tradition behind Mark 10:45? I will come back to this question later.

---

15. E.g., Fitzmyer, *Romans*, 390; Dunn, *Romans 1-8*, 240-41; Käsemann, *Commentary on Romans*, 128; Schlier, *Römerbrief*, 137; Wengst, *Christologische Formeln und Lieder des Urchristentums*, 101-4; Tödt, *Son of Man in the Synoptic Tradition*, 160-61.

16. Dunn claims, "Paul has shaped the two clauses to match the context, and indeed to provide a bridge between the two sections of his argument [that Jesus was handed over for our trespasses and that he was raised for our justification]"; Dunn, *Romans 1-8*, 240-41.

Romans 8:32

In contrast to Rom 4:25, the subject of Rom 8:32 is not Jesus but God: "He who did not withhold his own Son, but *gave him up for all of us* [ὑπὲρ ἡμῶν πάντων παρέδωκεν αὐτόν], will he not with him also give us everything else?" Paul in Rom 8:32 probably reflects the early church tradition behind Jesus' Passion predictions (Mark 8:31; 9:31; 10:33–34), using the so-called "divine passive" with God as the implied subject of the verb παραδίδωμι ("to hand over").[17] The early church tradition behind Jesus' Passion predictions fits Paul's theocentric argument in Rom 8:28–39 (cf. Rom 9–11) better than the early church tradition behind Mark 10:45.

1 Corinthians 15:3

Similar to Rom 4:25, Paul in 1 Cor 15:3 seems to replace a Semitizing poetic expression such as δοῦναι τὴν ψυχὴν αὐτοῦ λύτρον ἀντὶ πολλῶν ("to give his life a ransom for many") with a concise polished Greek sentence [Χριστὸς] ἀπέθανεν ὑπὲρ τῶν ἁμαρτιῶν ἡμῶν ("Christ died for our sins"). While admitting that the latter "recalls the Semitic style of the Gospels," Barrett claims that it is not "too readily to be described as a Semitism; the short independent propositions, not subordinated to one another, reflect the nature of proclamation."[18] While agreeing with Barrett, I maintain that the *verbal* and *formal*—not to mention the *conceptual* similarity—between the early church tradition behind Mark 10:45 and 1 Cor 15:3 should not be taken for granted. Paul in 1 Cor 15:3 could have modified the early church tradition behind Mark 10:45.

2 Corinthians 4:11

After speaking of "the treasure in jars of clay" (2 Cor 4:7), Paul makes an interesting statement in 2 Cor 4:11, "For while we live, we are always being *given up* to death *for Jesus' sake*, so that the life of Jesus may be made visible in our mortal flesh." Paul seems to create this statement in correspondence with the early church tradition behind Mark 10:45;

---

17. Cf. αὐτὸς ἁμαρτίας πολλῶν ἀνήνεγκεν καὶ διὰ τὰς ἁμαρτίας αὐτῶν παρεδόθη ("he bore the sins of many, and because of their sins he was given over"); while Mark 8:31 does not include the verb παραδίδωμι, the same "divine passive" idea is reflected in the use of the impersonal verb δεῖ ("it is necessary").

18. Barrett, *Commentary on the First Epistle to the Corinthians*, 338–39.

since Jesus is *given up* to death *for our sake*, we also are to be *given up for Jesus' sake*.[19] Paul may be echoing here the early church tradition behind Mark 10:45.[20] As Hooker notes, "If Christ died for all, this means not only that all have died, but that they must continue to work out the meaning of dying with Christ. The acceptance of Jesus as Messiah means a willingness to share his experiences. In this sense, at least, the sufferings of Christ are no substitute for ours, but a pattern to which we need to be conformed."[21] Paul creates a peculiar expression "baptized into Moses" (1 Cor 10:2) in parallel with the phrase "baptized into Christ" (1 Cor 12:13; cf. Rom 6:3; Gal 3:27). Likewise, in 1 Thess 5:5, Paul creates a new expression "sons of the Day" when he emphasizes the new identify of Christian believers due to the Christ-event (cf. 1 Thess 4:14). Although Paul does not cite explicitly the early church tradition behind Mark 10:45 in 2 Cor 4:11, he could be echoing it, when he links Christ's atoning death with the present suffering of Christians.

Galatians 2:20

In Gal 2:20 (cf. Eph 5:2, 25), Paul follows what seems to be a pattern of his citation of the early church tradition behind Mark 10:45—"Christ *gave up* himself *for us*." Paul's use of the first person pronoun "me" in Gal 2:20 cannot be evidence against his reference to the early church tradition. Although Paul uses first person pronouns in Gal 2:18–21, he clearly is not making some personal statements that only apply to him! Paul here is rather using first person pronouns in support of his earlier argument in Gal 2:15–16.[22] While speaking of himself in Gal 2:19–20, Paul is really saying here, "We have been crucified with Christ; and it is no longer we who live, but it is Christ who lives in us. And the life we now live in the flesh we live by faith in the Son of God, who loved us and gave himself for us."

---

19. Similarly, Hooker, *From Adam to Christ*, 50.

20. Paul also could be alluding to the early church tradition behind Mark 8:34 (cf. Matt 16:24; Luke 9:23) concerning the cost of Christian discipleship in addition to the early church tradition behind Mark 10:45.

21. Hooker, *From Adam to Christ*, 54.

22. "We have come to believe in Christ Jesus, so that we might be justified by faith in Christ, and not by doing the works of the law, because no one will be justified by the works of the law."

Paul's allusions to the early church tradition behind Mark 10:45 in Rom 4:25; 8:32; 1 Cor 15:3; 2 Cor 4:11; Gal 2:20 suggest that he also echoes the same early church tradition in his statement Χριστὸς ὑπὲρ ἡμῶν ἀπέθανεν ("Christ died for us") in Rom 5:8 and the corresponding phrase οἱ πολλοί ("the many") in Rom 5:15, 19.

Paul's Presentation of Jesus' Atoning Death and Isa 53

I want to discuss here the possibility that Paul derived the idea of Jesus' atoning death exclusively from Isa 53 without any influence from the early church tradition. Paul in Rom 3:25 says: "God presented him [Christ Jesus] as *a sacrifice of atonement* [ἱλαστήριον], through faith in his blood. He did this to demonstrate his justice, because in his forbearance he had left the sins committed beforehand unpunished" (NIV)." Paul in Rom 5:8–9 says: "But God proves his love for us in that while we still were sinners *Christ died for us*. Much more surely then, now that we have been justified *by his blood*, will we be saved through him from the wrath of God." The exact meaning of ἱλαστήριον in Rom 3:25 has been highly disputed; however, as Wenham points out, "what is indisputable is that Paul is speaking here in sacrificial terms."[23] Wenham also notes that Paul creatively uses the Old Testament imagery of the atoning sacrifice to present "the death of Jesus not only as a new Passover bringing 'redemption' to the people of God as well as to individuals enslaved in sin, but also as the fulfilment of the Day of Atonement."[24] With this in mind, I will discuss now whether or not Paul could have derived the idea of Jesus' atoning death exclusively from Isa 53 without any influence from the early church tradition.

While Paul undeniably refers to Isa 53 in his elucidation of Jesus' atoning death, I contend that Paul did not create such a link by himself—on the basis of his own reflection of the Scripture—but reflects the early church tradition behind Mark 10:45 for the following reasons. Firstly, the multiple connections between the early church tradition behind Mark 10:45 and Pauline material—that I have discussed so far—could not have been simply due to their mutual dependence on Isa 53. Particularly, Paul in Rom 5:15, 19 (cf. Eph 2:20) emphasizes that Jesus freely chose—τὸ χάρισμα ("the free gift"); ἡ δωρεὰ ἐν χάριτι τῇ τοῦ ἑνὸς

---

23. Wenham, *Paul*, 150; Wenham helpfully summarizes the Old Testament background of Paul's use of the word ἱλαστήριον in Rom 3:25; ibid., 151–53.

24. Ibid., 153.

ἀνθρώπου Ἰησοῦ Χριστοῦ ("the free gift in the grace of the one man Jesus Christ")—to give himself for the many out of his obedience. This emphasis on the voluntary nature of Jesus' atoning death is explicit in Mark 10:45 but not in Isa 53—cf. Isa 53:10.[25] The voluntary nature of Jesus' atoning death is only implied in the Words of Institution (Mark 14:22-25). On the contrary, in Jesus' Passion predictions (Mark 8:31; 9:31; 10:33-34), the passive aspect of Jesus' passion and death—as an innocent victim—is emphasized.

Secondly, while Isa 53 depicts the vicarious suffering of the Servant of Yahweh, the portrayal of his death as אשם ("guilt [reparation] offering") in its immediate literary context is different from the implied portrayal of Jesus' death as a ransom in Rom 5 (cf. Rom 3:24). As the evidence in Jewish intertestamental literature shows, which I will discuss shortly, the typical (or characteristic) way of reading Isa 53 did not involve the Servant's atoning death as in the case of that of the Son of Man in Mark 10:45. Hooker argues that the historical Jesus could not have identified his mission with that of the Suffering Servant in Isa 53 and such identification was first made by Paul. As we will see later, Paul or any other contemporary Christian probably did not derive the idea of Jesus' atoning death exclusively from the Suffering Servant in Isa 53 without any association with the early church tradition behind Mark 10:45. If Paul and the Evangelist independently reflected the early church tradition behind Mark 10:45, how exactly did such a tradition interpret Jesus' death in relation to that of the Suffering Servant in Isa 53?

It goes beyond the scope of this study to probe this question in detail. Peter Stuhlmacher's suggestion based on Grimm's dissertation[26] provides valuable insights on this question. As Stuhlmacher observes, "While there is only a partial connection between our saying [Mark 10:45] and Isaiah 53, the Hebrew text of Isa 43:3-4 and Mark 10:45 have remarkably significant things in common."[27] Stuhlmacher claims,

---

25. "Yet *it was the will of the LORD* to crush him with pain. When you make his life an offering for sin, he shall see his offspring, and shall prolong his days; through him *the will of the LORD* shall prosper."

26. Grimm, "Weil ich dich liebe," 231-77.

27. Stuhlmacher explains, "The true verbal equivalent of λύτρον, namely כפר, occurs in Isa 43:3-4; the repeated תחת ["instead of"] corresponds exactly to ἀντί (πολλῶν), and the striking saying about the Son of man who will give his life finds an interesting equivalent in אדם ואתן: the Son of man in Mark 10:45 takes the place of the people whom Yahweh will give as a ransom for Israel's life (תחתיך or תחת נפשך)";

"Mark 10:45 (Matt 20:28) stands at the point where these two texts from Deutero-Isaiah [Isa 53:10–12 and Isa 43:3–4] intersect; but Isa 43:3–4 delivers the primary accent," interpreting Mark 10:45 in the light of both passages.[28] The early church could have brought together the ransom imagery in Isa 43:3–4 and the language of Isa 52:13—53:12 in understanding Jesus' atoning death.[29] There is no convincing reason to suppose that it was Paul who first made the connection between Jesus' atoning death and the Suffering Servant.

There is an exceptionally strong case for the *authenticity* of Mark 10:45. If Paul did not derive the idea of Jesus' atoning death exclusively from Isa 53 but had access to some early church traditions, the early church tradition behind Mark 10:45 most likely played a central role in his understanding of Jesus' atoning death along with the early church tradition behind the Words of Institution and Jesus' Passion predictions. The following diagram visualizes the rather complex direction of influence concerning Paul's understanding of Jesus' atoning death:

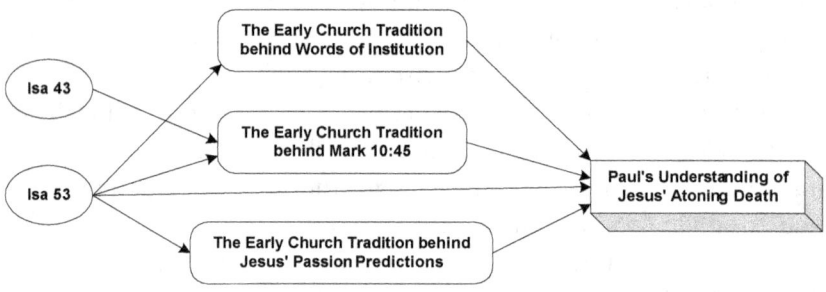

Stuhlmacher, *Reconciliation, Law, and Righteousness*, 22–23; cf. Isa 43:3–4 ("For I am the LORD your God, the Holy One of Israel, your Savior. I give Egypt as your ransom [λύτρον], Ethiopia and Seba in exchange for you. Because you are precious in my sight, and honored, and I love you, I give people in return for you, nations in exchange for your life").

28. Stuhlmacher clarifies: "Isa 52:13—53:12 describes Israel's substitutionary suffering for the nations (= the many). Jesus also takes on this substitutionary suffering of Israel as God's Servant when he gives his life as a ransom for many. His self-sacrifice offers his life vicariously not only for Israel but also for the nations of the world, that is, for all people far from God. ἀντὶ πολλῶν is clearly meant inclusively"; ibid., 24–25.

29. The connection between Mark 10:45 and both Isa 43:3–4 and 52:13—53:12 will be revisited in Appendix 2 ("Jesus and the Suffering Servant").

Paul's Presentation of Jesus' Atoning Death
and First-Century AD Judaism

I want to discuss here the possibility that Paul derived the idea of Jesus' atoning death exclusively from first-century AD Judaism without any influence from the early church tradition. The question of whether or not the idea of the Messiah's atoning death existed in Second Temple Judaism before the rise of Christianity goes beyond the scope of this study. I can make only some preliminary comments here concerning the possibility that Paul derived the idea of Jesus' atoning death exclusively from first-century AD Judaism. On the basis of the following considerations, I contend that Paul more likely derived the idea of Jesus' atoning death from the early church tradition than exclusively from first-century AD Judaism.

Firstly, despite a number of references to Isa 53 in Jewish intertestamental literature, there was no widespread Jewish expectation in Second Temple Judaism that the Messiah would die to provide atonement for sin. Having surveyed Jewish intertestamental literature (e.g., *1 En.* 47.1–4; 62.1–16; 63.1–11; Wis 2; 5; 1QIsa^a [1QIsaiah^a]; 4Q540 [4QTLevi^c]; 4Q541 [4QTLevi^d?]; *T. Benj.* 3.8; 4Q491c [4QWar Scroll^a/4QM^a Frag. 11 Col. I]), Hengel concludes that Isa 52:13—53:12 had multifaceted manifestations in Second Temple Judaism, predominantly with the emphasis on the Servant's exaltation and judgment over pagan nations.[30] John the Baptist's question to Jesus, "Are you the one who was to come, or should we expect someone else?" (Matt 11:3; Luke 7:20), most likely indicates that Jesus' ministry of healing, preaching the good news (Luke 7:21–23) and, later on, the Passion did not accord with the messianic expectations shared by his Jewish contemporaries—e.g., the restoration of Israel (cf. Acts 1:6).

---

30. Hengel, "Effective History of Isaiah 53 in the Pre-Christian Period," 145–46; similarly, McKnight, *Jesus and His Death*, 170. Koester similarly notes, "The concept of a suffering and dying Messiah is never found in the tradition of Israel and would be a very strange thing in this tradition. That 'the Messiah suffered' is purely based on a later Christian misunderstanding, and it is entirely wrong, if one wants to base such assumption on the text of Isaiah 53; the one who dies here is not the Messiah but the 'Suffering Servant,' who is Moses or a prophet like Moses"; Koester, *Paul & His World*, 105; having examined selected Jewish intertestamental literature, Hannah concludes, "It hardly needs to be stated, however, that nowhere in these three messianic readings of Isaiah's Servant songs, the *Similitudes*, the third *Sibylline Oracle* and the Isaiah Targum, is vicarious suffering attributed to the Messiah"; Hannah, "Isaiah within Judaism of the Second Temple Period," 32.

As Barrett highlights, there are some references to the self-sacrifice of Jewish martyrs as ransom for their nation in Maccabees (2 Macc 7.37; 4 Macc 6.27–29; 17.22; 18.4). None of these martyrs—Eleazar, the seven brothers, and their mother—however, were considered to be the Messiah. Hofius refutes the view that the Targum to Isa 53 speaks of a Messiah "forgiving sins."[31] Chilton similarly comments on Targum Isaiah 53, "The chapter is developed to refer to the Messiah and the '*righteous*' (v. 2) who depend on him, but in no sense can the Messiah (or the 'servant,' cf. 52:13) be said to suffer. Indeed the point of the interpretation is to emphasize the triumph of the Messiah (cf. 52:13–15) at the expense of '*all the kingdoms*' (v. 3a; cf. vv. 7, 11, 12)."[32] Based on these considerations, it is difficult to imagine that Paul derived the concept of Jesus' atoning death exclusively from first-century AD Judaism without any influence from the early church tradition.

Secondly, even if the idea of the Messiah's vicarious suffering or atoning death were not totally foreign to first-century AD Judaism, there is no convincing reason to think that Paul derived such an idea exclusively from first-century AD Judaism without any influence from the early church tradition. Despite the general lack of the notion of the Messiah's vicarious suffering in Second Temple Judaism, however, Hengel claims, "already in the pre-Christian period, traditions about suffering and atoning eschatological figures were available in Palestinian

---

31. Hofius summarizes the Targum Isaiah in two statements: "1. The Messiah works for and effects through His intercessions (Isa 53:4a,b, 6c–7b, 11f, 12e,f) the forgiveness of sins for those sinners in Israel who are willing to repent. 2. The Messiah fulfills this for them because they are ready to learn his teachings in the Torah and prepared to be led to an obedience of the Torah (Isa 53:5d,e, 11e,f, 12c–f)." Hofius explains: "The Messiah *works for* and is a *means towards* the forgiveness of sins, but he does not *grant* nor *guarantee* forgiveness. The one who forgives them is, according to *Targum Jonathan* Isa 53—as in the Isaiah Targum as a whole—God Himself and God alone. A Messiah who forgives out of his own perfect might and who dispenses forgiveness 'through word and deed' is *not* the Messiah of the fourth servant song of the Targum"; my translation of "1. Der Messias erwirkt und vermittelt durch seine Fürbitte den umkehrwilligen Sündern Israels die Vergebung ihrer Sünden (53,4a.b. 6c–7b. 11f. 12e,f). 2. Er erwirt und vermittelt sie ihnen, weil sie sich durch seine Lehre in der Tora unterweisen und zum Tora-Gehorsam anleiten lassen (53,5d.e. 11e.f. 12c–f). Der Messias *erwirt* und *vermittelt* die Sündenvergebung, aber er *wirkt* und *gewährt* sie nicht. Der Vergebende ist nach TargJon Jes 53 vielmehr—wie im gesamten Jesaja-Targum—Gott selbst und Gott allein. Einen Messias, der die Sünde kraft eigener Machtvollkommenheit vergibt und Sündenvergebung ‚durch Wort und Tat' spendet, kennt der Targum zum vierten Gottesknechtslied *nicht*"; Hofius, *Neutestamentliche Studien*, 104.

32. Chilton, *Isaiah Targum*, 103–5.

The Son of Man Sayings as Sources of Paul's Adam Christology 111

Judaism, and that Jesus and the early church could have known and appealed to them." Hengel continues, "This would explain how first Jesus himself and then his disciples after Easter could presuppose that their message of the various atoning death of the Messiah (cf. 1 Cor 15:3–5) would be understood among their Jewish contemporaries."[33] Due to the lack of evidence for traditions about suffering and atoning eschatological figures in pre-Christian Palestinian Judaism, we cannot be certain concerning whether or not the historical Jesus or the early church appealed to them in understanding his messianic mission, solely based on first-century AD Judaism.[34] If that is the case, it is even more uncertain whether or not Paul could have appealed to such Palestinian Jewish traditions for his predominantly Gentile readership, solely based on first-century AD Judaism. Unless one assumes that Paul was completely isolated from the early church and had absolutely no access to the early church tradition, it is difficult to suppose that Paul derived the idea of Jesus' atoning sacrifice exclusively from first-century AD Judaism without any influence from the early church tradition.

Many scholars recognize the Evangelist's allusion to Isa 53 and its related early church tradition in Mark 10:45[35] and Paul's allusion to Isa 53 and its related early church tradition in Rom 4:25; 8:32.[36] On the contrary, the probability that Paul knew about the specific early church tradition behind Mark 10:45, however, has not been seriously considered. As I discussed earlier, the concise Semitic-like form of Mark 10:45 in comparison with 1 Tim 2:5–6 supports its *authenticity*. If Paul alludes to the early church tradition behind Mark 10:45 in Rom 4:25; 8:32; 1 Cor 15:3; 2 Cor 4:11; Gal 2:20, as I have argued, the *verbal* and *conceptual* similarity between the early church tradition behind Mark 10:45 and Rom 5:15, 19 (concerning ἀντὶ πολλῶν in the former

---

33. Hengel, "Effective History of Isaiah 53 in the Pre-Christian Period," 146.

34. One may argue for the *historicity* and the *authenticity* of Mark 10:45, based on what John P. Meier calls "the criterion of discontinuity," referring to the "words or deeds of Jesus that cannot be derived either from Judaism at the time of Jesus or from the early Church after him"; Meier, *Marginal Jew*, 171.

35. E.g., Gnilka, *Evangelium nach Markus (Mk 8:27—16:20)*, 104; Collins, *Mark*, 500–504; Donahue and Harrington, *Gospel of Mark*, 313; Evans, *Mark 8:27—16:20*, 119–25; Stein, *Mark*, 487–89.

36. E.g., Fitzmyer, *Romans*, 389, 532; Schreiner, *Romans*, 243; Moo, *Romans*, 243, 459–60; Barrett, *Commentary on the Epistle to the Romans*, 95; Käsemann, *Commentary on Romans*, 128–29.

and ὑπὲρ ἡμῶν and οἱ πολλοί in the latter) cannot be taken for granted. Paul most likely incorporates the early church tradition behind Mark 10:45—which reflects the early church "Ransom Christology"—into his Adam Christology in Rom 5:15, 19, when he compares and contrasts the universal consequences of Adam's trespass and Christ's act of righteousness. Paul says in Rom 5:19, "For just as by the one man's disobedience *the many* (οἱ πολλοί) were made sinners, so by the one man's obedience *the many* (οἱ πολλοί) will be made righteous." Paul's incorporation of the early church tradition behind Mark 10:45 into his Adam Christology in Rom 5:15, 19 is not surprising, considering Paul's creative use of various authoritative traditions elsewhere.[37] An exceptionally strong case can be made for Paul's dependence on the early church tradition behind Mark 10:45.

MATT 19:28//LUKE 22:30

The Authenticity of Matt 19:28//Luke 22:30

Matthew 19:23–27; 29–30 (cf. Luke 18:24–30) contain virtually the same content as Mark 10:23–31. Matthew inserts Matt 19:28 in the context of Mark 10:23–31. In contrast, Luke inserts Luke 22:28–30 in the following literary context:

Content	Luke	Mark
The Lord's Supper	Luke 22:7–23	Mark 14:12–26
Becoming great by serving others	Luke 22:24–27	Mark 10:42–45
Reward of the faithful disciples	*Luke 22:28–30*	
Jesus' prediction of Peter's denial	Luke 22:31–38	Mark 14:27–31

The close parallel between the second part of Matt 19:28 and that of Luke 22:30 indicates that both Matthew and Luke here depend on the same early church tradition that is not attested in Mark:

Matt 19:28	ὅταν καθίσῃ ὁ υἱὸς τοῦ ἀνθρώπου ἐπὶ θρόνου δόξης αὐτοῦ, καθήσεσθε καὶ ὑμεῖς ἐπὶ δώδεκα θρόνους κρίνοντες τὰς δώδεκα φυλὰς τοῦ Ἰσραήλ.
Luke 22:30	ἵνα ἔσθητε καὶ πίνητε ἐπὶ τῆς τραπέζης μου ἐν τῇ βασιλείᾳ μου, καθήσεσθε ἐπὶ θρόνων τὰς δώδεκα φυλὰς κρίνοντες τοῦ Ἰσραήλ.

---

37. Cf. Gal 4:21–31; 1 Cor 7:8–16; 9:3–14; 10:1–22; 2 Cor 3:7–18; Rom 10:5–8; 1 Thess 4:13—5:11.

It is difficult either to identify the exact original form of this Son of Man saying or to discern its *historicity*. As many commentators recognize, however, the fact that both Matthew and Luke attest it in two completely different literary contexts indicates that it could not have been created out of nothing (*ex nihilo*).[38] It most likely is *authentic* to the early church from which Matthew and Luke derive the saying of Jesus, independently of each other.[39]

Paul's Allusion to the Early Church Tradition behind Matt 19:28//Luke 22:30

I contend that Paul alludes to the early church tradition behind Matt 19:28//Luke 22:30 on the basis of a *verbal* and *formal* similarity between Matt 19:28//Luke 22:30 and Paul's Adam Christology with respect to the verb κρίνω ("to judge") in Matt 19:28//Luke 22:30 and 1 Cor 6:2 (cf. Rom 5:17). Paul nowhere in his letters mentions the exact phrase "*judging* (κρίνοντες) the twelve tribes of Israel" as in Matt 19:28//Luke 22:30. Interestingly, however, Paul rebukes the Corinthians, who brought their dispute to civil court: "Do you not know that the saints will *judge* (κρινοῦσιν) the world? And if the world is to be judged by you, are you incompetent to try trivial cases?" (1 Cor 6:2). John Nolland suggests that, as Matthew expands the scope of Jesus' eschatological judgment from "the twelve tribes of Israel" (Matt 19:28) to "all the nations" (Matt 25:32), Paul could have known the tradition behind Matt 19:28//Luke 22:30 and modified it with "a worldwide perspective for the gospel" (1 Cor 6:2; cf. 2 Tim 2:12).[40]

38. E.g., Nolland, *Gospel of Matthew*, 797; Luz, *Matthew 8–20*, 511; Davies and Allison, *Matthew 19–28*, 58; Evans, *Luke and Scripture*, 160; Nolland, *Luke 18:35— 24:53*, 1063–64; Hempel, *Menschensohn und historischer Jesus*, 148–50; Fitzmyer, *Gospel According to Luke X–XXIV*, 1414; Marshall, *Gospel of Luke*, 815–17.

39. Verheyden examines various sayings with the motif of the judgment of Israel in Matthew and Luke and concludes, "The Source [Q], at least in the section that we have just been examining, can only be understood in the context of Israel's refusal, where Israel is very probably to be defined in a broader sense than that of the actual historical Israel. The Source speaks of regret and also disillusionment and frustration, following the failure of a mission"; my translation of "La Source, du moins dans la partie quie nous venons d'examiner, ne peut se comprendre que sous le signe du refus d'Israël, mais d'un Israël dont la définition, selon toute probabilité, est beaucoup plus large que la réalité historique. La Source parle de regret, et plus encore de désillusion et de frustration, suite à l' échec d'une mission"; Verheyden, "Jugement d'Israël dans la Source Q," 219.

40. Nolland, *Luke 18:35—24:53*, 1068; cf. 2 Tim 2:12—εἰ ὑπομένομεν, καὶ συμβασιλεύσομεν ("if we endure, we will also reign with him").

When describing the role of the believers in the new eschatological age, Paul in Rom 5:17 expresses a similar idea: "those who receive the abundance of grace and the free gift of righteousness" will "*exercise dominion* (βασιλεύσουσιν) in life through the one man, Jesus Christ." The fact that both the early church tradition behind Matt 19:28//Luke 22:30 and Paul portray the unique eschatological role of the faithful followers of Jesus strongly suggests that they share a common source.[41] One may argue that, since the verb κρίνω is not used in Rom 5:17, I can claim a *conceptual* similarity but not a *verbal* and *formal* similarity between the early church tradition behind Matt 19:28//Luke 22:30 and Paul's Adam Christology in Rom 5:17. While this criticism is valid in a strict sense, I still argue for the *verbal* and *formal* similarity for the following reason.

Both the early church tradition behind Matt 19:28//Luke 22:30[42] and Paul in 1 Cor 6:2 and Rom 5:17 undoubtedly allude to the vision in Dan 7.[43] As Nolland notes:

> [In Dan 7:26] *dyn'* is literally "the judgment," while *ytb* is "will sit." The phrase is typically translated "the court will sit in judgment" (NRSV), and the beneficiaries of the judgment are "the people of the saints of the Most High" of v. 27. But in v. 22 *dyn'* ("judgment") is given to "the saints of the Most High"—"the

---

41. Although Paul uses the future tense βασιλεύσουσιν in Rom 5:17, he seems to describe in Rom 5:12–21 what Christ has already accomplished and its consequences in contrast to Adam's trespass and its consequences. The idea of *ruling* in life in the context of Rom 5:12–21 seems to carry the characteristic tension in the Pauline theology, "already but not yet." If this observation is right, it contrasts with the definitely futuristic statement of *judging* in Matt 19:28//Luke 22:30; 1 Cor 6:2.

42. While suggesting that Matt 19:28 overall reflects the original Jesus tradition (from Q) better than Luke 22:28–30, some commentators consider "the Son of Man" in Matt 19:28 as Matthean redaction (cf. Matt 25:31); e.g., Davies and Allison, *Matthew 19–28*, 55; Evans, *Luke and Scripture*, 167; Fitzmyer, *Gospel According to Luke X–XXIV*, 1413; Marshall, *Gospel of Luke*, 817. While considering the phrase ἐν τῇ παλιγγενεσίᾳ ("at the renewal of all things") as Matthean redaction, I consider the phrase ὁ υἱὸς τοῦ ἀνθρώπου as traditional—rather than Matthean redaction out of nothing (*ex nihilo*)—at least for two reasons. Firstly, Jesus elsewhere in the Gospels characteristically refers to himself as "the Son of Man." Secondly, both Matthew and Luke show elsewhere their tendency to change the phrase "the Son of Man" to a first person pronoun in order to explicitly identify it with Jesus—e.g., Luke 22:27b (cf. Mark 10:45), Matt 5:11 (cf. Luke 6:22), Matt 10:32 (cf. Luke 12:8).

43. Evans observes that the early church tradition behind Matt 19:28//Luke 22:30 interprets Dan 7:9 in light of Ps 122:5 ὅτι ἐκεῖ ἐκάθισαν θρόνοι εἰς κρίσιν θρόνοι ἐπὶ οἶκον Δαυιδ ("For there the thrones for judgment were set up, the thrones of the house of David"); Evans, *Luke and Scripture*, 164.

saints of the Most High" is a decoded equivalent for "one like a Son of Man" of v. 13. And if *l* is taken here as meaning "to" rather than "for," then the sense could be represented as "[the role of] judgment is given to the Son of Man." If the opening words of v. 26 are read from this perspective, then what is literally "the judgment will sit" can be taken to mean that the Son of Man will sit in judgment—thus exercising rather than benefiting from the judging function referred to with *dyn'*. Such an interpretative approach may have been prompted by or may in turn have prompted a link with Ps 110.[44]

When we consider the allusion to Dan 7 in Matt 19:28//Luke 22:30, the relationship between the Son of Man and his followers in Matt 19:28//Luke 22:30 becomes more intelligible. Although the Son of Man in Matt 19:28//Luke 22:30 is not "a decoded equivalent" for the new eschatological people of God—the followers of Jesus, the Son of Man still represents them as their leader. Likewise, Paul evidently alludes to Dan 7:9–27 in 1 Cor 6:2 and Rom 5:17, in which he addresses the eschatological ruling of Jesus' followers as their privilege:

Matt 19:28	καθήσεσθε καὶ ὑμεῖς ἐπὶ δώδεκα θρόνους κρίνοντες τὰς δώδεκα φυλὰς τοῦ Ἰσραήλ. ("[You who have followed me] will also sit on twelve thrones, *judging* [κρίνω] the twelve tribes of Israel.")
1 Cor 6:2	ἢ οὐκ οἴδατε ὅτι οἱ ἅγιοι τὸν κόσμον κρινοῦσιν. ("Do you not know that the saints will *judge* [κρίνω] the world?")
Rom 5:17	εἰ γὰρ τῷ τοῦ ἑνὸς παραπτώματι ὁ θάνατος ἐβασίλευσεν διὰ τοῦ ἑνός, πολλῷ μᾶλλον οἱ τὴν περισσείαν τῆς χάριτος καὶ τῆς δωρεᾶς τῆς δικαιοσύνης λαμβάνοντες ἐν ζωῇ βασιλεύσουσιν διὰ τοῦ ἑνὸς Ἰησοῦ Χριστοῦ. ("If, because of the one man's trespass, death *exercised dominion* [βασιλεύω] through that one, much more surely will those who receive the abundance of grace and the free gift of righteousness *exercise dominion* [βασιλεύω] in life through the one man, Jesus Christ.")

---

44. Nolland, *Gospel of Matthew*, 800.

Commentators are divided in deciding whether the precise sense of the verb κρίνω in Matt 19:28//Luke 22:30 means either "to judge"[45] or "to rule."[46] The basis of the former view is that the verb κρίνω never means "to rule" in Greek.[47] The support of "to rule" is found in the function of judges in the Old Testament (Judg 3:10; cf. 1 Sam 8:20). However, as it will become clear shortly, these two senses are not contradictory but intricately related to each other. As Nolland suggests, "we may want to think in terms of judicial function of OT kings (e.g., 2 Sam 15:1-6; 1 Kgs 3:16-28) or of the broad sense of judging associated with the judges raised up by God (e.g., Judg 3:9, 15; 6:11-18)."[48] Judging obviously is one of the important royal functions. More importantly, while κρίνω in general does not mean "to rule," κρίνω in Matt 19:28//Luke 22:30 encompasses that meaning due to the obvious intertextual link with Dan 7:9-27. Commentators seem to overlook the fact that the role of *judging* and that of *ruling* in Dan 7:9-27 are intricately linked with each other—as both roles signify the eschatological reward of "the holy people of the Most High." "The holy ones of the Most High" not only will *judge* (Dan 7:26) the apostate king who will persecute them—Antiochus IV (Dan 7:25)—but also *rule* over all the other kingdoms (Dan 7:27).

Dan 7:26 [LXX-Θ]	καὶ τὸ κριτήριον καθίσει καὶ τὴν ἀρχὴν μεταστήσουσιν τοῦ ἀφανίσαι καὶ τοῦ ἀπολέσαι ἕως τέλους. ("And the court sat in judgment, and they shall remove his rule, to obliterate and to destroy completely" [NETS].)
Dan 7:27 [LXX-Θ]	καὶ ἡ βασιλεία καὶ ἡ ἐξουσία καὶ ἡ μεγαλωσύνη τῶν βασιλέων τῶν ὑποκάτω παντὸς τοῦ οὐρανοῦ ἐδόθη ἁγίοις ὑψίστου καὶ ἡ βασιλεία αὐτοῦ βασιλεία αἰώνιος καὶ πᾶσαι αἱ ἀρχαὶ αὐτῷ δουλεύσουσιν καὶ ὑπακούσονται. ("And the kingdom and the authority and the greatness of the kings, which are under the whole heaven, was given to the holy ones of the Most High, and his kingdom is an everlasting kingdom, and all dominions shall be slaves and heed him" [NETS].)

---

45. E.g., Luz, *Matthew 8-20*, 517; France, *Gospel of Matthew*, 744.

46. E.g., Davies and Allison, *Matthew 19-28*, 56; Evans, *Luke and Scripture*, 167; Fitzmyer, *Gospel According to Luke X-XXIV*, 1415.

47. Luz claims, "That κρίνω could mean 'to rule' is a philological fiction that is clearly false"; Luz, *Matthew 8-20*, 517. Similarly, France points out, "In NT Greek there is no other example of the verb 'judge' being used in the sense of 'rule,' so that the normal sense of the verb should probably be understood here [in Matt 19:28]"; France, *Gospel of Matthew*, 744.

48. Nolland, *Luke 18:35—24:53*, 1067; similarly, Marshall, *Gospel of Luke*, 818.

Although we cannot be certain about the exact form of the early church tradition behind Matt 19:28//Luke 22:30, it may have included both the role of *judging* and that of *ruling* concerning the eschatological reward of the faithful followers of Jesus in line with Dan 7:9-27. Paul probably highlights the role of *judging* in 1 Cor 6:2, on the one hand—as the Evangelists do in Matt 19:28//Luke 22:30—and the role of *ruling* in Rom 5:17, on the other hand, in accordance with his rhetorical purposes. This becomes obvious when we consider the context of Paul's argument in 1 Cor 6:1-7 and that in Rom 5:12-21. In 1 Cor 6:1-7, Paul rebukes the Corinthian believers who brought their dispute to a secular court. It makes sense that Paul would have focused on the role of *judging* in this particular context. Likewise, in Rom 5:12-21, Paul contrasts the *dominion* of death and sin with the *ruling*—rather than *judging*—of Jesus' followers in life, in relation to the figure of Adam and that of Christ. It is interesting to note that it is not life—as opposed to the *dominion* of death—which rules but Jesus' followers who rule in life. If Paul is not depending on the early church tradition behind Matt 19:28//Luke 22:30 in Rom 5:17 (*ex traditione*) but creating the antithesis out of nothing (*ex nihilo*), we would expect the *ruling* of life—instead of the *ruling* of Jesus' followers in life—as the natural logical opposite of the *dominion* of death. It is obvious why Paul would have focused on the role of Jesus' followers' eschatological *ruling*—rather than *judging*—in this particular context. Such selective citation of an authoritative tradition should not surprise us when we consider Paul's citation method of authoritative traditions elsewhere.

Paul's Incorporation of the Early Church Tradition behind Matt 19:28//Luke 22:30 Into His Adam Christology

In my discussion of the previous topic, I already explained in detail how Paul creatively incorporates the early church tradition behind Matt 19:28//Luke 22:30 into his Adam Christology in Rom 5:17. To sum up, Paul incorporates the early church tradition behind Matt 19:28//Luke 22:30 into his Adam Christology in Rom 5:17 in which he contrasts the reign of *death* and *sin* through Adam's transgression—the Old Age—with the reign of Jesus' followers in *life*—the New Age.

Paul's Presentation of Jesus' Followers' Eschatological Ruling and Dan 7

I want to discuss here the possibility that Paul derived the idea of Jesus' followers' eschatological ruling exclusively from Dan 7 without any influence from the early church tradition. The upfront way Paul asks a rhetorical question in 1 Cor 6:2 ("Do you not know that the saints will judge the world?") signifies the fact that he depends on some authoritative tradition with which his readers are already familiar. If not, Paul may have given his readers some exegetical justification for his interpretation of the Scripture (Dan 7), as he does in 1 Cor 10:1-22. For the reasons I have discussed earlier, I identify this authoritative tradition with the early church tradition behind Matt 19:28//Luke 22:30.

Paul's Presentation of Jesus' Followers' Eschatological Ruling and First-Century AD Judaism

I want to discuss here the possibility that Paul derived his idea of Jesus' followers' eschatological ruling exclusively from first-century AD Judaism without any influence from the early church tradition. In his illuminating article, Evans provides many interesting parallels in Jewish intertestamental literature to the early church tradition behind Matt 19:28//Luke 22:30.[49] Only a few of them, however, directly concern the righteous' participation in the divine judgment in the *eschaton*. For example, *1 En.* 1.9 writes, "Behold, the Lord comes with ten thousand of his holy ones, to execute judgment upon all."[50] The phrase "his holy ones" probably refers to angelic hosts (cf. Jude 14-15) rather than "the righteous" or "the elect" (*1 En.* 1.8). In *1 En.* 108.12, God promises in the last days, "I shall bring them out into the bright light, those who have loved my holy name, and seat each one by one upon the throne of his honor."[51] While the righteous sit on heavenly thrones in this passage, their role as *judges* (or *rulers*) is not explicitly stated here. It could simply refer to their rewards or honorific status without implying their eschatological judgment along with God—cf. Wis 5.16; 1QS 4.7, 8; 1QH^a

---

49. Evans, *Luke and Scripture*, 155-60.

50. Isaac, "1 Enoch," 13-14.

51. Ibid., 89; this contrasts with the *Similitudes* of Enoch (*1 En.* 37-71) in which, as Leslie W. Walck points out, "only the Lord of Spirits and the Elect One/Son of Man are seated on thrones"; Walck, "Son of Man in the Parables of Enoch and the Gospels," 323.

The Son of Man Sayings as Sources of Paul's Adam Christology 119

9.23-25.[52] There are three more intertestamental references (Wis 3.8[53]; *T. Ab.* 13.1-8; *Sib. Or.* 2.174-176[54]; cf. *1 En.* 62.15[55]) and a rabbinic reference (*Midrash Tanhuma*) that deserve our attention.

Firstly, Wis 3.8 mentions the righteous' reign over nations along with God as their eschatological reward. As Walter T. Wilson points out, "The affliction of the righteous may seem to be punishment, but is in reality divine testing; after death they are forever at peace with God, sharing in God's rule." Interestingly, Wis 3.4 also mentions *immortality* (ἀθανασία) as another eschatological reward of the righteous.[56] Paul's idea of Christians' "dominion in life" (Rom 5:17) has a certain parallel with Wis 3.1-9. While Paul emphasizes "dominion in life *through the one man, Jesus Christ*" (Rom 5:17), Wis 3.1-9 does not mention any messianic figure. While Paul most likely was familiar with a general paradigm of Jewish eschatological thinking, similar to that reflected in Wis 3.1-9, it is difficult to suppose that Paul derived the concept of Jesus' followers' eschatological ruling exclusively from first-century AD Judaism without any influence from the early church tradition.

Secondly, "the twelve tribes of Israel" in *T. Ab.* 13.1-8 are not the *objects* of judgment but the *agents* of the second judgment in the three tribunal system—the first by Abel and the third by God himself. Also,

---

52. *1 En.* 108.12 belongs to the editor's conclusion in the appendix of *1 Enoch* (chapters 105-8), which most likely did not come into being until the final stage of its compilation at the end of the first century AD.

53. "They (the righteous) *will govern* (κρινοῦσιν) nations and *rule* (κρατήσουσιν) over peoples, and the Lord *will reign* (βασιλεύσει) over them forever."

54. "Later the faithful chosen Hebrews will rule (ἄρξουσιν) over exceedingly mighty men, having subjected them as of old, since power will never fail"; Collins, "Sybilline Oracles," 349.

55. "The Lord of the Spirits will abide over them; they shall eat and rest and rise with that Son of Man forever and ever"; Isaac, "1 Enoch," 44. Walck finds an interesting parallel between Luke 22:28-30 and *1 En.* 62.15. As Walck observes, "The image of eating and drinking in his kingdom in the Lukan passage bears some similarity to the image of feasting and dwelling under the benevolent rule of the Son of Man in *1 En.* 62.15." This image is unique to L; Luke possibly knew about *1 En.* 62.15 and reflected this knowledge in Luke 22:28-30. However, as Walck himself acknowledges, "The righteous and elect [in *1 En.* 62.15] do not pass judgment, although they enjoy the benefits of vindication"; Walck, "Son of Man in the Parables of Enoch and the Gospels," 323. This fundamental difference makes any direct influence of *1 En.* 62.15 on Luke 22:28-30 doubtful.

56. "For though in the sight of others they were punished, their hope is full of immortality (ἀθανασία)."

the text does not clearly explain the relationship between the messianic figure—Abel—and "the twelve tribes of Israel." Any exclusive influence of *T. Ab.* 13.1–8 from Paul or the early church tradition behind Matt 19:28//Luke 22:30 seems unlikely. Thirdly, if *Sib. Or.* 2.174–76 reflects an earlier Jewish source, as Collins suggests,[57] Paul could have derived his idea of Christians judging the world with Christ from the Jewish tradition behind *Sib. Or.* 2.174–76.[58] However, there is no mention of any messianic figure in *Sib. Or.* 2.174–76, not to mention his role at the eschatological judgment. It is difficult to suppose the exclusive influence on Paul from such a tradition. These references possibly reflect some earlier Jewish traditions that influenced Paul in some limited aspects. It is difficult, however, to establish their direct and exclusive literary relationship with Paul.

Evans introduces an interesting piece of rabbinic evidence that illuminates the origin of the early church tradition behind Matt 19:28// Luke 22:30.[59] Evans himself translates *Midrash Tanhuma Qedoshim* §1 (on Lev 19:1–2):

> [71.5] And it says: "I kept looking until thrones were set up" (Dan 7:9) . . . [72.4] Our rabbis say: "What does 'thrones' mean in the world to come? The Holy One, blessed be He, will sit and the angels will give [5] thrones to the great ones of Israel, and they will sit. And the Holy One, blessed be He, will sit with them [or with the elders] as presiding judge. They will judge the peoples [6] of the world, as it says: 'Yahweh comes in judgment with the elders of his people and his princes' (Isa 3:14). Here it is not written [7] 'against,' but 'with' the elders [and his princes], teaching that the Holy One, blessed be He, sits with the elders and princes of Israel to judge the peoples [8] of the world. And whose are these thrones? (They belong to) the house of David and to the elders of Israel, as it says: 'There sit thrones [9] for judgment, thrones for the house of David'" (Ps 122:5). Said Rabbi Phineas in the

---

57. Collins claims, "[In Sibylline Oracles 2] it shows clear signs of Christian redaction but is probably not an original Christian composition. Rather the Christian Sybillist modified the eschatological conclusion of the Jewish work by interpolations. The extent of the redactor's work is difficult to determine exactly. One passage, 2.154–76 is surely Jewish, as it culminates in the universal rule of the Hebrews (175)"; Collins, "Sybilline Oracles," 330.

58. "Later the faithful chosen Hebrew will rule over exceedingly mighty men, having subjected them as of old, since power will never fail"; ibid., 349.

59. Evans, *Luke and Scripture*, 162–64.

name of Rabbi Hilkiah [10] in the name of Rabbi Reuben: "When you say, 'there sit thrones for judgment, thrones for the house of David,' what can 'The ancient of days sat down' (Dan 7:9) [11] mean, if not that He sits between them as presiding Judge and with them judges the peoples? [12] Therefore, it is written: 'until thrones were placed'" (Dan 7:9).[60]

As we can see here, the reference to plural "thrones" in Dan 7:9 sparks rabbis' speculations concerning who sit on those heavenly thrones. Rabbi Tanhuma (late fourth century AD) concludes that "the great ones of Israel" will sit on them and judge "the peoples of the world" along with Yahweh himself (72.5–6). Rabbi Tanhuma supports his view, arguing that, in Isa 3:14, the preposition עם ("with") is used instead of the preposition על ("against") (72.7). It is a linguistically clever argument, because as Evans observes, "The Hebrew text actually says exactly opposite. Isaiah is threatening judgment against Israel's elders and princes for devouring God's vineyard and looting the poor (cf. Isa 3:14b). He is not foretelling a time when God will sit with Israel's leaders and judge the nations."[61]

What is important for us is the exegetical motivation behind *Midrash Tanhuma Qedoshim* §1 71–72. The "one like a son of man" (Dan 7:13)—who represents "the holy ones of the Most High" (Dan 7:27)—is given authority (שלטן), honor (יקר), and kingdom (מלכו) (Dan 7:14; cf. Dan 7:27). In Dan 7:9–27, however, neither the "one like a son of man" nor "the holy ones of the Most High" is specifically associated with the plural thrones in Dan 7:9. As a matter of fact, the author of Daniel nowhere clarifies who sit on those thrones. The rabbinic tradition behind *Midrash Tanhuma Qedoshim* §1 71–72 speculates that "the great ones of Israel" will sit on those thrones. Despite its late date, there could have been some earlier Jewish tradition behind this rabbinic text, contemporary to the early church or the historical Jesus. Possibly, the early church or the historical Jesus knew about this Jewish tradition and adapted it in the early church tradition behind Matt 19:28//Luke 22:30. Even if such a Jewish tradition never existed, we can imagine the possible exegetical motivation behind associating the "thrones" in Dan 7:9 with "the holy ones of the Most High" in Dan 7:27, as it is reflected in Matt 19:28//Luke 22:30 and *Midrash Tanhuma Qedoshim* §1 71–72. As Kazen suggests, "It

60. Ibid., 162–63.
61. Ibid., 164.

is thus likely that the vindication of the Son of Man in the Jesus tradition was originally understood in line with Daniel 7 and applied to Jesus and his followers collectively."[62] Relatedly, Nolland points out: "The idea that the Messiah would be involved in judging Israel has little place in Jewish tradition, but the Qumran community would have been at home with the idea since it considered Jewish life to be largely under the control of the forces of darkness; and the idea is reflected in the John the Baptist materials as we have them."[63] It is not difficult to see why judging Israel—in contrast to judging Gentile oppressors—was not a common idea in Second Temple Judaism, being found only in the early church tradition behind Matt 19:28//Luke 22:30.

Could Paul have exclusively depended on the Jewish tradition behind *Midrash Tanhuma Qedoshim* §1 71–72 without any influence from the early church tradition behind Matt 19:28//Luke 22:30? The late date of *Midrash Tanhuma* and the lack of its close parallel contemporary to Paul make such a possibility doubtful. Could Paul have independently come up with the idea that those in Christ will *judge* or *reign* with him in his eschatological judgment exclusively from Dan 7:9? This is unlikely, considering the rhetorical tone of Paul's question, "Do you not know that the saints will judge the world?" (1 Cor 6:2). Paul clearly is depending on an already established authoritative tradition to support his argument. When we consider the *verbal* and *formal* similarity between the early church tradition behind Matt 19:28//Luke 22:30 and Paul—which we have observed so far—Paul more likely depended on the early church tradition behind Matt 19:28//Luke 22:30 in 1 Cor 6:2 and Rom 5:17.

The fact that both Matthew and Luke attest a common tradition in two different literary contexts suggests that Matt 19:28//Luke 22:30 is *authentic*. I have argued for a *verbal* and *formal* similarity between the early church tradition behind Matt 19:28//Luke 22:30 and Paul's Adam Christology in Rom 5 and 1 Cor 15. Although Paul attests the verb κρίνω only in 1 Cor 6:2 and uses the verb βασιλεύω in Rom 5:17, he most likely refers to the same early church tradition that relates the eschatological reward of the faithful followers of Jesus to that of "the holy ones of the Most High" (Dan 7:9–27). Such a tradition evidently included both the role of *judging* (Dan 7:26) and that of *ruling* (Dan 7:27). Paul creatively uses the early church tradition behind Matt 19:28//Luke 22:30 and

62. Kazen, "Son of Man as Kingdom Imagery," 106.
63. Nolland, *Gospel of Matthew*, 801; cf. Matt 3:7–12.

applies it to the situation (*Sitz im Leben*) of his readers in 1 Cor 6:1–8 and Rom 5:12–21 (cf. 1 Cor 15:20–23).

CONCLUSION

I have discussed Mark 10:45 and Matt 19:28//Luke 22:30 with a set of topics relevant to the relationship between the early church traditions behind them and Paul's Adam Christology. Regardless of their *historicity*, both sayings most likely are *authentic* to the early church. Paul reflects the early church tradition behind Mark 10:45 not only in Rom 5:8, 15, 19 but also in Rom 3:24; 4:25; 8:32; 1 Cor 15:3; 2 Cor 4:11; Gal 2:20 (cf. Eph 5:2, 25). As I have argued, there is no convincing reason to doubt that Paul knew about the early church tradition behind Mark 10:45, which interprets Jesus' atoning death with the image of "ransom" in Isa 43:3–4 and the language of Isa 52:13—53:12, related to the Suffering Servant. Paul builds the stark contrast in Rom 5:12–21 between the destruction of humanity due to Adam's transgression (or disobedience) and the salvation of humanity due to Christ's self-sacrifice (or obedience), by incorporating this early church tradition into his Adam Christology. Likewise, Paul's use of the verb βασιλεύω in Rom 5:17—cf. κρίνω in 1 Cor 6:2—in describing the eschatological rule of the followers of Jesus most likely reflects the early church tradition behind Matt 19:28//Luke 22:30, linked with Dan 7:9–27. Paul incorporates the early church tradition behind Matt 19:28//Luke 22:30 into his Adam Christology in Rom 5:12–21 in order to contrast the reign of *death* and *sin* through Adam's transgression (or disobedience) with the reign of Jesus' followers in *life* with the gift of *righteousness* through Christ's atoning sacrifice (or obedience). Paul in Rom 5 incorporates the Synoptic Son of Man saying traditions behind Mark 10:45 and Matt 19:28//Luke 22:30 into his Adam Christology.

4

Conclusion

THE PURPOSE OF THIS study is to compare and contrast the early church Christology and Paul's Christology, with two foci. The first focus is the relationship between the early church Adam-Jesus typology—reflected in the Synoptic Gospels and Hebrews—and Paul's Adam Christology. The second focus is the relationship between the Synoptic Son of Man saying traditions and Paul's Adam Christology. On the basis of the findings of this study, I contend that Paul uses the early church tradition as a source of his Adam Christology, particularly, its Adam-Jesus typology and Son of Man saying traditions. In chapter 1, after providing a concise literature survey of works related to the subject of this study, I defined a few key terms and stated a number of presuppositions in order to limit the scope of this study.

In chapter 2, I discussed Phil 2:6–11, Heb 2:5–9, and Mark 14:62 in relation to four topics. They were (a) the *authenticity* of each passage, (b) the early church Adam-Jesus typology in each passage, (c) Paul's allusion to the early church Adam-Jesus typology, and (d) Paul's creative use of the early church Adam-Jesus typology. On the basis of the findings of chapter 2, I contend that each passage contains some traditional elements that reflect the early church Adam-Jesus typology, which Paul further develops in Phil 2:6–11; Rom 5:12–21; 1 Cor 15.

In chapter 3, I investigated the relationship between two Synoptic Son of Man saying traditions—Mark 10:45 and Matt 19:28//Luke 22:30—and Paul's Adam Christology looking at five topics. These were (a) the *authenticity* of each Son of Man saying, (b) Paul's allusion to the early church tradition behind each Son of Man saying, (c) Paul's incorporation of it into his Adam Christology, (d) Paul's presentation of Jesus' atoning death/followers' eschatological ruling and the Scriptures, and (e) Paul's presentation of Jesus' atoning death/followers' eschatological ruling and first-century AD Judaism. As I have argued, regardless of their *historicity*, both Mark 10:45 and Matt 19:28//Luke 22:20 most likely are *authentic* to the early church. Paul incorporates the early church tradition behind Mark 10:45 into Rom 5:15, 19 when he develops his explicit and sophisticated Adam Christology (cf. Rom 3:24; 4:25; 8:32; 1 Cor 15:3; 2 Cor 4:11; Gal 2:20; Eph 5:2, 25). Paul's goal in Rom 5:15, 19 is to contrast the destruction of humanity due to Adam's transgression (or disobedience) with the redemption of humanity due to Christ's self-sacrifice (or obedience). Paul incorporates the early church tradition behind Matt 19:28//Luke 22:30 in Rom 5:17, when he contrasts the reign of *death* and *sin*—through Adam's transgression (or disobedience)—and the believers' reign in *life* with the gift of *righteousness*—through Christ's atoning sacrifice (or obedience). Although Paul uses the verb βασιλεύω in Rom 5:17—rather than the verb κρίνω (cf. 1 Cor 6:2)—he most likely refers to the early church tradition behind Matt 19:28; Luke 22:30, which links the eschatological role of Jesus' followers with that of "the holy ones of the Most High" in Dan 7:27.

If the findings of this study are valid, Paul uses the early church tradition as a source of his Adam Christology, particularly, its Adam-Jesus typology and Son of Man saying traditions. I am not arguing for a single coherent Adam Christology—as a firmly established doctrine—but the existence of a multifaceted and rudimentary Adam-Jesus typology. The early church seems to have employed its Adam-Jesus typology in order to elucidate Jesus' eschatological *authority* (similar to Adam's authority over God's creation in Gen 1:26–28), *obedience* (in contrast to Adam's disobedience), Jesus' *solidarity* with his followers (similar to Adam as the representative of humankind), and Jesus' *sanctification* of his followers (in contrast to the consequences of Adam's transgression). This list highlights the obvious *dialectic* nature of the early church Adam-Jesus typology, which undermines any assumption that Adam and Christ must be completely "equal" for Adam-Christ typology to work.

This study illuminates two axes in Paul's theology: *tradition* and *revelation*. Seyoon Kim in *The Origin of Paul's Gospel* concludes that Paul's Adam Christology is grounded in his Damascus Christophany.[1] In his more recent monograph *Paul and the New Perspective*, Kim

---

1. Kim, *Origin of Paul's Gospel*, 267.

concludes, "I would like to modify my fundamental thesis: Paul's gospel originated from both the Damascus revelation and the Jesus tradition."[2] Kim describes "an interplay to produce various Pauline theological conceptions," using filial relationships as a metaphor.[3] The findings of this study broadly support Kim's conclusion, for Paul uses the early church tradition as a source of his Adam Christology in addition to his Damascus revelation. When expounding Christology, Paul frequently refers to various authoritative traditions such as the Old Testament, contemporary Jewish exegetical traditions, and the early church tradition. Parallel to his creative use of authoritative traditions elsewhere, Paul develops his explicit and sophisticated Adam Christology in Rom 5 and 1 Cor 15 from the early church Adam-Jesus typology (reflected in Phil 2:6–11; Heb 2:5–11; Mark 14:62) and the two Son of Man saying traditions (Mark 10:45 and Matt 19:28; Luke 22:30). In this regard, it is more appropriate to call Paul "a follower of Jesus" than "the founder of Christianity" as David Wenham concludes.[4]

---

2. Kim, *Paul and the New Perspective*, 296; similarly, Witherington, *Paul's Narrative Thought World*, 154.

3. Kim considers Paul's Damascus Christophany as father, the Jesus tradition as mother, the Old Testament as a grandparent, and the pre-Pauline Christian kerygma as an older sibling; Kim, *Paul and the New Perspective*, 296–67.

4. Wenham, *Paul*, 408–10; similarly, Thompson, *Clothed with Christ*, 240; Häusser, *Christusbekenntnis und Jesusüberlieferung bei Paulus*, 361–64.

Appendix 1

The Early Church Adam-Jesus Typology in Luke 3:38—4:1

LUKE'S GENEALOGY OF JESUS (Luke 3:23-38) begins with Jesus and ends with the fascinating phrase Ἀδὰμ τοῦ θεοῦ ("Adam, [son] of God"). There is no doubt that Adam-Jesus typology is working behind this particular phrase and Luke's overall genealogy. Despite that fact, I have decided to include my discussion of Luke 3:38—4:1 in an appendix because of its speculative nature. While admitting that the early church Adam-Jesus typology in Luke 3:38—4:1 is not as transparent as that in Phil 2:6-11; Heb 2:5-11; Mark 14:62, I consider it as an interesting piece of evidence worthy of exploration. In parallel with chapter 2, I will discuss now the *authenticity* of Luke 3:38—4:1, the early church Adam-Jesus typology in Luke 3:38—4:1, and Paul's use of the early church Adam-Jesus typology.

To begin with, I consider Luke 3:21-22 and Luke 4:1-13 as *authentic* on the basis of their parallels in Mark 1:9-13 and Matt 3:13-4:11. It is difficult, however, to judge the *authenticity* of Luke's genealogy of Jesus in Luke 3:23-38. Certainly, there are more redactional components in Luke 3:23-38 than Luke 3:21-22; 4:1-13. Unlike anywhere else in this study, we are dealing with the material unique to Luke ("L"). As I stated in chapter 1, I do not automatically consider the material unique to Mathew ("M") or Luke ("L") as the Evangelist's creation out of nothing (*ex nihilo*). I contend that certain components in Luke 3:38—4:1 are traditional, which I will explain shortly.

While a number of scholars have argued for the early church Adam-Jesus typology in Mark 1:9-13, none of them has won general consensus. Space does not allow me here to discuss every argument in detail. The most common argument seems to be the view that the use of the word θηρία ("wild beasts") in Mark 1:13 presents Jesus as a new Adam, overcoming Satan's temptations—in contrast to Adam in Gen 3—and living in peaceful co-existence with wild beasts.[1] This is unlikely for two reasons. Firstly, as John Paul Heil points out, the chiastic structure of Mark 1:12–13 suggests confrontation rather than peaceful co-existence between Jesus and the wild beasts. Based on his observation of this chiastic structure, Heil translates καί in Mark 1:13c as "but" rather than "and."[2] The following table visualizes the chiastic structure in Mark 1:12–13.

	Mark 1:12–13
A	Καὶ εὐθὺς τὸ πνεῦμα αὐτὸν ἐκβάλλει εἰς τὴν ἔρημον (12).
B	καὶ ἦν ἐν τῇ ἐρήμῳ τεσσεράκοντα ἡμέρας πειραζόμενος ὑπὸ τοῦ Σατανᾶ (13a),
B′	καὶ ἦν μετὰ τῶν θηρίων (13b),
A′	καὶ οἱ ἄγγελοι διηκόνουν αὐτῷ (13c).

Secondly, as Jeffrey B. Gibson suggests, "Mark 1:13b is an *allusion to the particular catenation of ideas embodied in such writings as* Ps 91:11–13, *T. Iss.* 7.7, *T. Benj.* 5.2, and *T. Naph.* 8.4."[3] The *conceptual* parallels between Mark 1:13 and these passages are striking. In Ps 91:11–13; *T. Naph.* 8.4, angels stand against wild beasts. In *T. Iss.* 7.7; *T. Benj.* 5.2; *T. Naph.* 8.4, each patriarch exhorts his readers to do good so that the evil spirits (or the devil) may flee from them and wild beasts may fear them (or may be subdued by them). Greek *Life of Adam and Eve* 10–12[4]

---

1. E.g., Häusser, *Christusbekenntnis und Jesusüberlieferung bei Paulus*, 249; Focant, *Évangile Selon Marc*, 70–71; Marcus, "Son of Man As Son of Adam," 55–56; Donahue and Harrington, *Gospel of Mark*, 66; Moloney, *Gospel of Mark*, 38–39; Mell, "Jesu Taufe Durch Johannes (Markus 1,9–15)," 161–78; Bauckham, "Jesus and the Wild Animals (Mark 1:13)," 3–21; Parkman, "Adam Christological Motifs in the Synoptic Traditions," 120; Sahlin, "Adam-Christologie im Neuen Testament," 12–14; Jeremias, "Adam," 141–43.

2. Heil, "Jesus with the Wild Animals in Mark 1:13," 65; Gibson similarly claims, "In Mark 1:13b 'the wild beasts' and angels stand over against one another . . . therefore an explanation of Mark 1:13b wholly in terms of a *Urzeit-Endzeit*/Paradise typology is incomplete and inadequate"; Gibson, *Temptations of Jesus in Early Christianity*, 66–67.

3. Ibid., 67.

4. "And Seth and Eve went into the regions of Paradise. As they were going, Eve saw her son and *a wild beast* (θηρίον) attacking him . . . And Eve cried out to the beast and

The Early Church Adam-Jesus Typology in Luke 3:38—4:1 129

is another important piece of evidence that suggests the confrontation between Jesus and the wild beasts in Mark 1:13 rather than their peaceful coexistence, in which, as Rivka Nir notes, "Seth's battle with the beast should be understood as a struggle between the 'image of God' and Satan, and viewed in a Christian context."[5] Cumulative evidence suggests that Mark 1:13 highlights Jesus' continual faithful obedience to God even in midst of Satan's hostile temptation rather than his re-acquisition of the access to Paradise—that Adam lost in Gen 3—by portraying his peaceful co-existence with the wild beasts.[6]

While there is no trace of the implicit primitive Adam-Jesus typology of the early church in Mark 1:9–13, it is implied in Luke's version of the description of Jesus' baptism and temptation in Luke 3:21—4:13. Immediately after depicting Jesus' baptism in Luke 3:21–22, the Evangelist introduces an extensive genealogy of Jesus in Luke 3:23–38,[7] tracing his root to Adam who is called "son of God" (Luke 3:38)—in contrast to Matthew's genealogy only to Abraham. Since three topics—*authenticity*, Adam-Jesus typology, and Paul's use of it—are closely related to one another in this case, I will discuss them simultaneously and sum them up later.

The phrase πλήρης πνεύματος ἁγίου ("full of the Holy Spirit") in Luke 4:1 provides a crucial piece of evidence that the Evangelist incorporates the implicit primitive Adam-Jesus typology of the early church in his description of Jesus' baptism and temptation in Luke 3:21—4:13. Evans acutely observes that Luke's pneumatology provides the key to understand Adam-Jesus typology in Luke 3:21—4:13.[8] While Luke already

---

said, '*O you evil beast* (θηρίον πονηρόν), do you not fear to attack the image of God?' . . . Seth said to *the beast* (τὸ θηρίον), 'Shut your mouth and be silent, and keep away from the image of God until the day of judgment' . . . Then *the beast* (τὸ θηρίον) fled and left him wounded and went to its dwelling"; Johnson, "Life of Adam and Eve," 273–75.

5. Nir, "Struggle between the 'Image of God' and Satan in the Greek Life of Adam and Eve," 327–29.

6. Fitzmyer considers the latter view as "highly eisegetical"; Fitzmyer, *Gospel According to Luke I–IX*, 512.

7. Robbins points out: "The structural intrusion of this genealogy [Luke 3:23–38] completely overpowers the surroundings of this story [Luke 4:1–13; cf. Matt 4:1–11] in Q. 'Son of God' is play-dough in the quick and skilful hand of this author. With the words 'Adam son of God' still ringing in their ears, the readers will *hear* the devil ask 'If you are the (a) Son of God' but they will *perceive* in the encounter *a new Adam*"; Robbins, *Testing of Jesus in Q*, 90.

8. Evans, *Luke and Scripture*, 38.

associates Jesus' identity as the Son of God with the Holy Spirit in Luke 1:35 and Luke 3:22, it may not have been by accident that Luke mentions Adam's sonship (Luke 3:38) right before describing the fullness of the Spirit in Jesus (Luke 4:1) and emphasizing his Sonship (Luke 4:3, 9). Evans raises an interesting question, "On what ground could Jesus be called the 'Son of God?'" in relation to Adam who also is called "son of God."[9] The phrase πλήρης πνεύματος ἁγίου (Luke 4:1) immediately following the phrase [Ἀδάμ] τοῦ θεοῦ (Luke 3:38) suggests the following typology[10]:

Adam: first son of God	"Then the LORD God formed man from the dust of the ground, and breathed (נפח; ἐμφυσάω) into his nostrils the breath of life (נשמת היים; πνοὴ ζωῆς); and the man became a living being (נפש; ψυχὴ ζῶσα)" (Gen 2:7)
	"[Adam] the son of God (τοῦ θεοῦ)" (Luke 3:38)
Jesus: second Son of God	"The angel said to her, 'The Holy Spirit (πνεῦμα ἅγιον) will come upon you, and the power of the Most High will overshadow you; therefore the child to be born will be holy; he will be called Son of God (υἱὸς θεοῦ)'" (Luke 1:35)
	"Jesus, full of the Holy Spirit (πλήρης πνεύματος ἁγίου), returned from the Jordan and was led by the Spirit in the desert" (Luke 4:1)

The following table visualizes various semantic relationships among the words נפח, נשמת, and רוח:

Gen 2:7	"Then the LORD God formed man from the dust of the ground, and breathed (נפח; ἐμφυσάω) into his nostrils the breath of life (נשמת היים; πνοὴ ζωῆς); and the man became a living being (נפש; ψυχὴ ζῶσα)"
Ezek 37:9	"Then he said to me, 'Prophesy to the breath (הרוח; τὸ πνεῦμα), prophesy, mortal, and say to the breath (הרוח; τὸ πνεῦμα): Thus says the Lord GOD: Come from the four *winds* (רוחות; πνεύματοι), O breath (הרוח), and breathe (נפח; ἐμφυσάω) upon these slain, that they may live"
Prov 1:23	"Give heed to my reproof; I will pour out my thoughts (רוחי; ἐμῆς πνοῆς ῥῆσις) to you; I will make my words known to you"

---

9. Ibid., 38–39.
10. Similarly, ibid., 38–45.

Although the Hebrew word נשמה ("breath"; cf. πνοή ["wind"] in the LXX)—instead of רוח ("breath, wind, spirit"; cf. πνεῦμα ["breath, spirit"] in the LXX)—is used in Gen 2:7, נשמה clearly refers to the Spirit of God in the creation of Adam. The closest parallel to the breath of God in Gen 2:7 can be found in Ezek 37:9. The LXX of Prov 1:23 also shows that the Hebrew word רוח can be translated as πνοή rather than πνεῦμα. The comparison between Gen 2:7 and Ezek 37:9 shows the intrinsic association between the verb נפח and the noun נשמה / רוח. Since the writer of Ezekiel evidently alludes to the creation of Adam in Gen 2:7 in his description of the resurrection of the dead bodies in Ezek 37:9, we can suppose that נשמה and רוח can be used interchangeably in relation to the life-giving breath of God. The comparison between Ezek 37:9 and Prov 1:23 shows that the Hebrew word רוח is not always translated as πνεῦμα but sometimes as πνοή, which once again supports the semantic association between נשמה and רוח in Hebrew.

Although Luke nowhere quotes Gen 2:7 in Luke 3:21—4:13, as Paul does in 1 Cor 15:45, the Adam-Jesus typology embedded in Luke 3:38—4:1 suggests that the Spirit of God has to do with Adam's and Jesus' status as the Son of God. Evans notes, "If it was by virtue of his Spirit-generation [cf. Luke 1:35] that Jesus was regarded as the 'Son of God,' then Luke likewise must have regarded Adam as 'son of God' by virtue of his generation by the Spirit (or breath) of God."[11] This is not the place to discuss the pre-existence of Christ. While I do not suppose that the early church authors held an adoptionist Christology, it is not necessary to rule out the possibility of the existence of the early church Adam-Jesus typology behind Luke 3:38—4:1, on the basis of the doctrine of the pre-existence of Christ.[12] Evans states, "It is clear therefore that Luke's notion

---

11. Ibid., 39; Philo expresses a similar view in *Virt.* 37.203-4: "And he [Adam] was also thought worthy of a soul, which was derived from no being who had as yet come into existence by being created, but God breathed into him as much of his own power as mortal nature was capable of receiving . . . But the father of this man was not mortal at all, and the sole author of his being was God . . ."; Yonge, *Works of Philo*, 660–61.

12. As I have discussed in chapter 2, the pre-existence of Christ does not necessarily negate the existence of the implicit primitive Adam-Jesus typology of the early church in Phil 2:6–11. In his Graham Stanton Lecture at the British New Testament Conference 2011 in Nottingham, UK, Professor Andrew T. Lincoln gave a paper entitled "Luke and Jesus' Conception: A Case of Double Paternity?" in which he claims that the Evangelist presents *both* Joseph (despite Mary's virgin birth; cf. Luke 1:27, 32; 2:4, 7, 11, 27, 33, 41–51; 3:23–38; 4:22) *and* God as the father of Jesus. He argues that the Evangelist's depiction of double paternity has parallels in both the Old Testament (cf. Jer 1:5; Isa 44:2)

of the divine sonship of Adam was neither unique nor unintelligible to first-century readers of Scripture."[13] Evans claims, "Luke's pneumatology not only provides the basis for understanding why he calls both Adam and Jesus sons of God; it also clarifies why Jesus was successful in facing Satanic temptation and Adam was not."[14]

As I already have mentioned, Luke's genealogy of Jesus in Luke 3:23–38 is unique and may not have been *authentic* to the early church. Likewise, the phrase πλήρης πνεύματος ἁγίου ("full of the Holy Spirit") only appears in Luke 4:1 but not in Mark 1:12 and Matt 4:1. Considering its frequent appearance in Luke-Acts (Luke 1:15, 41, 67; Acts 2:4; 4:8, 31; 6:3, 5; 7:55; 11:24; 13:9), it probably is "a Lucan theologoumenon," as Fitzmyer suggests.[15] Both the phrase "full of the Holy Spirit" (Luke 4:1) and the genealogy of Jesus (Luke 3:23–38) are possibly Lukan redaction. Apart from these potential Lukan elements, I consider the rudimentary Adam-Jesus typology behind Luke 3:38—4:1 as *authentic* to the early church, on the basis of its parallel in Paul. I argue that Paul alludes to the early church Adam-Jesus typology behind Luke 3:38—4:1, on the basis of its *conceptual* similarity and dissimilarity to Paul's Adam Christology in 1 Cor 15:45, which I will explain in the following.

There is a *conceptual* similarity between the Adam-Jesus typology in Luke 3:38—4:1 and 1 Cor 15:45. Paul attests a similar Adam-Jesus typology to that in Luke 3:38—4:1, referring to Christ as ὁ ἔσχατος Ἀδάμ ("the last Adam") in 1 Cor 15:45. Paul quotes Gen 2:7 from the LXX but he also incorporates new expressions such as ὁ ἔσχατος Ἀδάμ and πνεῦμα ζῳοποιοῦν into the second half, based on his midrash-like interpretation of Gen 2:7.[16] The following chart visualizes the *verbal* and *formal* parallel between 1 Cor 15:45 and Gen 2:7.

---

and Greco-Roman literature (cf. Plutarch, *Theseus* 2.3.36; *Romulus* 2–4; *Alexander* 2, 3; Suetonius, *Divus Augustus* 2, 4, 94; Dio Cassius, *Hist. Rom.* 45.1; Diogenes Laertius, *Lives of Eminent Philosophers* 3; Olympiodorus, *Life of Plato* 1; Philostratus, *Vit. Apoll.* 1.6; Iamblichus, *Vit. Pyth.* 2). The Evangelist seems to employ the implicit primitive Adam-Jesus typology of the early church in Luke 3:38—4:1 in conjunction with his portrayal of Jesus' divine paternity.

13. Evans, *Luke and Scripture*, 40.

14. Ibid.

15. Fitzmyer, *Gospel According to Luke I–IX*, 513; similarly, Johnson, *Gospel of Luke*, 73.

16. Similarly, Fitzmyer, *First Corinthians*, 598; Schrage, *Erste Brief an die Korinther (1Kor 15:1—16:24)*, 156; as Schrage observes: "For Paul, in any case, it is only Christ

1 Cor 15:45	... ἐγένετο ὁ πρῶτος ἄνθρωπος Ἀδὰμ εἰς ψυχὴν ζῶσαν, ὁ ἔσχατος Ἀδὰμ εἰς πνεῦμα ζῳοποιοῦν. ("... 'The first man, Adam, became a living being'; the last Adam became a life-giving spirit.").
Gen 2:7	... ἐγένετο ὁ ἄνθρωπος εἰς ψυχὴν ζῶσαν. ("... the man became a living being" [NETS].)

The fact that Adam (cf. Gen 2:7) is the reference point of Christ' identity in Luke 3:38—4:1 and 1 Cor 15:45 indicates that both texts have Adam-Jesus typology in mind.

While Luke and Paul share a similar Adam-Jesus typology with each other in Luke 3:38—4:1 and 1 Cor 15:45, there is also a fundamental difference between the two. The gist of Paul's use of Adam-Jesus typology in 1 Cor 15:45 is not the contrast between Adam's *disobedience* and Jesus' *obedience*, as in Luke 3:38—4:1, but the contrast between "a physical body" and "a spiritual [resurrection] body." Also, while Paul's Adam Christology in 1 Cor 15:45 begins with Christ's resurrection, Luke's Adam-Jesus typology begins with Jesus' receiving of the Holy Spirit (Luke 3:21–22; 3:38—4:1). Considering the *conceptual* similarity and dissimilarity between Luke 3:38—4:1 and 1 Cor 15:45, which I have discussed, Paul and the Evangelist probably reflect the implicit primitive Adam-Jesus typology of the early church, independently of each other.

Could Luke have depended on Paul instead of their common dependence on the early church Adam-Jesus typology? Alternatively, could Luke have influenced Paul as they were travelling companions in Acts? I am not holding any particular position on the issue of the authorship of Luke-Acts for this study. Generally speaking, Paul's dependence on the Evangelist is less likely than the other way around, since Paul's letters pre-date Luke-Acts. The fact that there is nothing distinctively Pauline in Luke 3:38—4:1 apart from the rudimentary Adam-Jesus typology suggests their independent reliance on the early church Adam-Jesus typol-

---

who rises from the dead and thereby becomes the life-bringing Spirit and now present in the Spirit (cf. 2 Cor 3:17), who mediates eschatological life as the last Adam as beginner and author of eschatological humanity (2 Cor 5:17; Rom 8:10–11; cf. John 20:22–23). And this new-creating Spirit contrasts with ψυχὴ ζῶσα"; my translation of "Für Paulus jedenfalls ist es allein der von den Toten auferweckte, dadurch zum lebendigmachenden Geist gewordene und nun im Geist gegenwärtige Christus (vgl. 2Kor 3,17), der als ἔσχατος Ἀδάμ und d.h. als Anfänger und Urheber der endzeitlichen Menschheit eschatologisches Leben vermittelt (2Kor 5,17; Rom 8,10f; vgl. Joh 20,22f). Und diesem neu-und lebenschaffenden Geist steht gegenüber die ψυχὴ ζῶσα; ibid., 304.

ogy. While admitting Luke's potential theologizing of the other aspects of the Testing Story in Luke 4:1–13, I contend that the implicit Adam-Jesus typology in Luke 3:38—4:1 is *authentic* to the early church on the basis of the *conceptual* similarity and dissimilarity between Adam-Jesus typology in Luke 3:38—4:1 and 1 Cor 15:45.

Paul at times creates new expressions in citing an authoritative tradition for his rhetorical purposes as in the case of the phrase "baptized into Moses" (1 Cor 10:2) and the phrase "sons of the Day" (1 Thess 5:5). In explaining the nature of the resurrection body in 1 Cor 15:35–49, Paul contrasts "a physical body" and "a spiritual body" in 1 Cor 15:42–44. In order to strengthen this contrast, Paul cites Gen 2:7, adding the adjective πρῶτος ("first") to the word ἄνθρωπος ("man"). As Stanley points out, "In the context of 1 Cor 15, the addition brings to formal expression the fundamental contrast between Adam and Christ as the πρῶτος and ἔσχατος Adam (v. 45b) that forms the backbone of the ensuing argument."[17] In 1 Cor 15:45, immediately after citing Gen 2:7, Paul claims, "*The last Adam* (ὁ ἔσχατος Ἀδάμ) became *a life-giving spirit* (πνεῦμα ζῳοποιοῦν)." Paul creates a new expression ὁ ἔσχατος Ἀδάμ in 1 Cor 15:45 to explicate his Adam Christology. The expression πνεῦμα ζῳοποιοῦν is a *hapax legomenon* in the Greek Bible and clearly is a Pauline neologism (cf. John 5:21; 6:63).[18]

By creating these unique phrases in 1 Cor 15:45, Paul associates "a physical body" with Adam who is called ψυχή ζῶσα and "a spiritual body" with Christ who is called πνεῦμα ζῳοποιοῦν. Dunn points out:

> As the first Adam came into existence (ἐγένετο) at creation, the beginning of the old age, so the last Adam (as such) came into existence at the resurrection, the beginning of the age to come. The same point is implicit elsewhere in Paul—particularly Rom 8:29, where Christ's Adamic role as eldest brother in a new family of men begins with his birth from the dead (cf. Col 1:18), and Phil 3:21, where a share in the lost Adamic glory is finally attained

---

17. Stanley, *Paul and the Language of Scripture*, 208. When assuring the Corinthian believers of their future bodily resurrection, Paul contrasts σῶμα ψυχικόν ("a physical body") and σῶμα πνευματικόν ("a spiritual body") in 1 Cor 15:44. Immediately after that, Paul contrasts Adam and Christ, calling the latter ὁ ἔσχατος Ἀδάμ ("the last Adam") in 1 Cor 15:45. Although the contrast here does not concern Christ's eschatological authority *per se*, it shows that Paul in 1 Cor 15:42–49 is picking up the Adam-Christ typology in 1 Cor 15:20–28.

18. Even in John 5:21; 6:63, Jesus is not exactly identified with "a life-giving spirit" as in 1 Cor 15:45.

by transformation of our lowly body to be like Christ's resurrection body . . . Christ's role as second man, as last Adam, does not begin either in some pre-existent state, or at incarnation, but at his resurrection. For Paul, the resurrection marks the beginning of the representative humanity of the last Adam.[19]

Dunn correctly observes that Paul creatively uses Gen 2:7 to highlight the resurrection of Christ and its eschatological implication—the bodily resurrection of those in Christ.[20] Nonetheless, Paul's citation of Gen 2:7 in 1 Cor 15:45 in parallel with the rudimentary Adam-Jesus typology in Luke 3:38—4:1 indicates that he is not creating his neologism in 1 Cor 15:45 out of nothing (*ex nihilo*) but on the basis of the early church Adam-Jesus typology associated with Gen 2:7. Paul as a creative theologian seems to have developed the implicit primitive Adam-Jesus typology of the early church and compared Adam and Jesus—as the first and the second Son of God—based on their association with the breath/Spirit of God, identifying Christ with "a life-giving spirit." Paul possibly alludes to the early church Adam-Jesus typology behind Luke 3:38—4:1 and creatively uses it in developing his Adam Christology in 1 Cor 15:45.

I will sum up now my discussion so far. Luke's genealogy of Jesus in Luke 3:23–38 or the phrase "full of the Holy Spirit" may not be *authentic*. However, the rudimentary Adam-Jesus typology operating behind the Evangelist's description of Jesus' baptism and temptation may be *authentic* to the early church. Although the Evangelist nowhere cites Gen 2:7 in Luke 3:21—4:13, it provides a relevant background for the Adam-Jesus typology in Luke 3:38—4:1. The fact that Paul in 1 Cor 15:45 quotes Gen 2:7 when he contrasts Adam and Christ may not have been coincidental. Luke in Luke 3:38—4:1, on the one hand, compares Adam's and Jesus' association with the Spirit in Luke 3:38—4:1. Paul in 1 Cor 15:45, on the other hand, contrasts the physical (or perishable) body of Adam who is "a living being" with the spiritual (or imperishable) body of Christ who is "a life-giving spirit." Both of them may have derived their Adam-Jesus typology from the implicit primitive Adam-Jesus typology of the early church rather than creating it out of nothing (*ex nihilo*).

---

19. Dunn, *Christology in the Making*, 108.

20. Caution should be made in that, as I pointed out in chapter 2, Dunn's claim that the early church Adam-Jesus typology reflected in Phil 2:6–11 negates the pre-existence of Christ is unwarranted; ibid., 120.

Appendix 2

Jesus and the Suffering Servant

THERE HAS BEEN CONSIDERABLE debate in New Testament scholarship concerning Jesus and the Suffering Servant of Isa 53 as the background of Mark 10:45. While this subject is important in its own right, it is only indirectly related to this study. Therefore, I will discuss briefly the relationship between the early church tradition behind Mark 10:45 and Isa 53 in the following.

Barrett argues that there is no definite linguistic link between Mark 10:45 and Isa 53.[1] Based on the evidence in Jewish intertestamental literature such as 2 Macc 7.37; 4 Macc 6.27–29; 17.22; 18.4, Barrett claims, "The self-sacrifice of the martyrs, who acted as intercessors before God, would form a means of atonement for Israel . . . It would not be an exaggeration to say that the martyrs are here described as λύτρον ἀντὶ πολλῶν."[2] Barrett concludes, "A creative mind working upon it [Jewish tradition concerning martyrdom] could *produce* a saying such as that recorded by Mark [10:45]."[3] Hooker also rejects any connection between the Son of Man in Mark 10:45 and the Suffering Servant in Isa 53 on the basis of her two observations.[4] Firstly, the context of Mark 10:35–45 and that of Isa 53 are radically different from each other; the Servant in Isa 53 is not a servant of people—in contrast to the Son of Man in Mark 10:45—but a servant of Yahweh. Secondly, the actual word λύτρον in Mark 10:45 does not appear in the LXX of Isa 53.

---

1. Barrett, "Background of Mark 10:45," 2–7.
2. Ibid., 12.
3. Ibid., 15.
4. Hooker, *Jesus and the Servant*, 74–79.

Hooker's first argument—that the early church tradition behind Mark 10:45 could not have identified Jesus with the Suffering Servant in Isa 53 because the Servant is the servant of Yahweh ("a title of great honour"[5]) and not that of men—is unwarranted, for the Servant "serves many [πολλοί; people of Yahweh] well" (Isa 53:11–12 in the LXX). The Servant in Isa 53 is not only the servant of Yahweh but also that of the many. Hooker's second argument—that the actual word λύτρον (Mark 10:45) does not appear in the LXX of Isa 53—is stronger than her first argument. As Hooker points out:

> There is, however, not the slightest evidence to show that these two terms [λύτρον in Mark 10:45 and אשם in Isa 53:10] were ever connected: the λύτρον, as we have seen, was the redemption of a person or thing by purchase; the אשם was the repayment of something wrongfully withheld, together with a guilt-offering by means of expiation: the one is a business transaction; the other involves a sacrifice for sin. Some scholars have stressed the substitutionary element implied by the word ἀντί in Mark 10:45. The אשם, however, was never a substitute: it was payment, together with compensation and a guilt-offering.[6]

As Hooker observes, אשם in the Hebrew Scripture stands for "guilt-offering" and is distinct from the concept of λύτρον. Hooker, however, does not make much out of the fact that the LXX translates what parallels אם־תשים אשם נפשו in the MT (literally, "if you [singular] lay down his life as a guilt-offering") as ἐὰν δῶτε περὶ ἁμαρτίας (literally, "if ever you [plural] give [his life an offering] for sin"), which demonstrates the translator's interpretive freedom. In her more recent publication, Hooker points out:

> This redemption of his people is now to be fulfilled, according to Mark 10:45, by the Son of Man surrendering his own life as a "ransom." Isa 53:10–11, however, contains a different idea. This

---

5. Hooker, "Isaiah in Mark's Gospel," 48; Hooker also emphasizes that the verb διακονέω is used in Mark 10:45, while the verb δουλεύω is used in Isa 53:11–12 (LXX). There is no great semantic difference between the two verbs to suppose that there is no allusion to Isa 53:11–12 in Mark 10:45.

6. Hooker, *Jesus and the Servant*, 77. As Collins points out, the term λύτρον (both in the singular and the plural) occur in the LXX (cf. Exod 21:29; 30:11–16; Num 35:31–34; Lev 19:20; 25:24, 51–52; 27:31; Prov 6:35, 13:8; Isa 45:13); Collins, *Mark*, 500–502; cf. Num 3:12 ("I hereby accept the Levites from among the Israelites as *substitutes* [λύτρα] for all the firstborn that open the womb among the Israelites. The Levites shall be mine").

passage speaks of God's Servant being made a "guilt offering," which involved making restitution to the injured party and offering a sacrifice as a means of expiation. This is a very different image [from that in Mark 10:45], and it is taken over in the LXX version, which translates that term [אשם] by the phrase "for sin."[7]

The phrase περὶ ἁμαρτίας in Isa 53:10 does not simply "take over" אשם ("guilt-offering") but reflects an interpretative move that associates אשם with the imagery of חטאת ("sin/purification offering"[8]) related to the Day of Atonement.[9]

Although both חטאת ("sin/purification offering") and λύτρον ("a ransom") refer to something vicarious, they convey quite different imagery from each other. As I pointed out in chapter 3, section 1, while there is no "ransom" idea in Isa 53, it is present in Isa 43. As Stuhlmacher suggests, either the historical Jesus or the early church could have merged the "ransom" idea of Isa 43:3–4 with the language of Isa 53 in understanding Jesus' atoning death. I identify this particular connection as a *conceptual* similarity between the early church tradition behind Mark 10:45 and Deutero-Isaiah. In addition to this *conceptual* similarity, there are multiple *verbal* and *formal* parallels between the early church tradition behind Mark 10:45 and Isa 53, which make Barrett's and Hooker's view—that there is no connection between Mark 10:45 and Isa 53—unconvincing. The following chart visualizes the *verbal* and *formal* similarities behind the early church tradition between Mark 10:45 and Isa 53.

---

7. Hooker, "Isaiah in Mark's Gospel," 48.

8. Milgrom challenged the consensus interpretation of as חטאת "sin offering" and argued for "purification offering"; Milgrom, "Sin-Offering or Purification-Offering?" 237–39. It goes beyond the scope of this study to determine the precise meaning of חטאת. What is important for our discussion is the fact that the LXX translator brings in the imagery of חטאת in translating אשם in Isa 53:10.

9. Cf. *Tg. Isa* 53:10 ("Yet *before* the LORD *it was a pleasure to refine and to cleanse the remnant of his people, in order to purify their* soul *from sins* [לנקאה מחובין נפשהון]; *they* shall see *the kingdom of their Messiah, they shall increase sons and daughters, they* shall prolong days; *those who perform the law of* the LORD shall prosper in his *pleasure* [the innovative wording of the Targum in italics]"; Chilton, *Isaiah Targum*, 104–5).

Isa 53:11-12 [LXX]	Mark 10:45
δίκαιον εὖ δουλεύοντα πολλοῖς ("[the] righteous one who *serves* many *well*"¹⁰)	διακονῆσαι ("*to serve*")
ἀνθ' ὧν παρεδόθη εἰς θάνατον ἡ ψυχὴ αὐτοῦ ("because *his soul was given over* to death" [NETS].)	δοῦναι τὴν ψυχὴν αὐτοῦ ("*to give his life*") Cf. Mark 10:33 παραδοθήσεται ("*will be handed over*")
–	λύτρον ("ransom")
Αὐτὸς ἁμαρτίας πολλῶν ἀνήνεγκεν ("he bore the sins of *many*" [NETS].)	ἀντὶ πολλῶν ("for *many*")
διὰ τὰς ἁμαρτίας αὐτῶν παρεδόθη ("because of *their* sins he *was given over*" [NETS].)	Cf. Mark 10:33 παραδοθήσεται ("*will be handed over*")

Hooker acknowledges these undeniable *verbal* and *formal* similarities between the early church tradition behind Mark 10:45 and Isa 53 with respect to the phrase δοῦναι τὴν ψυχὴν αὐτοῦ ἀντὶ πολλῶν.¹¹ Hooker also admits that πολλῶν in Mark 10:45 is a "Semitism" reflecting an earlier Aramaic tradition and the word πολύς occurs three times in the LXX of Isa 53:11–12, translating the Hebrew word רב.¹² Hooker, nevertheless, maintains that πολλῶν in Mark 10:45 is "in no way dependent upon the possibility of a reference to Isa 53:11[–12]."¹³ I agree with her that πολλῶν in Mark 10:45 alone cannot be the evidence of its allusion to Isa 53. Considering both the *conceptual* similarity and the *verbal* and *formal* similarities between the early church tradition behind Mark 10:45 and Isa 53 (and Isa 43), however, Hooker's conclusion that

10. My literal translation; NETS translation "a righteous one who is well subject to many" does not reflect the active voice of the participle δουλεύοντα in Isa 53:11 [LXX].

11. Hooker, *Jesus and the Servant*, 78–79.

12. As Boring points out, "'Many' in the Semitic sense often is not contrasted with 'all' but with 'few,' and is the functional equivalent of 'all'—as in Qumran usage, where 'the many' means 'everyone' (e.g., 1QS 6.1, 7–25) and as recognized by the paraphrase in 1 Tim 2:6. The word 'many' (πολλοί) seems to be an important point of contact with Isa 53, where it occurs three times in 53:11–12 in the context of the Servant's giving his life for the sins of others"; Boring, *Mark*, 303; similarly, Donahue and Harrington, *Gospel of Mark*, 313.

13. Hooker, *Jesus and the Servant*, 78.

there is no connection "in thought or in language" between Mark 10:45 and Isa 53 is unconvincing.[14]

As Dunn points out, it is difficult to refute that "Isa 53 provided the first generation Christians with an important scriptural means of understanding the death of Jesus." Dunn supports this claim, "The fact that the reference [Rom 4:25] is a formulaic allusion rather than a carefully argued scriptural proof strongly suggests that the use of Isa 53 was widespread in earliest Christian apologetic and exercised a major influence on earliest Christian thought."[15] Following Barrett, Hooker attributes the background of Mark 10:45 to the "one like a son of man" in Dan 7 and its subsequent influence on the ideology of Jewish martyrdom attested in Jewish intertestamental literature.[16] Considering the context of first-century AD Judaism, Evans seems to provide a more convincing explanation of the background of Mark 10:45 than Hooker: "The Danielic elements do not necessarily compete with or contradict the underlying elements from Isaiah. The two scriptural traditions complement each other, with the Suffering Servant of Isa 53 redefining the mission and destiny of the 'son of man' in Dan 7 . . . This shows that Jesus' hermeneutic was dynamic and experientially oriented. It also reflects the Jewish

---

14. Similarly, France, *Gospel of Mark*, 420–21; as Gnilka notes: "The word [Mark 10:45] is not understandable without the background of Isa 53:10–12. Although neither the Isaiah text is cited, nor the destiny of the Servant of God is applied to Jesus on the whole, the presentation of the representative atoning death for many is borrowed in free form from there"; my translation of "Das Wort ist ohne den Hintergrund von Jes 53,10–12 nicht verstehbar. Obwohl weder der Jesajatext zitiert noch das Schicksal des Gottesknechtes insgesamt auf Jesus übertragen ist, wird die Vorstellung vom stellvertretenden Sühnetod für die Vielen in freier Form von dort entlehnt"; Gnilka, *Evangelium nach Markus (Mk 8:27—16:20)*, 104. Also, as Collins observes: "The figure spoken about here is defined as the servant of God (ὁ παῖς μου) in Isa 52:13, just as Jesus as the Son of Man comes to serve. In addition, in 53:11, he is described as a just man 'who serves many well' (δίκαιον εὖ δουλεύοντα πολλοῖς). As the Son of Man gives his life (δοῦναι τὴν ψυχὴν αὐτοῦ), the servant's soul or life is 'handed over to death' (παρεδόθη εἰς θάνατον ἡ ψυχὴ αὐτοῦ). A similarity with a difference is that the servant is cast in the image of the scapegoat by his portrayal as one who has borne the sins of many (καὶ αὐτὸς ἁμαρτίας πολλῶν ἀνήνεγκεν), whereas the Son of Man [voluntarily] gives his life as a ransom in behalf of many (λύτρον ἀντὶ πολλῶν)"; Collins, *Mark*, 500; similarly, Gnilka, *Evangelium nach Markus (Mk 8:27—16:20)*, 104.

15. Dunn, *Romans 1–8*, 241; similarly, Donahue and Harrington, *Gospel of Mark*, 315.

16. Hooker focuses on the contrast between the "one like a son of man" to be served in Dan 7:14 and "the Son of Man" to serve in Mark 10:45; Hooker, *Son of Man in Mark*, 142.

interpretative principle of two passages interpreting each other (*gezerah shawa*)."[17]

In contrast to Barrett's view that Mark 10:45 is a work of "a creative mind," Hooker considers it as *authentic*. Hooker claims, "We have here, not a 'fusion' between the term 'Son of man' and some other concept, but an expression of something which is involved in being Son of man." She goes on, "This interpretation may be due to either Jesus or the early church, but if we accept the view that Jesus used the term 'Son of man' of himself at all, then it seems reasonable to suppose that the insight was his."[18] Hooker more recently suggests that it may have been Paul who first identified Jesus with the Suffering Servant.[19] Considering the findings of chapter 3, Paul is not the first theologian who identified Jesus with the Isaianic Suffering Servant but he depends on the early church tradition behind Mark 10:45 in Rom 5:15, 19 and elsewhere. While rightly identifying the examples of Israel's martyr ideology in Second Temple Judaism, Barrett's conclusion that "a creative mind working upon it could *produce* a saying such as that recorded by Mark [10:45]" dismisses both the *verbal* and the *conceptual* parallels between the early church tradition behind Mark 10:45 and Isa 53. It is much more likely the case that either the historical Jesus or the early church interpreted Jesus' atoning death in the matrix of the "ransom" idea of Isa 43 and in the language of the Suffering Servant of Isa 53—reflected in Mark 10:45 and Pauline material (Rom 4:25; 5:15, 19; 8:32; 1 Cor 15:3; 2 Cor 4:11; Gal 2:20), independently of each other.

---

17. Evans, *Mark 8:27—16:20*, 123-24.
18. Hooker, *Son of Man in Mark*, 146-47.
19. Hooker concludes her article, "To the question that has been put to me, 'Did the use of Isaiah 53 to interpret his mission begin with Jesus?' I remain convinced that the answer is 'No.' To the question 'Where, then did it begin?' I am far more ready than I was forty years ago to suggest that it may well have been with Paul"; Hooker, "Did the Use of Isaiah 53 to Interpret His Mission Begin with Jesus?" 103.

Bibliography

Aageson, James W. *Witten Also for Our Sake: Paul and the Art of Biblical Interpretation.* Louisville, KY: Westminster John Knox, 1993.

Albl, Martin C. *"And Scripture Cannot Be Broken": The Form and Function of the Early Christian Testimonia Collections.* Supplements to Novum Testamentum 96. Leiden: Brill, 1999.

Attridge, Harold W. *The Epistle to the Hebrews: A Commentary on the Epistle to the Hebrews.* Hermeneia. Philadelphia: Fortress, 1989.

Barrett, C. K. "The Background of Mark 10:45." In *New Testament Essays: Studies in Memory of T. W. Manson,* 1–18. Manchester: Manchester University Press, 1959.

———. *A Commentary on the Epistle to the Romans.* Black's New Testament Commentaries. London: Black, 1957.

———. *A Commentary on the First Epistle to the Corinthians.* Black's New Testament Commentaries. London: Black, 1971.

Basevi, Claudio and Juan Chapa. "Philippians 2:6–11: The Rhetorical Function of a Pauline 'Hymn.'" In *Rhetoric and the New Testament: Essays from the 1992 Heidelberg Conference,* edited by Stanley E. Porter and Thomas H. Olbricht, 338–56. Sheffield, UK: JSOT, 1993.

Bauckham, Richard. *Jesus and the Eyewitnesses: The Gospel as Eyewitness Testimony.* Grand Rapids: Eerdmans, 2006.

———. "Jesus and the Wild Animals (Mark 1:13): A Christological Image for an Ecological Age." In *Jesus of Nazareth: Lord and Christ,* edited by Joel B. Green and Max Turner, 3–21. Grand Rapids: Eerdmans, 1994.

———. "The Son of Man: 'a Man in My Position' or 'Someone?'" *JSNT* 23 (1985) 23–33.

———. "The Worship of Jesus in Philippians 2:9–11." In *Where Christology Began,* edited by Ralph P. Martin and Brian J. Dodd, 128–39. Louisville, KY: Westminster John Knox, 1998.

Baum, Armin D. *Der mündliche Faktor und seine Bedeutung für die synoptische Frage: Analogien aus der antiken Literatur, der Experimentalpsychologie, der Oral Poetry-Forschung und dem rabbinischen Traditionswesen.* Tübingen: Francke, 2008.

Baumert, Norbert. *Der Weg des Trauens: Übersetzung und Auslegung des Briefes an die Galater und des Briefes an die Philipper.* Paulus neu gelesen. Würzburg: Echter, 2009.

Beare, F. W. *A Commentary on the Epistle to the Philippians.* Black's New Testament Commentaries 11. London: Black, 1969.

Benko, S. "Pagan Criticism of Christianity during the First Two Centuries." *ANRW* 2.23.2 (1980) 1055–1118.

Berger, Klaus. "Hellenistischen Gattungen im Neuen Testament." *ANRW* 2.25.2 (1984) 1031–1432.

Black, Mathew. "Πᾶσαι ἐξουσίαι αὐτῷ ὑποταγήσονται." In *Paul and Paulinism: Essays in Honour of C. K. Barrett*, edited by M. D. Hooker and S. G. Wilson, 74–82. London: SPCK, 1982.

Blomberg, Craig L. "Better Things in This Case: The Superiority of Today's New International Version in Hebrews." *BT* 55 (2004) 310–18.

Bock, Darrell L. "The Use of Daniel 7 in Jesus' Trial, with Implications for His Self-Understanding." In *"Who is This Son of Man?": The Latest Scholarship on a Puzzling Expression of the Historical Jesus*, edited by Larry W. Hurtado and Paul L. Owen, 78–100. Library of New Testament Studies 390. London: T. & T. Clark, 2011.

Bockmuehl, Markus. "'The Form of God' (Phil 2:6): Variations on a Theme of Jewish Mysticism." *JTS* 48.1 (1997) 1–23.

Boring, M. Eugene. *Mark: A Commentary*. New Testament Library. Louisville, KY: Westminster John Knox, 2006.

Borsch, Frederick H. *The Son of Man in Myth and History*. New Testament Library. London: SCM, 1967.

Bowker, John. "The Son of Man." *JTS* 28 (1977) 19–48.

Brawley, R. *Text to Text Pours Forth Speech: Voices of Scripture in Luke–Acts*. Indianapolis, IN: Indiana University Press, 1995.

Breytenbach, Cilliers. *Versöhnung: Eine Studie zur paulinischen Soteriologie*. Wissenschaftliche Monographien zum Alten und Neuen Testament 60. Neukirchen-Vluyn: Neukirchener, 1989.

Brown, Raymond E. *An Introduction to the New Testament*. Anchor Bible Reference Library. New York: Doubleday, 1997.

Bruce, F. F. *The Epistles to the Hebrews*. New International Commentary on the New Testament 58. Grand Rapids: Eerdmans, 1990.

Brucker, Ralph. *"Christushymnen" oder "Epideiktische Passagen?": Studien zum Stilwechsel im neuen Testament und seiner Umwelt*. Forschungen zur Religion und Literatur des Alten und Neuen Testaments 176. Göttingen: Vandenhoeck & Ruprecht, 1997.

Bultmann, Rudolf. *Theology of the New Testament*. Translated by Kendrick Grobel. Vol. 1. London: SCM, 1951. Translation of *Theologie des Neue Testaments*. Neue theologische Grundrisse. Tübingen: Mohr Siebeck, 1948.

Burkett, Delbert. *Rethinking the Gospel Sources: From Proto-Mark to Mark*. New Testament Guides. London: T. & T. Clark, 2004.

———. *The Son of Man Debate: A History and Evaluation*. Society for New Testament Studies Monograph Series 107. Cambridge: Cambridge University Press, 1999.

Byrne, Brendan. *Romans*. Sacra Pagina Series 6. Collegeville, PA: Liturgical, 2007.

Byrskog, Samuel. *Story as History—History as Story: The Gospel Tradition in the Context of Ancient Oral History*. Wissenschaftliche Untersuchungen zum Neuen Testament I 123. Tübingen: Mohr Siebeck, 2000.

Caneday, Ardel B. "The Eschatological World Already Subjected to the Son: The οἰκουμένη of Hebrews 1:6 and the Son's Enthronement." In *A Cloud of Witnesses: The Theology of Hebrews in Its Ancient Context*, edited by Daniel R. Driver, Richard Bauckham, Trevor H. Hart, and Nathan MacDonald, 28–39. Library of New Testament Studies 387. London: T. & T. Clark, 2008.

Casey, P. Maurice. *From Jewish Prophet to Gentile God*. Louisville, KY: Westminster John Knox, 1991.

———. *The Solution to the "Son of Man" Problem*. Library of New Testament Studies 343. London: T. & T. Clark, 2007.

Chilton, Bruce D. *The Isaiah Targum: Introduction, Translation, Apparatus and Notes*. Aramaic Bible 11. Wilmington, DE: Glazier, 1987.
Collins, Adela Yarbro. *Mark: A Commentary*. Hermeneia. Minneapolis: Fortress, 2007.
Collins, J. J. *The Scepter and the Star: The Messiahs of the Dead Sea Scrolls and Other Ancient Literature*. Anchor Bible Reference Library. New York: Doubleday, 1995.
———. "Sybilline Oracles: A New Translation and Introduction." In *OTP* 1:317–472.
Cortés, J. B., and F. M. Gatti. "The Son of Man or the Son of Adam." *Bib* 49 (1968) 457–502.
Cousar. Charles B. *Philippians and Philemon: A Commentary*. New Testament Library. Louisville, KY: Westminster John Knox, 2009.
Cullmann, Oscar. *The Christology of the New Testament*. Translated by Shirley C. Guthrie and Charles A. M. Hall. New Testament Library. London: SCM, 1963. Translation of *Die Christologie des Neuen Testaments*. Tübingen: Mohr Siebeck, 1957.
Davies, W. D., and D. C. Allison. *A Critical and Exegetical Commentary on the Gospel according to Saint Matthew*. Vol. 3. International Critical Commentary. 1988. Reprint. Edinburgh: T. & T. Clark, 1997.
Davila, James R. *The Provenance of the Pseudepigrapha: Jewish, Christian, or Other?* Journal for the Study of Judaism Supplement Series 105. Leiden: Brill, 2005.
Deane, Scott A. "Obedience and Humility of the Second Adam: Philippians 2:6–11." *JRR* 7.1 (1997) 4–12.
De Boer, Martinus C. "Paul's Use of a Resurrection Tradition in 1 Cor 15:20–28." In *The Corinthian Correspondence*, edited by R. Bieringer, 640–51. Bibliotheca Ephemeridum Theologicarum Lovaniensium 125. Leuven: Leuven University Press, 1996.
Deichgäber, R. *Gotteshymnus und Christushymnus in den frühen Christenheit*. Studien zur Umwelt des Neuen Testaments 5. Göttingen: Vanderhoeck & Ruprecht, 1967.
Dewey, K. E. "Peter's Curse and Cursed Peter (Mark 14:53–54; 66–72)." In *The Passion in Mark: Studies on Mark 14–16*, edited by W. Kelber, 96–114. Philadelphia: Fortress, 1976.
Dobschütz, Ernst von. "Zur Erzählerkunst des Markus." *ZNW* 27 (1928) 193–98.
Donahue, John R. "Introduction: From Passion Traditions to Passion Narrative." In *The Passion in Mark: Studies on Mark 14–16*, edited by W. Kelber, 1–20. Philadelphia: Fortress, 1976.
Donahue, John R. and Daniel L. Harrington. *The Gospel of Mark*. Sacra Pagina Series 2. Collegeville, PA: Liturgical, 2002.
Dunn, James D. G. *Christology in the Making: A New Testament Inquiry into the Origins of the Doctrine of the Incarnation*. Philadelphia: Westminster John Knox, 1980.
———. *Jesus Remembered*. Christianity in the Making 1. Grand Rapids: Eerdmans, 2003.
———. *Romans 1–8*. Word Biblical Commentary 38A. Nashville: Thomas Nelson, 1988.
———. "'Son of God' as 'Son of Man' in the Dead Sea Scrolls?: A Response to John Collins on 4Q246." In *The Scrolls and the Scriptures: Qumran Fifty Years Later*, edited by Stanley E. Porter and Craig A. Evans, 198–210. Journal for the Study of the New Testament Supplement Series 26. Sheffield, UK: JSOT, 1997.
———. *The Theology of Paul the Apostle*. Grand Rapids: Eerdmans, 1998.
Eddy, Paul Rhodes, and Gregory A. Boyd. *The Jesus Legend: A Case for the Historical Reliability of the Synoptic Jesus Tradition*. Grand Rapids: Baker, 2007.

Ellingworth, Paul. *The Epistle to the Hebrews: A Commentary on the Greek Text*. New International Greek Testament Commentary. Grand Rapids: Eerdmans, 1993.

Evans, Craig A. *Mark 8:27—16:20*. Word Biblical Commentary 34B. Nashville: Thomas Nelson, 2001.

———. "'Peter Warming Himself': The Problem of an Editorial 'Seam.'" *JBL* 101 (1982) 245–49.

Evans, Craig A., and James A. Sanders, *Luke and Scripture: The Function of Sacred Tradition in Luke-Acts*. Minneapolis: Fortress, 1993.

Farmer, William R. "The Case for the Two-Gospel Hypothesis." In *Rethinking the Synoptic Problem*, edited by David Alan Black and David R. Beck, 97–135. Grand Rapids: Baker, 2001.

Fee, Gordon D. *Paul's Letter to the Philippians*. New International Commentary on the New Testament 50. Grand Rapids: Eerdmans, 1995.

Fitzmyer, Joseph A. "The Aramaic Background of Philippians 2:6–11." *CBQ* 50 (1988) 470–83.

———. *First Corinthians: A New Translation with Introduction and Commentary*. Anchor Yale Bible Commentaries 32. New Haven, CT: Yale University Press, 2008.

———. *The Gospel According to Luke I-IX: Introduction, Translation, and Notes*. Vol. 1. Anchor Bible Commentaries 28A. New York: Doubleday, 1981.

———. *The Gospel According to Luke X-XXIV: Introduction, Translation, and Notes*. Vol. 2. Anchor Bible Commentaries 28B. New York: Doubleday, 1985.

———. *Romans: A New Translation with Introduction and Commentary*. Anchor Yale Bible Commentaries 33. New Haven, CT: Yale University Press, 1993.

———. "4Q246: The 'Son of God' Document from Qumran." *Bib* 74 (1993) 153–74.

Flusser, David. *Judaism and the Origins of Christianity*. Jerusalem: Magnes, 1988.

Focant, Camille. *L'évangile selon Marc*. Commentaire Biblique Nouveau Testament 2. Paris: Cerf, 2004.

Fortuna, R. T. "Jesus and Peter at the High Priest's House: A Test Case for the Question of the Relation between Mark's and John's Gospels." *NTS* 24 (1978) 371–83.

Fowl, Stephen E. *Philippians*. Two Horizons New Testament Commentary 11. Grand Rapids: Eerdmans, 2005.

———. *The Story of Christ in the Ethics of Paul: An Analysis of the Function of the Hymnic Material in the Pauline Corpus*. Journal for the Study of the New Testament Supplement Series 36. Sheffield, UK: JSOT, 1990.

France, R. T. *The Gospel of Mark: A Commentary on the Greek Text*. New International Greek Testament Commentary. Grand Rapids: Eerdmans, 2002.

Garland, David E. "The Composition and Unity of Philippians: Some Neglected Literary Factors." *NovT* 27 (1985) 141–73.

———. *1 Corinthians*. Baker Exegetical Commentary on the New Testament. Grand Rapids: Baker, 2003.

Garrett, Susan R. *The Temptations of Jesus in Mark's Gospel*. Grand Rapids: Eerdmans, 1998.

Gerhardsson, Birger. "The Secret of the Transmission of the Unknown Jesus Tradition." *NTS* 51 (2005) 1–18.

Gibson, Jeffrey B. *The Temptation of Jesus in Early Christianity*. Sheffield, UK: JSOT, 1995.

Gnilka, Joachim. *Das Evangelium nach Markus (Mk 8:27—16:20)* Evangelisch-Katholischer Kommentar zum Neuen Testament 2. Vol 2. Neukirchen-Vluyn: Neukirchener, 1978.

Goodacre, Mark. *The Synoptic Problem: A Way through the Maze*. Biblical Seminar 80. London: T. & T. Clark, 2001.
Goulder, Michael. *Luke: A New Paradigm*. 2 Vols. Journal for the Study of the New Testament Supplement Series 20. Sheffield, UK: JSOT, 1989.
Grimm, W. "Weil ich dich liebe: Die Verkundigung Jesu und Deuterjesaja." In *Arbeiten zum Neuen Testament und Judentum*, Vol. 1, edited by Otto Betz, 231–77. Bern: Lang, 1976.
Gundry, Robert H. *Mark: A Commentary on His Apology for the Cross*. 2 Vols. Grand Rapids: Eerdmans, 1993.
Gunkel, H., and J. Begrich. *Einleitung in die Psalmen: Die Gattungen der religiösen Lyrik Israels*. Göttingen: Vandenhoeck & Ruprecht, 1966.
Habermann, Jürgen. *Präexistenzaussagen im Neuen Testament*. Europäische Hochschulschriften 362. Frankfurt: Lang, 1990.
Hampel, Volker. *Menschensohn und historischer Jesus: Ein Rätselwort als Schlüssel zum messianischen Selbstverständnis Jesu*. Neukirchen-Vluyn: Neukircher, 1990.
Hannah, Darrell D. "Isaiah within Judaism of the Second Temple Period." In *Isaiah in the New Testament*, edited by Steve Moyise and Maarten J. J. Menken, 7–34. London: T. & T. Clark, 2005.
———. "The Throne of His Glory: The Divine Throne and Heavenly Mediators in Revelation and the Similitudes of Enoch." *ZNW* 94.1–2 (2003) 68–96.
Hare, D. R. A. *The Son of Man Tradition*. Minneapolis: Fortress, 1990.
Häusser, Detlef. *Christusbekenntnis und Jesusüberlieferung bei Paulus*. Wissenschaftliche Untersuchungen zum Neuen Testament II 210. Tübingen: Mohr Siebeck, 2006.
Hay, David M. *Glory at the Right Hand: Psalm 110 in Early Christianity*. Society of Biblical Literature Monograph Series 18. Nashville: Abingdon, 1973.
Hays, Richard B. *Echoes of Scripture in the Letters of Paul*. New Haven, CT: Yale University Press, 1989.
Heil, John Paul. "Jesus with the Wild Animals in Mark 1:13." *CBQ* 68.1 (2006) 63–78.
Hellermann, J. H. *Reconstructing Honor in Roman Philippi: Carmen Christi as Cursus Pudorum*. Society for New Testament Studies Monograph Series 132. Cambridge: Cambridge University Press, 2005.
Hengel, Martin. *Between Jesus and Paul: Studies in the Earliest History of Christianity*. Translated by John Bowden. Minneapolis: Fortress, 1983.
———. "The Effective History of Isaiah 53 in the Pre-Christian Period." In *The Suffering Servant: Isaiah 53 in Jewish and Christian Sources*, edited by Bernd Janowski and Peter Stuhlmacher, 75–146. Grand Rapids: Eerdmans, 2004.
———. *The Son of God: The Origin of Christology and the History of Jewish-Hellenistic Religion*. Translated by John Bowden. Philadelphia: Fortress, 1976.
———. *Studies in Early Christology*. Edinburgh: T. & T. Clark, 1995.
Higgins, A. J. B. *Jesus and the Son of Man*. London: Lutterworth, 1964.
Hofius, Otfried. *Der Christushymnus Philipper 2,6–11: Untersuchungen zu Gestalt U. Aussage eines urchristlichen Psalms*. Wissenschaftliche Untersuchungen zum Neuen Testament I 17. Tübingen: Mohr Siebeck, 1976.
———. *Neutestamentliche Studien*. Wissenschaftliche Untersuchungen zum Neuen Testament I 132. Tübingen: Mohr Siebeck, 2000.
Holloway, Paul A. *Consolation in Philippians: Philosophical Sources and Rhetorical Strategy*. Society for New Testament Studies Monograph Series 112. Cambridge: Cambridge University Press, 2001.

Hooker, Morna D. "Adam Redivivus: Philippians 2 Once More." In *The Old Testament in the New Testament: Essays in Honour of J. L. North*, edited by Steve Moyise, 220–34. Journal for the Study of the New Testament Supplement Series 189. Sheffield, UK: JSOT, 2000.

———. "Christ, the 'End' of the Cult." In *The Epistle to the Hebrews and Christian Theology*, edited by Daniel R. Driver, Richard Bauckham, Trevor A. Hart, and Nathan MacDonald, 189–212. Grand Rapids: Eerdmans, 2009.

———. "Did the Use of Isaiah 53 to Interpret His Mission Begin with Jesus?" In *Jesus and the Suffering Servant: Isaiah 53 and Christian Origins*, edited by W. H. Bellinger Jr. and W. R. Farmer, 88–103. Harrisburg, PA: Trinity, 1998.

———. *From Adam and Christ: Essays on Paul*. Cambridge: Cambridge University Press, 1990.

———. *The Gospel According to Saint Mark*. Black's New Testament Commentaries. Peabody, MA: Hendrickson, 1991.

———. "Isaiah in Mark's Gospel." In *Isaiah in the New Testament*, edited by Steve Moyise and Maarten J. J. Menken, 35–50. London: T. & T. Clark, 2005.

———. *Jesus and the Servant*. London: SPCK, 1959.

———. "Philippians 2:6–11." In *Jesus und Paulus: Festschrift für Werner Georg Kümmel zum 70 Geburstag*, edited by E. E. Ellis and E. Grässer, 151–64. Göttingen: Vandenhoeck & Ruprecht, 1978.

———. *The Son of Man in Mark*. London: SPCK, 1967.

Hoover, Roy W. "The *Harpagmos* Enigma: A Philological Solution." *HTR* 64 (1971) 95–119.

Hultgren, Stephen. "The Origin of Paul's Doctrine of the Two Adams in 1 Corinthians 15.45–49." *JSNT* 25.3 (2003) 343–70.

Hurst, L. D. "Christ, Adam, and Preexistence Revisited." In *Where Christology Began*, edited by Ralph P. Martin and Brian J. Dodd, 84–95. Louisville, KY: Westminster John Knox, 1998.

———. *The Epistle to the Hebrews: Its Background of Thought*. Society for New Testament Studies Monograph Series 65. Cambridge: Cambridge University Press, 1990.

Hurtado, Larry W. "Jesus as Lordly Example in Philippians 2:5–11." In *From Jesus to Paul: Studies in Honour of Francis Wright Beare*, edited by P. Richardson and J. C. Hurd, 113–26. Waterloo, ON: Wilfrid Laurier University Press, 1984.

———. *Lord Jesus Christ: Devotion to Jesus in Earliest Christianity*. Grand Rapids: Eerdmans, 2003.

———. "Pre-Existence." In *DPL*, 743–46.

———. "Summary and Concluding Observations." In *"Who is This Son of Man?": The Latest Scholarship on a Puzzling Expression of the Historical Jesus*, edited by Larry W. Hurtado and Paul L. Owen, 159–77. Library of New Testament Studies 390. London: T. & T. Clark, 2011.

Isaac, E. "1 (Ethiopic Apocalypse of) Enoch: A New Translation and Introduction. " In *OTP* 1:13–89.

Jeremias, Joachim. "Adam." In *TDNT* 1:141–43.

———. *New Testament Theology: The Proclamation of Jesus*. Translated by John Bowden. Vol. 1. New Testament Library. London: SCM, 1971. Translation of *Neuetestamentliche Theologie: Die Verkündigung Jesu*. Gütersloh: Gütersloher, 1970.

———. "Zur Gedankenführung in den paulinischen Briefen." In *Studia Paulina in honorem J. de Zwaan*, edited by J. W. Sevenster and W. C. van Unnik, 146–54. Haarlem, Netherlands: Bohn, 1953.
Johnson, Luke Timothy. *The Gospel of Luke*. Sacra Pagina Series 3. Collegeville, PA: Liturgical, 1991.
———. *Hebrews: A Commentary*. New Testament Library. Louisville, KY: Westminster John Knox, 2006.
Johnson, M. D. "Life of Adam and Eve: A New Translation and Introduction." In *OTP* 2:249–95.
Juel, Donald. *Messiah and Temple: The Trial of Jesus in the Gospel of Mark*. Society of Biblical Literature Dissertation Series 31. Atlanta: SBL, 1977.
Käsemann, Ernst. *Commentary on Romans*. Translated by Geoffrey W. Bromiley. London: SCM, 1980. Translation of *An Die Römer*. 4th ed. Tübingen: Mohr Siebeck, 1980.
Kazen, Thomas. "Son of Man as Kingdom Imagery: Jesus between Corporate Symbol and Individual Redeemer Figure." In *Jesus from Judaism to Christianity: Continuum Approaches to the Historical Jesus*, edited by Tom Holmén, 87–108. Library of New Testament Studies. 352. London: T. & T. Clark, 2007.
Kennel, Gunter. *Frühchristliche Hymn?: Gattungskritische Studien zur Frage nach den Liedern der frühen Christenheit*. Wissenschaftliche Monographien zum Alten und Neuen Testament 71. Neukirchen-Vluyn: Neukirchener, 1995.
Kim, Seyoon. *The Origin of Paul's Gospel*. 2nd ed. Wissenschaftliche Untersuchungen zum Neuen Testament II 4. Tübingen: Mohr Siebeck, 1984.
———. *Paul and the New Perspective: Second Thoughts on the Origin of Paul's Gospel*. Wissenschaftliche Untersuchungen zum Neuen Testament I. 140. Tübingen: Mohr Siebeck, 2002.
———. *The 'Son of Man' as the Son of God*. Wissenschaftliche Untersuchungen zum Neuen Testament I 30. Tübingen: Mohr Siebeck 1983.
Kister, Menahem. "'First Adam' and 'Second Adam': 1 Cor 15:45–49 in the Light of Midrashic Exegesis and Hebrew Usage." In *The New Testament and Rabbinic Literature*, edited by Reimund Beringer, Florentino García Martínez, Didier Pollefeyt, and Peter J. Tomson, 351–65. Supplements to the Journal for the Study of Judaism 136. Leiden: Brill, 2010.
Koester, Helmut. *Paul & His World: Interpreting the New Testament in Its Context*. Minneapolis: Fortress, 2007.
Kraus, Wolfgang. *Der Tod Jesu als Heiligtumsweihe: Eine Untersuchung zum Umfeld der Sühnevorstellung in Römer 3, 25–26a*. Wissenschaftliche Monographien zum Alten und Neuen Testament 66. Neukirchen-Vluyn: Neukirchener, 1991.
Kreitzer, L. J. "Adam and Christ." In *DPL*, 9–15.
———. "When He at Last Is First!" In *Where Christology Began*, edited by Ralph P. Martin and Brian J. Dodd, 111–27. Louisville, KY: Westminster John Knox, 1998.
Krentz, Edgar. "Epideiktik and Hymnody: The New Testament and Its World." *BR* 90 (1995) 50–97.
Lane, William L. *Hebrews 1–8*. Word Biblical Commentary 47. Nashville: Thomas Nelson, 1991.
Lattke, Michael. *Hymnus: Materialien zu einer Geschichte der antiken Hymnologie*. Novum Testamentum et Orbis Antiquus 19. Göttingen: Vandenhoeck & Ruprecht, 1991.

Levison, John R. *Portraits of Adam in Early Judaism: From Sirach to 2 Baruch.* Journal for the Study of the Pseudepigrapha Supplement Series 1. Sheffield, UK: JSOT, 1998.

Lindars, Barnabas. *Jesus Son of Man.* Edinburgh: SPCK, 1983.

———. *The Theology of the Letter to the Hebrews.* New Testament Theology. Cambridge: Cambridge University Press, 1991.

Lohmeyer, Ernst. *Der Brief an die Philipper.* Kritisch-exegetischer Kommentar über das Neue Testament 11. Göttingen: Vandenhoeck & Ruprecht, 1953.

———. *Kyrios Jesus: Eine Untersuchung zu Phil 2:5–11.* Heidelberg: Carl Winter Universitätsverlag, 1928.

Löhr, Hermut. "Anthropologie und Eschatologie im Hebräerbrief: Bemerkungen zum theologischen Interesse einer frühchristlichen Schrift." In *Eschatologie und Schöpfung: Festschrift für Erich Gräßer zum siebzigsten Geburtstag,* edited by Helmut Merklein, Michael Wolter, and Marting Evang, 169–99. Beihefte zur Zeitschrift für die neutestamentliche Wissenschaft und die Kunde der älteren Kirche Beiheft 89. Berlin: de Gruyter, 1997.

Long, Thomas G. *Hebrews.* Interpretation. Louisville, KY: Westminster John Knox, 1997.

Longenecker, Richard N. "Christological Materials in the Early Christian Communities." In *Contours of Christology in the New Testament,* edited by Richard N. Longenecker, 47–76. McMaster New Testament Series. Grand Rapids: Eerdmans, 2005.

Lüdemann, Gerd. *Paulus, der Gründer des Christentums.* Lüneberg: Klampen, 2001.

Lukaszewski, Albert L. "Issues Concerning the Aramaic Behind ὁ υἱὸς τοῦ ἀνθρώπου: A Critical Review of Scholarship." In *"Who is This Son of Man?": The Latest Scholarship on a Puzzling Expression of the Historical Jesus,* edited by Larry W. Hurtado and Paul L. Owen, 1–27. Library of New Testament Studies 390. London: T. & T. Clark, 2011.

Luz, Ulrich. *Matthews 8–20.* Hermeneia. Minneapolis: Fortress, 2001.

Malina, Bruce J. and Jerome H. Neyrey. *Portraits of Paul: An Archaeology of Ancient Personality.* Louisville, KY: Westminster John Knox, 1996.

Marcus, Joel. *Mark 8–16: A New Translation with Introduction and Commentary.* Anchor Yale Bible Commentaries 27A. New Haven, CT: Yale University Press, 2008.

———. "Mark 14:61: 'Are You the Messiah-Son-of-God?'" *NovT* 31.2 (1989) 125–41.

———. "Mark—Interpreter of Paul." *NTS* 46 (2000) 473–87.

———. "Son of Man as Son of Adam." *RB* 110.1 (2003) 38–61.

———. "Son of Man as Son of Adam Part II: Exegesis." *RB* 110.3 (2003) 370–86.

Marshall, I. Howard. "The Christ-Hymn in Philippians 2:5–11." *TynBul* 19 (1968) 104–27.

———. *The Epistle to the Philippians.* Epworth Commentaries. London: Epworth, 1991.

———. *The Gospel of Luke: A Commentary on the Greek Text.* New International Greek Testament Commentary. Grand Rapids: Eerdmans, 1978.

Marshall, John W. "Paul's Ethical Appeal in Philippians." In *Rhetorica and the New Testament: Essays from the 1992 Heidelberg Conference,* edited by Stanley E. Porter and Thomas H. Olbricht, 357–74. Sheffield, UK: JSOT, 1993.

Martin, Ralph P. *Carmen Christi.* 2nd ed. 1967. Reprint. Grand Rapids: Eerdmans, 1983.

———. "Carmen Christi Revisited." In *Where Christology Began,* edited by Ralph P. Martin and Brian J. Dodd, 1–5. Louisville, KY: Westminster John Knox, 1998.

———. *A Hymn of Christ: Philippians 2:5–11 In Recent Interpretation & In the Setting of Early Christian Worship.* Downers Grove, IL: InterVarsity, 1997.

Martin, Ralph P. and Gerald F. Hawthorne. *Philippians.* 2nd ed. Word Biblical Commentary 43. Nashville: Thomas Nelson, 2004.

Martínez, Florentino García. *The Dead Sea Scrolls Translated: The Qumran Texts in English*. 2nd ed. Grand Rapids: Eerdmans, 1996.
McKnight, Scot. *Jesus and His Death: Historiography, the Historical Jesus, and Atonement Theory*. Waco, TX: Baylor University Press, 2005.
Meier, John P. *A Marginal Jew: Rethinking the Historical Jesus. Volume One: the Roots of the Problem and the Person*. Anchor Bible Reference Library. New York: Doubleday, 1991.
Mell, Ulrich. "Jesus Taufe durch Johannes (Markus 1,9-15)—zur narrativen Christologie vom neuen Adam." *BZ* 40.2 (1996) 161-78.
Milgrom, Jacob. "Sin-Offering or Purification-Offering?" *VT* 21 (1971) 237-39.
Moule, C. F. D. "Further Reflexions on Philippians 2:5-11." In *Apostolic History and the Gospel: Biblical and Historical Essays Presented to F. F. Bruce and His 60th Birthday*, edited by W. W. Gasque and R. P. Martin, 264-76. Exeter, UK: Paternoster, 1970.
Müller, Ulrich B. "Jesus als 'der Menschensohn.'" In *Gottessohn und Menschensohn: exegetische Studien zu zwei Paradigmen biblischer Intertextualität*, edited by Dieter Sänger, 91-129. Biblisch-theologische Studien 67. Neukirchen-Vluyn: Neukirchener, 2004.
Murphy-O'Connor, J. "Christological Anthropology in Phil 2:6-11." *RB* 83 (1976) 25-50.
Nir, Rivka. "The Struggle between the 'Image of God' and Satan in the Greek Life of Adam and Eve." *SJT* 61.3 (2008) 327-39.
Nolland, John. *The Gospel of Matthew*. New International Greek Testament Commentary. Grand Rapids: Eerdmans, 2005.
———. *Luke 9:21—18:34*. Word Biblical Commentary 35B. Nashville: Thomas Nelson, 1993.
———. *Luke 18:35—24:53*. Word Biblical Commentary 35C. Nashville: Thomas Nelson, 1993.
Oakes, Peter. *Philippians: From People to Letter*. Society for New Testament Studies Monograph Series 110. Cambridge: Cambridge University Press, 2001.
O'Brien, Peter T. *The Epistle to the Philippians: A Commentary on the Greek Text*. New International Greek Testament Commentary. Grand Rapids: Eerdmans, 1991.
Park, M. Sydney. *Submission within the Godhead and the Church in the Epistle to the Philippians: An Exegetical and Theological Examination of the Concept of Submission in Philippians 2 and 3*. Library of New Testament Studies 361. London: T. & T. Clark, 2007.
Parker, Robert C. T. "Hymn." In *The Oxford Classical Dictionary*, edited by Simon Hornblower and Antony Spawforth, 735-36. Oxford: Oxford University Press, 2003.
Parkman, Joel William. "Adam Christological Motifs in the Synoptic Traditions." PhD diss., Baylor University, 1994.
Pate, C. Marvin. *Adam Christology as the Exegetical & Theological Substructure of 2 Corinthians 4:7—5:21*. New York: University Press of America, 1991.
Perrin, Norman. "Mark XIV.62: The End Product of a Christian Pesher Tradition?" *NTS* 13 (1965-66) 150-55.
Pöhlmann, W. "*Morphe*." In *EDNT* 2:442-43.
Reed, Jeffrey T. *A Discourse Analysis of Philippians: Method and Rhetoric in the Debate over Literary Integrity*. Journal for the Study of the New Testament Supplement Series 170. Studies in New Testament Greek 4. Sheffield, UK: JSOT, 1997.

Reumann, John. *Philippians: A New Translation with Introduction and Commentary*. Anchor Yale Bible Commentaries 33B. New Haven, CT: Yale University Press, 2008.

Riesner, Rainer. "Back to the Historical Jesus through Paul and His School (the Ransom Logion—Mark 10:45; Matthew 20:28." *JSHJ* 1.2 (2003) 171–99.

Risenfeld, H. "Unpoetische Hymnen im Neuen Testament? Zu Phil 2,1–11" In *Glaube und Gerechtigkeit: Festschrift für Rafael Gyllenberg*, edited by Jarmo Kiilunen, Vilho Riekkinen, and Heikki Räisänen, 153–68. Schrfiten der Finnischen Exegetischen Gessellschaft Series 38. Helsinki: Finnish Exegetische Gesellschaft, 1983.

Robbins, C. Michael. *The Testing of Jesus in Q*. Studies in Biblical Literature 108. New York: Lang, 2007.

Robbins, Vernon K. "Interfaces of Orality and Literature in the Gospel of Mark." In *Performing the Gospel: Orality, Memory, and Mark*, edited by Jonathan A. Draper, John Miles Foley, and Richard A. Horsley, 125–46. Minneapolis: Fortress, 2006.

Robinson, J. M., P. Hoffmann, and J. S. Kloppenborg, eds. *The Critical Edition of Q*. Hermeneia. Minneapolis: Fortress, 2000.

Roloff, J. "Anfänge der soteriologischen Deutung des Todes Jesu (Mark 10:45 und Luke 22:27)." *NTS* 19 (1972) 38–64.

Sahlin, Harald. "Adam-Christologie im neuen Testament." *ST* 41 (1987) 11–32.

Sanders, E. P. "Testament of Abraham: A New Translation and Introduction." In *OTP* 1:871–902.

Sanders, Jack T. *The New Testament Christological Hymns: Their Historical Religious Background*. Society for New Testament Studies Monograph Series 15. Cambridge: Cambridge University Press, 1971.

Schenk, W. "Der Philipperbrief in der neueren Forschung (1945–1985)." *ANRW* 2.25.4 (1985) 3280–3313.

Schlier, Heinrich. *Der Römerbrief: Kommentar*. Herders theologischer Kommentar zum Neuen Testament 6. Freiburg im Breisgau: Herder, 1977.

Schrage, Wolfgang. *Der erste Brief an die Korinther (1Kor 15:1—16:24)*. Vol. 4. Evangelisch-Katholischer Kommentar zum Neuen Testament 7.4. Neukirchen-Vluyn: Neukirchener, 2001.

Schöter, Jens. "Jesus and the Canon: The Early Jesus Traditions in the Context of the Origins of the New Testament Canons." In *Performing the Gospel: Orality, Memory, and Mark*, edited by Jonathan A. Draper, John Miles Foley, and Richard A. Horsley, 104–24. Minneapolis: Fortress, 2006.

Schreiner, Thomas R. *Romans*. Baker Exegetical Commentary on the New Testament 6. Grand Rapids: Eerdmans, 1998.

Schwindt, Rainer. "Zu Tradition und Theologie des Philipperhymnus." *SNTSU* 31 (2006) 1–60.

Scroggs, Robin. *The Last Adam: A Study in Pauline Anthropology*. Oxford: Blackwell, 1966.

Silva, Moisés. *Philippians*. Baker Exegetical Commentary on the New Testament. Grand Rapids: Baker, 2005.

Sim, David C. "Matthew and the Pauline Corpus: A Preliminary Intertextual Study." *JSNT* 31.4 (2009) 401–22.

Spicq, Ceslas. *Theological Lexicon of the New Testament*. Translated by James D. Ernest. 2 Vols. Peabody: Hendrickson, 1994. Translation of *Notes de Lexiographie Neo-Testamentaire*. Orbis Biblicus et Orientalis 22. Göttingen: Vandenhoeck & Ruprecht, 1982.

Stanley, Christopher D. *Paul and the Language of Scripture: Citation Technique in the Pauline Epistles and Contemporary Literature.* Society for New Testament Studies Monograph Series 74. Cambridge: Cambridge University Press, 1992.

Steenburg, Dave. "The Case Against the Synonymity of μορφή and εἰκών." *JSNT* 34 (1988) 77–86.

Stein, Robert H. *Mark.* Baker Exegetical Commentary on the New Testament. Grand Rapids: Baker, 2008.

Stuhlmacher, Peter. *Reconciliation, Law, & Righteousness: Essays in Biblical Theology.* Translated by Everett R. Kalin. Philadelphia: Fortress, 1986. Translation of *Versöhnung, Gesetz und Gerechtigkeit: Aufsätze zur biblischen Theologie.* Göttingen: Vandenhoeck & Ruprecht, 1981.

Subramanian, J. Samuel. *The Synoptic Gospels and the Psalms as Prophecy.* Library of New Testament Studies 351. London: T. & T. Clark, 2007.

Taylor, V. *New Testament Essays.* London: Epworth, 1970.

Theobald, M. "'Der Galaterbrief' und 'der Philipperbrief.'" In *Einleitung in das neue Testament,* edited by M. Ebner and S. Schreiber, 345–83. Kohlhammer Studienbücher Theologie 6. Stuttgart: Kohlhammer, 2008.

Thiselton, Anthony C. *The First Epistle to the Corinthians.* New International Greek Testament Commentary. Grand Rapids: Eerdmans, 2000.

Thompson, Michael B. *Clothed with Christ: The Example and Teaching of Jesus in Romans 12.1—15.13.* Journal for the Study of the New Testament Supplement Series 59. Sheffield, UK: JSOT, 1991.

Thurston, Bonnie B., and Judith Ryan. *Philippians & Philemon.* Sacra Pagina Series 10. Collegeville, PA: Liturgical, 2005.

Tödt, H. E. *The Son of Man in the Synoptic Tradition.* Translated by Dorothea M. Barton. New Testament Library. London: SCM, 1965. Translation of *Der Menschensohn in der synoptischen Überlieferung.* 2nd ed. Gütersloh: Gütersloher, 1963.

Tuckett, Christopher M. *The Revival of the Griesbach Hypothesis: An Analysis and Appraisal.* Society for New Testament Studies Monograph Series 44. Cambridge: Cambridge University Press, 1983.

———. "Synoptic Tradition in 1 Thessalonian?" In *The Thessalonian Correspondence,* edited by Raymond F. Collins, 160–82. Bibliotheca Ephemeridum Theologicarum Lovaniensum 87. Leuven: Leuven University Press, 1990.

Urbach, E. E. *The Sages.* 2 Vols. Jerusalem: Magnes, 1979.

Verheyden, Joseph. "Le Jugement d'Israël dans la Source Q." In *La Source des Paroles de Jésus (Q),* edited by Andreas Dettwiler and Daniel Marguerat, 191–220. Monde de la Bible 62. Genève: Labor et Fides, 2008.

Vermes, Geza. *Jesus and the World of Judaism.* London: SCM, 1983.

Vögtle, Anton. "'Der Menschensohn' und die paulinische Christologie." In *Studiorum Paulinorum Congressus Internationalis Catholicus* 1961, Vol. 1, 199–218. Rome: Pontifical Biblical Institute, 1963.

Walck, Leslie W. "The Son of Man in the Parables of Enoch and the Gospels." In *Enoch and the Messiah Son of Man: Revisiting the Book of Parables,* edited by Gabriele Boccaccini, 299–337. Grand Rapids: Eerdmans, 2007.

Walter, Nikolaus. "Der Brief an die Philipper." In *Die Briefe an die Philipper, Thessalonicher und an Philemon,* edited by E. Reinmuth, P. Lampe, and N. Walter, 11–101. Neue Testament Deutsch 8.2. Göttingen: Vandenhoeck & Ruprecht, 1998.

Wanamaker, C. A. "Philippians 2.6–11: Son of God or Adamic Christology." *NTS* 33 (1987) 179–93.

Watson, Francis. "'I Received from the Lord . . .': Paul, Jesus, and the Last Supper." In *Jesus and Paul Reconnected: Fresh Pathways into an Old Debate*, edited by Todd D. Still, 103–24. Grand Rapids: Eerdmans, 2007.

Wengst, Klaus. *Christologische Formeln und Lieder des Urchristentums*. Studien zum Neuen Testament 7. Gütersloh: Gerd Mohn, 1972.

———. *Humility: Solidarity of the Humiliated*. Translated by John Bowden. London: SCM, 1988. Translation of *Demut, Solidät der Gedemütigen*. München: Kaiser, 1987.

Wenham, David. *Paul: Follower of Jesus or Founder of Christianity?* Grand Rapids: Eerdmans, 1995.

Werner, Martin. *Der Einfluss paulinischer Theologie im Markusevangelium: Eine studie zur neutestamentlichen Theologie*. Giessen: Töpelmann, 1923.

Wildberger, H. "Selem." In *TLOT* 3:1080–85.

Williams, Demetrius K. *Enemies of the Cross of Christ: The Terminology of the Cross and Conflict in Philippians*. Library of New Testament Studies 223. London: T. & T. Clark, 2002.

Witherington III, Ben. *The Gospel of Mark: A Socio-Rhetorical Commentary*. Grand Rapids: Eerdmans, 2001.

———. *What's in the Word: Rethinking the Socio-Rhetorical Character of the New Testament*. Waco, TX: Baylor University Press, 2009.

Wolff, Christian. "Humility and Self-Denial in Jesus' Life and Message and in the Apostolic Existence of Paul." In *Paul and Jesus: Collected Essays*, edited by A. J. M. Wedderburn, 145–60. Journal for the Study of New Testament Supplement Series 37. 1989. Reprint. London: T. & T. Clark, 2004.

Wrede, William. *Paul*. London: Green, 1907.

Wright, N. T. *The Climax of the Covenant: Christ and the Law in Pauline Theology*. Minneapolis: Fortress, 1993.

———. "*Harpagmos* and the Meaning of Philippians 2:5–11." *JTS* 37 (1986) 321–52.

Yonge, C. D. *The Works of Philo: Complete and Unabridged*. Peabody, MA: Hendrickson, 1993.

Scripture Index

HEBREW BIBLE / OLD TESTAMENT

Genesis
1–3	45, 51, 53, 55, 61, 63, 70
1–2	2, 11
1:26–30	6, 65, 68, 81–83, 88–89
1:26–28	2, 60, 91, 95, 125
1:27	45–46, 49, 55
1:28	59
2:7	11–13, 91, 130–35
2:15	53
3	45, 128–29
3:4–5	51
3:5	51, 55, 58–59
3:7	7
3:16	7
3:21	7
3:23	37, 52–53

Exodus
20:4	52
21:29	137
25:9	50
25:40	50
30:11–16	137
31:13	70

Leviticus
19:1–2	120
19:20	137
20:8	70
20:18	36
21:15	70
22:9	70
22:16	70
22:32	70
25:24	137
25:51–52	137
27:31	137

Numbers
3:12	137
12:8	52
35:31–34	137
35:52	48

Deuteronomy
4:12	52
4:15	52
4:16	50, 52
4:17	50
4:18	50
4:23	52
4:25	52
5:8	52
19:15	93
32:8	75

Joshua
22:28	50

Judges
3:9	116
3:10	116

Ruth
2:7	67

1 Samuel
6:5	48
8:20	116

2 Samuel
7:12–14	77
7:14	75–76
15:1–6	116

1 Kings
3:16–28	116

2 Kings
16:10	50

1 Chronicles
28:11	50
28:12	50
28:18	50
28:19	50
29:12	77

2 Chronicles
7:6	26
23:17	48

Nehemiah
12:24	26
12:46	26
12:47	26

Job
4:15–17	52
4:16	52
24:24	67

Psalms
8	4, 10, 45, 60, 64, 67–70, 80, 83, 87–88, 91
8:4–6	64–65, 67–68, 70, 72, 84, 89, 91, 95
8:4	64–65, 67, 81–83, 89
8:5–7	63, 67
8:5	67, 83
8:6–7	67
8:6	60, 64–65, 67–68, 72, 80, 82, 84–86, 89
8:7	67, 79–80, 87
17:15	52
37:35	39
54:1	77
62:11	77
65:6	77
68:14	39
73:11	75
91:9	75
91:11–13	128
97:9	39
99:4	26
106:20	50
107:11	75
110	79, 83, 92, 115
110:1	68, 75, 78–84, 86–89, 91–92, 95
118:171	26
122:5	114, 120
139:6	11
144:12	50
148:14	26

Proverbs
1:23	130–31
6:35	137
13:8	137

Isaiah
3:14	120–21
9:5	77
14:14	75
40–55	37
40:10	77
42:1	37
42:19	37

Isaiah (*cont.*)

43	108, 138, 139, 141
43:3–4	107–8, 123, 138
44:2	131
44:13	50
45	60
45:13	137
45:22–25	27, 36, 59
45:23	59
48:20	37
49:3	37
49:5	37
49:6	37
50:10	37
52:7	110
52:11	110
52:12	110
52:13—53:12	36–37, 52, 123
52:13–15	110
52:13	36–37, 59, 110, 140
53	22, 36, 106–11, 136–41
53:4	110
53:5	110
53:6–7	110
53:10–12	101, 108–9, 140
53:10	107, 137–38
53:10–11	137
53:11–12	137, 139
53:11	59, 110, 139
53:12	36, 59, 103, 110

Jeremiah

1:5	131

Ezekiel

8:3	50
10:8	50
20:12	70
37:9	70, 130–31
37:28	70

Daniel

2–3	46
3:19	46–48
4:31	77
4:35	35
7	6, 10, 22, 76–77, 87, 114–15, 118, 122, 140
7:9–27	115–17, 121–23
7:9	81, 114, 118, 121–22
7:10	76
7:13–14	87
7:13	11, 38, 77–79, 81–83, 87–89, 91–92, 95, 121
7:14	77, 87, 121, 140
7:17	76
7:23	76
7:20	38
7:25	116
7:26	114, 116, 122
7:27	76, 116, 121–22, 125

Amos

5:26	48

Zephaniah

2:14	36

~

NEW TESTAMENT

Matthew

1:28–30	8
3:7–12	122
3:13—4:11	127
4:1–11	129
4:1	132
5:11	114
10:32	114
10:32–33	10
11:3	109
12:18	36
16:24	105
19:23–27	112

Matthew (cont.)

19:28	2, 3, 17, 22, 81, 96, 112–18, 120–26
19:29–30	112
20:25–28	37
20:28	97, 99, 101, 108
22:44	79, 85
23:11	37
24:43–44	10
25:31	114
25:32	113
26:26–29	96
26:63	72
26:64	72, 81

Mark

1:1	77
1:9–13	7, 8, 127, 129
1:12–13	128
1:12	132
1:13	127–29
2:7	8
2:10	2
2:17	16
2:23–26	2
2:27–28	2
3:1–6	8
8:31–33	16
8:31	86, 99, 103–4, 107
8:34	105
8:38	10
9:31	86, 99, 103–4, 107
9:35	37
10:2–12	8
10:23–31	112
10:33–34	86, 99, 103–4, 107
10:33	139
10:35–45	136
10:42–45	112
10:43–45	37
10:45	2, 3, 8, 17, 22, 36, 96–108, 111–12, 114, 123–26, 136–41
12:36	79, 85
13:26–27	10
14	73
14:12–26	112
14:22–25	99, 107
14:24	97
14:27–31	112
14:53–72	73, 74, 89
14:53–65	72, 74, 77
14:53–54	73
14:61–62	12, 74
14:61	72, 74–75, 89
14:62	2, 3, 10, 18, 23, 68, 72, 77–83, 86–89, 91–92, 94, 96, 124, 126, 127
14:66–72	73
15:39	79

Luke

1–2	31
1:15	132
1:27	131
1:32	75, 131
1:35	130–31
1:41	132
1:67	132
2:4	131
2:7	131
2:11	131
2:27	131
2:33	131
2:41–51	131
3:21—4:13	131, 135
3:21–22	127, 129, 133
3:22	130
3:23–38	127, 129, 131–32, 135
3:38—4:1	2, 127, 129, 131–35
3:38	129–30
4:1–13	127, 129, 132, 134
4:1	129–30, 132
4:3	130
4:9	130
4:22	131
6:22	114

Luke (cont.)

6:35	75
7:20	109
7:21–23	109
9:23	105
12:8–9	10
12:8	114
12:39–40	10
14:11	12
18:24–30	112
20:43	79
22:7–23	112
22:15–20	99
22:24–27	37, 112
22:27	97, 101, 114
22:28–30	112, 119
22:30	2, 3, 17, 22, 96, 112–18, 120–26
22:31–38	112
22:69	72, 81
22:70	72
24:26	42

John

3:12	39
5:18	33
5:21	134
6:63	134
13:5–7	37
18	73
18:12–27	73
20:22–23	133

Acts

1:6	109
2:4	132
3:13	36
3:26	36
4:8	132
4:27	36
4:31	132
6:3	132
7:55–56	81
7:55	132
11:24	132
13:9	132

Romans

1–8	57
1:1	62
1:3–4	12, 56, 57
1:4	56
1:18–32	8
3:22–25	102
3:24	98, 100, 102, 107, 123, 125
3:25	102, 106
4:14	35
4:15	16, 111
4:25	99, 100–101, 103–4, 106, 123, 140–41
5	2, 3, 7–8, 23–24, 53–55, 61, 63, 94–95, 101–2, 107, 122–24, 126
5:6	99–100, 102–103
5:8–9	106
5:8	99–100, 102–3, 106, 123
5:12–21	8, 57, 70–71, 114, 117, 123
5:12–17	69
5:12–14	5, 8
5:14	54–55
5:15	99–100, 102–3, 106, 111–12, 123, 125, 141
5:17	69, 71–72, 91, 94, 113–15, 117, 119, 122–23, 125
5:18–19	16
5:19	69, 71–72, 91, 94, 99–100, 102–3, 106, 111–12, 123, 125, 141
5:21	54
6:2–14	54
6:3	105
6:17	62
6:19	37, 62
6:20	62
7:6	37, 62
7:25	37, 62

Romans (cont.)

8:3–4	49, 56
8:3	56
8:10–11	133
8:12–14	49
8:17	69
8:21	62
8:27	47
8:28–39	104
8:29	33, 47, 49, 56, 134
8:32	100–101, 104, 106, 111, 123, 125, 141
9–11	30, 104
10:5–13	55, 101
10:5–8	112
10:6–8	42–43
11:33–36	29–32, 63
11:33	31
12:11	37, 62
14:18	37, 62
15:3	62
15:8	36
16:18	37, 62

1 Corinthians

1:17	35
6:1–8	123
6:1–7	117
6:2	113–15, 117–18, 122–23, 125
7:8–16	55, 100, 112
8:6	42
9:3–14	55, 101, 112
9:15	35
10:1–22	101, 112, 118
10:2	105, 134
10:13	47
11:3–16	47
11:3	47
11:7	47
11:23–25	12, 21
11:24–25	99
12–14	30
12:13	105
13	30, 32
13:1–13	63
15	2, 3, 7–8, 23–24, 54, 61, 65, 82, 94, 95, 122, 124, 126, 134
15:3–8	12
15:3–5	111
15:3	99–100, 104, 106, 111, 123, 125, 151
15:12–58	65
15:12	68
15:20–28	83, 85, 86–89, 134
15:20–23	68, 123
15:20	88–89
15:21–23	88
15:21–22	83
15:22	69, 83, 91
15:23	83
15:23–28	10, 87
15:24–28	56, 65, 68, 89
15:24–27	82
15:25–27	80, 85–89, 91
15:25	68, 78¬–79, 82–84, 89, 92, 94
15:26	83–84
15:27	64, 68, 71–72, 82–84, 89, 92, 94
15:28	80
15:35–49	134
15:40	39
15:42–49	134
15:42–44	134
15:43	69
15:45–49	3, 5, 11–13
15:44	134
15:45	2, 7–8, 83, 94, 131–35
15:49	33, 47
15:52	33
15:54–57	83

2 Corinthians

3:7–18	55, 101, 112
3:17	133
3:18	47–49, 56

2 Corinthians (*cont.*)

4:1	100
4:4	33, 47, 50
4:4–6	46
4:5	62
4:6	47
4:7–5:21	7
4:7–10	49
4:7	104
4:11	104–6, 111, 123–24, 151
5:1–10	7
5:1	39
5:14–15	98
5:15	99
5:17	133
8:9	42, 56
9:3	35
4:4	33, 47, 50
4:4–6	46
4:5	62
4:6	47
4:7–5:21	7
4:7–10	49
4:7	104
4:11	104–6, 111, 123–24, 151
5:1–10	7
5:1	39
5:14–15	98
5:15	99
5:17	133
8:9	42, 56
9:3	35

Galatians

1:10	62
2:15–16	105
2:18–21	105
2:19–20	105
2:20	98–100, 105–6, 111, 123, 125, 141
3:27	105
4:3	62
4:7	62
4:8	62

4:9	62
4:21–31	101, 112
4:25	62
5:1	62
5:13	62
2	16
4:4–5	12, 55
4:4	55
4:21–31	55
5:13	37

Ephesians

1:7	102
1:20–23	85–87
1:20–22	79, 85
1:20	85, 106
3:8	31
4:13	56
4:24	33, 56
5:2	100, 105, 123, 125
5:19–20	27
5:19	26
5:25	100, 105, 123, 125

Philippians

1:1	62
1:21	62
2	5, 27, 45
2:1–18	18, 24, 30–32, 37, 41, 43–44, 61–63, 94
2:1–5	62–63
2:5–11	24
2:6–11	8, 12, 18, 23–45, 48, 51–63, 91, 94, 96, 124, 126, 131, 135
2:5	62
2:6–8	24, 37, 56, 59, 62
2:6	33–35, 37, 45, 48, 50–52, 56–58
2:7	24, 35–37, 43, 48, 52–53, 56
2:8	28, 36, 38, 41, 62
2:9–11	56, 59–61, 63
2:9–10	36

Philippians (cont.)

2:9	38
2:10	39
2:12–18	49
2:22	37, 62
3:19	39
3:21	33, 49, 69, 134
1:14	102,

Colossians

1:15–20	26, 42
1:15	33, 47
1:18	134
3:9	33
3:10	56
3:16–17	27
3:16	26
3:24	37, 62
4:12	62

1 Thessalonians

1:9	37, 62
4:13—5:11	55, 101, 112
4:14	105
5:5	105, 134
5:10	99

1 Timothy

2:5–6	98–99, 111
2:6	98, 102, 139
3:16	26

2 Timothy

2:12	113

Hebrews

1:1—2:5	65
1:3	85–86
1:13—2:11	91
1:13—2:8	85, 87, 91
1:13	79–80, 83–85, 87–89
1:16	70
2:1–4	65
2:3	65
2:5–11	2, 18, 23, 63, 65, 71, 81–82, 94, 96, 126–27
2:5–9	63–65, 67–71, 82–83, 124
2:5–8	64
2:5	65, 67, 70–71
2:6–8	64, 66, 70, 83–86, 88–89
2:6	65, 68, 80
2:7	67
2:8	64, 67, 71, 85–87
2:8–9	64–65, 68
2:9	65–68, 70–71
2:10–11	63, 65, 68–72
2:10	69, 91
2:11	69, 91
2:17	69, 91
5:6	64
5:10	64
6:20	64
7:1	64
7:10	64
7:11	64
7:15	64
7:17	64
8:1	85
9:5	102
10:12–13	80, 85
12:2	42, 85

James

3:15	39

1 Peter

1:11	69
3:18–22	42
3:18	99
3:21–22	86–87
3:21	85
3:22–23	85
3:22	80, 85

Jude

14–15	118

Rev

5:12	42
5:13	39

APOCRYPHA

Judith

15.16	26

1 Maccabees

4.33	26

2 Maccabees

3.39	39
6.28	39
7.6	39
7.37	110, 136
9.12	33

4 Maccabees

6.27–29	110, 136
15.4	57
17.22	110, 136
18.4	110, 136

Sirach

44.1	26

Wisdom

2	109
3.1–9	119
3.4	119
3.8	119
5	109
5.16	118
10.1–2	60

BOOK OF ODES

Ode

8.52	39
8.54	39
8.55	39
8.57–88	39

OLD TESTAMENT PSEUDEPIGRAPHA

Apoc. Mos.

39.2	11

2 Bar.

14.18	60
54.21	93

1 En.

1.8	118
1.9	118
37–71	118
45.6	93
46.2–4	77
47.1–4	109
48.2	77
51.3	92
54.6	93
55.4	92
61.8	92
62.1–16	109
62.1–2	92
62.5	77
62.7	77
62.9	77
62.14	77
62.15	119
63.1–11	109
63.11	77
69.27	77
69.29	77

1 En. (cont.)

70.1	77
71.14	77
71.17	77
77.2	74
108.12	118–19

2 En.

58.6	93
65.6	93

Ezek. Trag.

	77

4 Ezra

6.46	60
6.53–54	60
13	77

L.A.E.

37.3	50
39.2–3	50
47.4	11
49.3	93

Sib. Or.

2.174–76	119–120
2.241–44	81
4.183–84	93
5.34	33
8.256–73	47
8.439–45	47
12.86	33

T. Benj.

3.8	109
5.2	128

T. Iss.

7.7	128

T. Jud.

45.5–6	93

T. Naph.

8.4	128

T. Ab.

13.1–8	93–94, 119–20
13.7	93

~

DEAD SEA SCROLLS

1QIsa^a	109

1QapGen

20.2	46–48
22.15–16	75

1QS

4.7	118
4.8	118
6.1	139
6.7–25	139

1QS^a

2.11–12	75

1QH^a

9.23–25	119
11.10	77

4Q174

1.11	75

4Q246

2	77
2.1	75
2.9	77

4Q491	77
4Q491^c	109
4Q540	109
4Q541	109

11QMelch

2.18	77

PHILO

Leg. 1

49	33

Legat.

55	57

Mos. 1

111	77

Virt.

37.203–4	131

JOSEPHUS

Ant.

11.5.6	34

MISHNAH, TALMUD, AND OTHER RABBINIC WORKS

b. Ket.

8a	49

m. Ber.

7.3	74

b. Ber.

7.3	74

y. Ber.

7.3	74

Midr. Teh.

Ps 139:6	11

m. Sanh.

4–7	74

Gen. R.

14.2–5	11
8.1	11

Midr. Tanh.

1.71.5–12	120

TARGUMIC TEXTS

Tg. Onq.

Ps 8:5	83

Tg. Isa.

52:13–15	110
52:13	110
53:2	110
53:3	110
53:4	110
53:5	110
53:6–7	110
53:7	110
53:10	138
53:11	110
53:12	110

Tg. Ps.-J.

Isa 53	110

CLASSICAL AUTHORS

Aeschylus
Persae
856   51

Homer
Od.
5.184–86   39

HELLENISTIC AND LATE ANTIQUITY AUTHORS

Ailios Aristides
Sacred Words   29

Alexander
Art of Engaging Rhetoric   29

Dio Cassius
Hist. Rom. 45.1   132
Hist. Rom. 51.20   51
Hist. Rom. 52.35   51

Diodorus Siculus
1.2   51

Diogenes Laertius
Lives of Eminent Philosophers 3   132

Heliodorus
4.6   34
7.11   34
7.20   34
8.7   34

Iamblichus
Vit. Pyth. 2   132

Menander Rhetor
Division of Epideictic Speeches   29

Olympiodorus
Life of Plato 1   132

Philostratus
Vit. Apoll. 1.6   132

Plutarch
De Alexandri magni fortuna aut virtute 8.330D   34
Marcus Cato 13.343F   34
De liberis educandis 15.12A   34
Amartorius 2.755B, C   34
Theseus 2.3.36   132
Romulus 2–4   132
Alexander 2–3   132

Ps.-Aristotle
De Mundo   29

P. Oxy.
1380   29

Plinius
Epistula 10.96   23–24

Quintilian
Institutes of Oratory 3.7.1   29
Institutes of Oratory 3.7.6–9   29

Strabo
Geography 10.4.21   34

Suetonius
Divus Augustus 2   132
Divus Augustus 4   132
Divus Augustus 94   132

Achilles Tatius
Leucippe and Clitophon
2.2.1—2.12.1   73
Vettius Valens
90.7   35
122.1   34

~

CHURCH FATHERS AND EARLY CHRISTIAN LITERATURE

Cyril of Alexandria
De Ador. 1.25   34

Eusebius
Hist. Eccl. 5.2.2   34
Hist. Eccl. 8.12.2   34
Vita Constantini 31.2   34

Ignatius
Epistle to the Trallians 9.1   39

Ps.-Clementine
Homily 17.7   47

www.ingramcontent.com/pod-product-compliance
Lightning Source LLC
Chambersburg PA
CBHW052059230426
43662CB00036B/1695